BROKEN HEARTS HELD BY GOD

"A devotional you can begin any time of the year"

Fidelia Israel

Copyright © 2025 by Fidelia Israel

First Published: September 2025

Second Edition (*revised layout*): January 2026

ISBN: 979-8-218-76960-4

Cover design by Fidelia Israel

Typeset by www.typesetting.ie

Scripture quotations are taken from the New American Standard Bible (NASB), New International Version (NIV), and New King James Version (NKJV).

You are welcome to share brief excerpts from this book for personal, small group, or church use, provided the material is not altered and proper credit is given to the author. For all other uses, including reproduction for sale, please request permission at brokenheartsheld@gmail.com.

Printed in USA

To all those who walk through storms but never let go of God's hand—
This book is for you.
For the broken but still believing.
For the weary but still walking.
For the ones who have whispered, "But God..." when life made no sense.
May you find strength in every page and hope in every line.

Table of Contents

Week 1 1
Monday: Your Deepest Pain. . . 1
Tuesday: When God Rewrites
  Your Story 2
Wednesday: Love That Keeps
  on Giving............... 3
Thursday: A Father's Grip 4
Friday: When My Foot Was
  Slipping 5
Saturday: Be the Light or Grab
  the Light............... 6
Sunday: The Power of
  Gathering............... 7

Week 2 8
Monday: Leave the Thinking
  to the Conductor 8
Tuesday: Spiritual Snaccident.. 9
Wednesday: Invest Eternally ... 10
Thursday: Let It Go 11
Friday: ReSet. ReAdjust.
  ReStart. ReFocus.......... 12
Saturday: Unsinkable? 13
Sunday: A Day to Refocus 14

Week 3 15
Monday: Anchored Faith 15
Tuesday: Pleasing the One
  Who Called You 16
Wednesday: The Holy Habit ... 16
Thursday: Grace for Every Step. 18
Friday: He Walks With Me ... 19
Saturday: The Divine
  Assignment 20
Sunday: Worship and
  Community 21

Week 4 22
Monday: When God Brings
  Someone to Mind 22
Tuesday: More Valuable Than
  Sparrows 23
Wednesday: Keep It Real...... 24
Thursday: But for Him 24
Friday: From Sip to Sacred ... 25
Saturday: Assignment from
  Above.................. 26
Sunday: The Power of
  Gathering............... 27

Week 5 28
Monday: Addiction.......... 28
Tuesday: Confidence in the
  Creator................. 29
Wednesday: Be the Bear 30
Thursday: Be the Gardener of
  Grace 31
Friday: Don't Lose Your Joy .. 32
Saturday: Focus on the Rose .. 33
Sunday: A Day to Refocus 34

Week 6 35
Monday: When Relationships
  Break 35
Tuesday: Only God Can Glue
  It Back Together.......... 36
Wednesday: When It Was
  Never Meant to Be........ 37
Thursday: Shake the Dust and
  Keep Moving 38
Friday: Frayed Edges and
  Faithful Friends 39
Saturday: Held in His Palms... 40
Sunday: Coming to Your House . 41

Week 7 42	*Saturday*: Quiet Time with God . 67
Monday: You Are Not Alone . . 42	*Sunday*: Worship and Fellowship . 68
Tuesday: Red Lights and Stop Signs.................... 43	**Week 11** 69
Wednesday: Don't Withhold Good 44	*Monday*: The Gift Found in Stillness 69
Thursday: When God Closes the Door................. 45	*Tuesday*: When Cracks Invite His Strength 70
Friday: Give the Day Back 46	*Wednesday*: You Are Wonderfully Made......... 71
Saturday: Extraordinary in the Ordinary............. 47	*Thursday*: A Covenant That Cannot Be Shaken 72
Sunday: Rest and Worship 48	*Friday*: Keepers of the Covenant 73
Week 8 49	*Saturday*: Commit and be Established................ 74
Monday: Prompted to pray 49	*Sunday*: The Power of Gathering................. 75
Tuesday: But for Him 50	
Wednesday: Keep It Real....... 51	**Week 12** 76
Thursday: Eternity Is Long.... 52	*Monday*: Undivided Attention . 76
Friday: Let Go of the Branch.. 53	*Tuesday*: Your 24/7 Father.... 77
Saturday: Decluttered Vision .. 54	*Wednesday*: Is Your Soul Parched?................ 78
Sunday: A Day to Refocus 54	*Thursday*: Refueling Like Jesus . 79
Week 9 56	*Friday*: Blooming in Due Time . 80
Monday: Insulated by Christ .. 56	*Saturday*: Eternal Investments . 81
Tuesday: Check Your Signal... 57	*Sunday*: Reflection & Renewal . 82
Wednesday: Stay Close to the Shepherd 58	**Week 13** 83
Thursday: Walk in His Strength. 59	*Monday*: Wait for the Walk Sign 83
Friday: Be Persistent.......... 60	*Tuesday*: Sighing at God's Requests................. 84
Saturday: You Are Valued 61	*Wednesday*: The Power of a Parent's Tear 85
Sunday: The Power of Gathering................. 62	*Thursday*: Seeing Clearly 85
Week 10 63	*Friday*: Don't Discard the Pot . 86
Monday: Clear Your Heart's Cache................... 63	*Saturday*: ASAP — Always Say a Prayer 87
Tuesday: Insulated by Grace .. 64	*Sunday*: A Day to Refocus 88
Wednesday: Strengthening the Signal................... 64	
Thursday: The Crushing That Refines 65	
Friday: Mindful of Me........ 66	

Table of Contents

Week 14	89	**Week 18**	115
Monday: God's Joy, My Strength	89	*Monday*: God of Impossibilities	115
Tuesday: Soul Doctors	90	*Tuesday*: He Hears Every Cry	116
Wednesday: My Trustworthy Father	91	*Wednesday*: Shine Anyway	117
Thursday: Rest, Refuel, Rejuvenate	92	*Thursday*: Addiction: — Mastered or Mindful?	118
Friday: Choose to Refuel	93	*Friday*: Touch the Hem	119
Saturday: In the Waiting Room	94	*Saturday*: God's Boot Camp	120
Sunday: A Day to Refocus	95	*Sunday*: Renew and Be Restored	121
Week 15	96	**Week 19**	122
Monday: Never Alone	96	*Monday*: Covenant of Love	122
Tuesday: Milk or Meat?	97	*Tuesday*: Eternal Friends	123
Wednesday: The Years Will Be Restored	98	*Wednesday*: Gift Giving Like God	123
Thursday: Don't Linger at Closed Doors	99	*Thursday*: Let It Go	124
Friday: Are You Living or Just Surviving?	100	*Friday*: Anchored in Gratitude	125
Saturday: The Beauty Around You	101	*Saturday*: Calm Beneath the Waves	126
Sunday: Worship and Renewal	102	*Sunday*: Worship and Community	127
Week 16	103	**Week 20**	128
Monday: Soaring in the Shadow	103	*Monday*: Foggy Drive	128
Tuesday: Hold On to the Lifeline	104	*Tuesday*: The Power of 'I'	129
Wednesday: Today's Assignment	105	*Wednesday*: Are You a Sower?	130
Thursday: Permission to Rest	105	*Thursday*: Simple Obedience, Great Reward	131
Friday: Listen to the Voice	106	*Friday*: Should I or Should I Not?	132
Saturday: The Test of Trials	107	*Saturday*: Anchored Calm	132
Sunday: Worship and Reflection	108	*Sunday*: Renewal and Readiness	133
Week 17	109	**Week 21**	134
Monday: Guided by His Eye	109	*Monday*: Welcome to Our Happy Mess	134
Tuesday: When Trust Gets Tested	110	*Tuesday*: Customized Wisdom	135
Wednesday: Running on Empty	111	*Wednesday*: The Temptation of Warm Bread	135
Thursday: Wisdom in the Wrinkles	111	*Thursday*: White as Snow	136
Friday: Rejection Redefined	112	*Friday*: Victim or Conqueror?	137
Saturday: The Scar Healed	113	*Saturday*: Broken Pieces	138
Sunday: Worship and Rest	114	*Sunday*: Worship and Community	139

Week 22 140
Monday: Flying Solo 140
Tuesday: Enter by the Narrow Gate 141
Wednesday: Blame Game 142
Thursday: Heart Check. 144
Friday: Monarch in a Storm. .. 145
Saturday: Which Clay Pot Are You? 146
Sunday: A Day to Refocus 147

Week 23 148
Monday: Inner Beauty Over Outward Appearance...... 148
Tuesday: Cleft of the Rock.... 149
Wednesday: The Chief Cupbearer Did Not Remember Joseph .. 150
Thursday: Writing on the Wall: Grateful 152
Friday: Safety Net 153
Saturday: No More Excuses... 154
Sunday: A Day of Worship and Renewal................ 155

Week 24 156
Monday: Blessed Assurance, Jesus Is Mine 156
Tuesday: Writing on the Canvas – Only What's Done for Christ Will Last .. 157
Wednesday: Representing the Savior Well.............. 158
Thursday: Don't Forget Your Humble Beginnings 159
Friday: Break Now the Bread of Life 161
Saturday: Giving Thanks in All Circumstances 162
Sunday: Reflection and Renewal.. 163

Week 25 164
Monday: Drifting 164
Tuesday: Enlighten.......... 165
Wednesday: Detective 165
Thursday: Love Like a Widow . 166
Friday: Choose Joy.......... 167
Saturday: When God Rewrites Your Story 168
Sunday: Reflection & Renewal. 169

Week 26 170
Monday: Lord, Plant My Feet on Higher Ground 170
Tuesday: Do Not 171
Wednesday: The King of Kings Calls Me His Own ... 172
Thursday: Stay in His Presence . 173
Friday: You Are Not Forgotten . 173
Saturday: I Will Not Be Shaken. 174
Sunday: A Day of Worship, Rest, and Renewal 175

Week 27 176
Monday: Bloom Where You're Planted................. 176
Tuesday: Whiter Than Snow .. 177
Wednesday: Decluttered by Grace . 178
Thursday: God's Love Bubbles Over! 179
Friday: Faith Wi-Fi 180
Saturday: Tears on the Pillow.. 181
Sunday: Renewal and Readiness............... 182

Week 28 183
Monday: Living Full — Even When Life Feels Empty 183
Tuesday: Reflected Accurately . 184
Wednesday: A Solo Walk of Praise.................. 185
Thursday: Eyes That See, Ears That Hear............... 186
Friday: Decluttering the Soul .. 187
Saturday: Same Sun, Different Growth................. 188
Sunday: The Power of Gathering . 189

Table of Contents

Week 29 191
Monday: When You Feel
   Misunderstood 191
Tuesday: Among the Weeds . . . 192
Wednesday: No Shadow in the
   Light 193
Thursday: A Pause 194
Friday: Weed Day 195
Saturday: The Right Season . . . 196
Sunday: The Sacred Rhythm
   of Sunday. 196

Week 30 198
Monday: Jesus Will See You
   Through 198
Tuesday: A Friend Like No Other. 199
Wednesday: Living for Others . . 200
Thursday: Don't Forget the
   Sacrifice 201
Friday: His Word is My Anchor . . 201
Saturday: Sitting or Serving? . . 202
Sunday: Worship and Fellowship . 203

Week 31 204
Monday: Killjoy or Joy-Filled? . 204
Tuesday: Radical Obedience . . . 205
Wednesday: When It Rains,
   It Pours 206
Thursday: The Eye of the Storm . . 206
Friday: When the Day Runs
   Wild 207
Saturday: Watch and Pray 208
Sunday: Worship and Fellowship . 209

Week 32 210
Monday: Perfect Peace 210
Tuesday: Surrounded by Favor . 211
Wednesday: Be Specific 211
Thursday: God Is Still at Work . 212
Friday: Revealed Treasures 213
Saturday: Same Soil, Different
   Growth 213
Sunday: Worship and Fellowship . 214

Week 33 216
Monday: From Acquaintance
   to Intimacy 216
Tuesday: When Health
   Becomes the Prayer 217
Wednesday: Shadow of Surrender . 218
Thursday: "I'll Be Praying for
   You" — A Sacred Promise . . 219
Friday: Release the Emotions . . 220
Saturday: Hands That Satisfy . . 221
Sunday: Renewal and Readiness . . 222

Week 34 223
Monday: Thanksgiving 223
Tuesday: Hope 224
Wednesday: Peace 225
Thursday: Grace 226
Friday: Forgiveness 227
Saturday: Motherhood 228
Sunday: A Day to Refocus 229

Week 35 230
Monday: Close Your Eyes:
   Who Is God to You? 230
Tuesday: Let Me Be Singing . . . 231
Wednesday: Do My Best, Not
   Be the Best 232
Thursday: Steward of His
   Creation 233
Friday: The Lord Stood By Me . 234
Saturday: What Are We
   Waiting For? 236
Sunday: A Day to Refocus 237

Week 36 238
Monday: Walk the Talk 238
Tuesday: Feeling Alone in a
   Sea of People 239
Wednesday: Hearers or Doers? . 240
Thursday: Shake the Dust and
   Keep Moving 242
Friday: The Joy 243
Saturday: Planted to Withstand . 244
Sunday: A Day to Refocus 245

Week 37 .... **247**
Monday: Eternity in Our Hearts. 247
Tuesday: Breathe on Me,
  O Breath of God 248
Wednesday: Emoji World:
  When LOL Meets G-O-D .. 250
Thursday: Keep Us Grounded,
  Lord 251
Friday: Be the Night Light 252
Saturday: Hear My Song, Lord . 253
Sunday: The Sacred Rhythm
  of Sunday................ 255

Week 38 .... **256**
Monday: When Doubt Creeps In . 256
Tuesday: A Bible That's
  Falling Apart 257
Wednesday: In His Time 259
Thursday: More Valuable Than
  Sparrows 260
Friday: Keep It Real 261
Saturday: Assignment from
  Above................... 262
Sunday: Worship and Fellowship . 263

Week 39 .... **264**
Monday: You Are Not Alone .. 264
Tuesday: Red Lights and Stop
  Signs.................... 265
Wednesday: Don't Withhold
  Good 266
Thursday: When God Closes
  the Door................. 267
Friday: Give the Day Back 269
Saturday: Extraordinary in the
  Ordinary 270
Sunday: A Day to Refocus 271

Week 40 .... **272**
Monday: Soul Temperature
  Check................... 272
Tuesday: Keep a Part of You
  Empty 273

Wednesday: Held in My
  Brokenness............... 274
Thursday: Don't Let the Storm
  Stop You 275
Friday: Trust Over Whys 276
Saturday: Even If... He Is
  With Me................. 277
Sunday: Worship and Fellowship . 279

Week 41 .... **280**
Monday: Daily Manna 280
Tuesday: Rooted in Truth..... 281
Wednesday: Refined to Reflect . 282
Thursday: Eternity Is Too
  Long to Stay Silent........ 283
Friday: Covenant of Love 284
Saturday: Gift Giving Like God. 285
Sunday: The Sacred Rhythm
  of Sunday................ 286

Week 42 .... **288**
Monday: Obedience Without
  the Bargain.............. 288
Tuesday: Should I or Should
  I Not?................... 289
Wednesday: The Temptation of
  Warm Bread............. 290
Thursday: Victim or a
  Conqueror? 291
Friday: Blame Game 293
Saturday: Deflated, But Not
  Defeated................. 295
Sunday: Worship and
  Fellowship 296

Week 43 .... **298**
Monday: What Are We
  Waiting For?............. 298
Tuesday: A Head-to-Toe
  Inventory of God's Design.. 299
Wednesday: Steward of His
  Creation 300

Table of Contents

Thursday: Put It in Grandma's Basket.................. 301	**Week 46** **326**
Friday: The Straw That Broke the Camel's Back 303	*Monday*: The Weight of the Calling 326
Saturday: The Curved End of the Staff 305	*Tuesday*: From a Lion's Mane to a Horse's Tail" 327
Sunday: The Sacred Rhythm of Sunday 306	*Wednesday*: When My Foot Slipped 328
Week 44 .... **308**	*Thursday*: For Such a Time as This 330
Monday: The Gift Found in Stillness 308	*Friday*: When the Door Is Shut . 331
Tuesday: When Cracks Invite His Strength 309	*Saturday*: No Experience Required................. 333
Wednesday: You Are Wonderfully Made........ 310	*Sunday*: Worship and Fellowship . 334
Thursday: A Covenant That Cannot Be Shaken 311	**Week 47** **336**
Friday: Keepers of the Covenant 312	*Monday*: Leave the Thinking to the Conductor 336
Saturday: Commit and be Established............... 313	*Tuesday*: Anchored Love 337
Sunday: The Power of Gathering................ 314	*Wednesday*: Held in the Hollow . 338
Week 45 .... **315**	*Thursday*: A Love That Doesn't Walk Away 339
Monday: The Weight of the Calling 315	*Friday*: Held When I Can't Hold On................ 340
Tuesday: Anxiety and the Killjoy 316	*Saturday*: Unshaken......... 341
Wednesday: When My Foot Slipped 318	*Sunday*: The Power of Gathering................ 342
Thursday: Don't Let the Little Foxes In 319	**Week 48** **343**
Friday: When the Door Is Shut 321	*Monday*: The War Within 343
Saturday: No Experience Required................. 323	*Tuesday*: Dressed to Stand 344
Sunday: Worship and Fellowship 324	*Wednesday*: Watch the Gates .. 345
	Thursday: Don't Fight Naked.. 345
	Friday: Still Standing 346
	Saturday: The Mind is a Battlefield............... 347
	Sunday: The Power of Gathering................ 348

Week 49 349
  Monday: When Doubt
    Creeps In 349
  Tuesday: A Bible That's
    Falling Apart 350
  Wednesday: Salute Your Mother. 352
  Thursday: More Valuable
    Than Sparrows........... 353
  Friday: Keep It Real 354
  Saturday: Assignment from
    Above 355
  Sunday: Worship and
    Fellowship 356

Week 50 358
  Monday: "But God..." 358
  Tuesday: The Power of the
    Pause 359
  Wednesday: Still Standing..... 360
  Thursday: Don't Rush the
    Process.................. 361
  Friday: When Your Child
    Breaks Your Heart 362
  Saturday: Refined, Not Ruined.. 363
  Sunday: Worship and Fellowship. 364

Week 51 365
  Monday: The Wheel of
    Teaching................. 365
  Tuesday: The Wheel of
    Fellowship 366
  Wednesday: The Wheel of
    Breaking the Bread........ 366
  Thursday: The Wheel of Prayer. 367
  Friday: Serving Side by Side... 368
  Saturday: The Power of
    Showing Up.............. 369
  Sunday: Let Us Not Give Up
    Meeting Together......... 370

Week 52 371
  Monday: The God Who
    Restores 371
  Tuesday: Held in the Potter's
    Hands.................... 372
  Wednesday: Give It to God —
    and Actually Go to Sleep... 373
  Thursday: After the Breaking,
    Comes the Blessing 374
  Friday: The Cracks Let the
    Light In 375
  Saturday: Wholeness Doesn't
    Mean Unbroken........... 376
  Sunday: The Power of
    Gathering................ 377

Special Weeks/Days 378
  Holy week devotionals: He Knew,
    and He Still Rode In....... 378
  When He Rode in on a Donkey .. 379
  Thanksgiving devotional: The
    Leper Who Returned....... 380
  Gratitude Inventory 381
  Christmas devotional: The Gift
    That Changed Everything .. 382
  New Year's eve devotional:
    Anchored in Gratitude...... 383
  New Year's day devotional:
    Let It Go 384

Preface

I never set out to write a book. I simply wanted to spend time with God. In the quiet corners of my day—during morning devotions, in between life's demands—I began journaling. Just me, God, and His Word.

Then came COVID. Like so many, I found myself navigating isolation. What started as a small Zoom exercise group turned into something unexpected: community. Somewhere between squats and stretches, I felt led to share short devotionals with the women in that group. I didn't think they were anything extraordinary—just whispers from God during my quiet time. But one message turned into another... and then another.

That's when the encouragement came:
"You should write a devotional."

More nudges followed—from my Bible study group, from friends who forwarded messages, and from family who saw how these words were touching lives. I didn't write because I had it all figured out. I wrote because I needed the reminders as much as anyone else.

And what I discovered is this:
God shows up in our broken places. He meets us in our "But God" moments—and rewrites our stories with grace.

This devotional isn't meant to impress. It's meant to walk with you—through joy, through loss, and through the ordinary days in between. The readings are organized by weeks and days, but you don't have to start on January 1st. Begin on any day you hold this book in your hands. What matters isn't the date on the calendar—it's the time you spend with Him.

Each entry is drawn from Scripture and paired with reflections from life's journey—real stories from my heart. Some will make you smile, others may stir your heart, but all are written with the hope that you'll be drawn closer to the One who heals, restores, and holds you through it all.

Some of the most profound truths aren't found in grand sermons, but in the quiet corners of our lives—between tears, triumphs, setbacks, and silent prayers. These pages were collected during storms, refined through personal pain, and anchored in God's Word.

So wherever you are—whether on a mountaintop or in a valley—I pray you'll see God's fingerprints on every page... and be reminded that even when we reach the end of ourselves, He steps in.

About the Author

Fidelia Israel is a wife, mother, and grandmother whose journey of faith has been shaped by both joys and trials. The seed for this devotional was planted during the COVID-19 pandemic, when a Zoom exercise group she organized became a place not only for physical movement but also for spiritual encouragement. What began as sharing a few reflections turned into a daily practice of writing, eventually blossoming into the book you now hold.

Fidelia's writing is warm, relatable, and rooted in Scripture. She desires that every reader—whether new to faith or walking with God for decades—will find encouragement in these pages. She lives with her husband, Daniel, and enjoys time with her children and grandchildren, who continue to inspire her faith and joy in the Lord. You can reach her at brokenheartsheld@gmail.com.

Acknowledgments

I am especially grateful for my Zoom exercise sisters—your encouragement and friendship have been a blessing in ways I never imagined.

To my parents, thank you for giving me a godly home, where my faith was nurtured and the power of prayer was not just taught, but lived. Your example laid the foundation for every word in this devotional.

To my husband, Daniel—thank you for standing by me for over 40 years with unwavering love and grace. You have been my greatest encourager, my sounding board, and the quiet strength behind every word written here. I thank God for the gift of walking this journey of life and faith with you.

To my steadfast encourager, Mark—thank you for your quiet support in my mission to publish this devotional. Your simple question, "So, do you have a date in mind?" was a gentle nudge that helped move this vision toward reality.

To my family and friends, your love, prayers, and gentle nudges to keep writing made this possible. And to every reader who chooses to spend part of their day with these devotionals—thank you.

Above all, I thank God, the giver of every good gift, for His unfailing love and for allowing me the privilege of writing these reflections for His glory.

WEEK 1

Monday

Your Deepest Pain

> *"He lifted me out of the pit of despair, out of the mud and the mire. He set my feet on solid ground and steadied me as I walked along."*
> Psalm 40:2 (NLT)

Craig Groeschel once said, "God often uses our deepest pain as the launching pad for our greatest calling." That quote hit me like a ton of bricks. Because pain has a way of making everything feel heavy, personal, and inescapable.

When we're hurting, whether emotionally, physically, or spiritually, our first instinct is to isolate and believe the lie: No one else has felt this. I've thought that myself, especially during moments of deep physical pain, like the time I experienced excruciating back pain that seemed to radiate to the depths of my soul. In that moment, I remember thinking, Lord, I don't think anyone has gone through this exact pain. No one could possibly understand.

And yet... He does.

Our Savior is no stranger to pain. He bore it, every ounce of it, for us. He understands the sting of rejection, the ache of loss, the weight of suffering. And He promises not just to walk with us through it, but to use it. He doesn't waste pain. He transforms it. He recycles our deepest hurt into a platform for ministry, compassion, and purpose.

Sometimes it's only in the depths of our desperation that we truly feel His embrace, not a casual hug, but an all-encompassing hold that steadies us when we're ready to collapse. And once you've experienced that divine embrace, you stop running to empty solutions. You run straight to the One who restores.

Maybe today you're in the thick of it, crushed, weary, and wondering how God could possibly use this season. Take heart. You're not disqualified. You're being refined. And from this place of pain, a powerful testimony can emerge, one that will point others to the God who lifted you out of the mud and set your feet on solid ground.

> **Prayer:**
> *Lord, I give You my deepest pain, the parts I don't even have words for. Remind me that You are near, even in the lowest valley. Use my struggle for Your glory and shape my calling through what I've endured. May I be a living testimony that You truly do bring beauty from ashes. Amen.*

TUESDAY

"When God Rewrites Your Story"

> *"But now, Lord, You are our Father;*
> *We are the clay, and You our potter,*
> *And all of us are the work of Your hand." Isaiah 64:8 (NASB)*

A radio personality posed a question in her blog: "How is God rewriting your story?" That question lingered in my heart long after I read it. As I sat with it, this truth stirred within me:

Every day, God edits my story and makes it better. That is the power of His forgiveness and acceptance.

Our stories are often marked by heartache, detours, and moments we wish we could erase, but God, in His magnanimous love, doesn't discard our chapters. He rewrites them. He takes the broken pages and pens redemption. His forgiveness isn't just about erasing sin; it's about restoring identity. His acceptance embraces us as we are, but it also gently transforms us into who He created us to be.

TUESDAY: *"When God Rewrites Your Story"*

So today, if you feel like your story is stuck, unfinished, or too messy to continue, come to Him. Surrender the pen. Let the Author of life take over.

When God writes your story, it doesn't mean there won't be valleys or storms. But it does mean there will be purpose, peace, and a glorious ending. Your role? Stay pliable. Trust the Potter. Let Him shape the narrative in His time and His way.

What parts of your story are you holding onto instead of surrendering to God?

Take a moment to pray and give those areas to Him today. Consider journaling the ways God has already rewritten painful chapters in your life.

Prayer:
Father, thank You for being the Author of my life. Forgive me for the times I tried to write my own story without You. I give You the pen today. Edit my heart, rewrite my past, and shape my future. I trust You to make my story beautiful, because You are good, and You love me more than I can comprehend. Amen.

WEDNESDAY

Love That Keeps on Giving

> *"For God so loved the world, that He gave His only begotten Son, that whosoever believeth in Him should not perish, but have everlasting life." John 3:16 (KJV)*

If you don't have love, you can't love others. It's that simple. But the kind of love we're called to give isn't human love; it's God's love. Human love is situational, conditional, and often temporary. It depends on how others treat us. If someone despises you, it's nearly impossible to love them in return. Our instinct is to withhold warmth and affection in the face of hostility.

But then, lift your eyes and look to the cross.

God's love is nothing like ours. While we were still sinners, far removed from His holiness, God looked at us with eyes full of compassion. He didn't wait for us to clean ourselves up or return His love. Instead, He sent His only Son, Jesus Christ, into a broken world to take upon Himself every ounce of hate, jealousy, bitterness, and sin. He bore it all on the cross so that our hearts could be filled with a love that never runs dry. Can you picture it? Imagine the depth of His love when all you had in return was rejection. Yet, He still chose to die for you.

How much more is His love for you now, when you choose to surrender your life to Him?

Prayer:
Lord, thank You for loving us with an everlasting love. Help us to love others not with our limited capacity, but with the overflow of Your love in our hearts. Let Your love in us be patient, kind, and unconditional—just as You are. Amen.

THURSDAY

A Father's Grip

"When you pass through the waters, I will be with you; And through the rivers, they will not overflow you. When you walk through the fire, you will not be scorched. Nor will the flame burn you." Isaiah 43:2 (NASB)

A father was gently holding his daughter's hand as she held a firecracker. The daughter rested in the fact that her father's protection was there. His hand didn't flinch. Her face showed peace.

THURSDAY: *A Father's Grip*

Using this example, I want to remind all of us that the challenges of this day are no big deal because our Heavenly Father is there to assist and protect. He never leaves our side. His promises are real.

Perhaps this morning you woke up with shoulders drooping, already weighed down by all that lies ahead. The meetings, the burdens, and the unknowns can make us feel like we're holding something dangerous in our hands, something too big to manage.

But that's what our Father in Heaven does. He doesn't let go. His grip is steady, even when flames are near. Your challenges today are not too much for Him. Lean into His grip. You are not alone.

> **Prayer:**
> *Lord, thank You that Your grip is stronger than any flame I face. Help me to rest in Your strength and walk boldly through today's fire. Amen.*

FRIDAY

When My Foot Was Slipping

"When I said, 'My foot is slipping,' your unfailing love, LORD, supported me." Psalm 94:18 (NIV)

This verse has stayed with me since the day I read it: "My foot is slipping," and "Your unfailing love supported me." I pondered it deeply, wondering how to visualize that moment of slipping. Then, like a lightbulb, an image came to mind.

Have you ever stood at the edge of the sea, hesitant to wade deeper, planting your feet firmly in the sand just as the waves rush toward you? I've done that many times. I twist my feet in, hoping the shifting sand won't carry me away because I'm not ready to go in deeper. That sensation—that moment of being unsure, a little unstable—is how life feels when we're not planted on Christ, our Rock.

Friday: *When My Foot Was Slipping*

There's also a memory from our trip to Israel. One of our group members, a frail woman, longed to be baptized in the River Jordan. But the riverbed was slippery. The pastor, understanding her weakness, told her to step on his feet so he could stabilize her and baptize her safely. His feet became her anchor. That moment, though small, was a picture of love—of support.

Now, imagine the far greater love of Christ. When our foot is slipping, when we're overwhelmed, confused, or faltering, His unfailing love is right there, supporting us. But are we reaching out for it?

Sometimes, we're partially surrendered, half in and half out, trying to balance ourselves instead of fully resting on His support. But partial surrender is no surrender at all.

Today, if you feel your grip on life is loosening, if you're weary and slipping, reach out. His love isn't conditional or limited. It's unfailing, steady, present, and ready to support.

> **Prayer:**
> *Lord, I admit that there are moments when I feel myself slipping emotionally, spiritually, or physically. Thank You for Your unfailing love that catches me every time. Help me surrender fully to You, plant my feet on the Rock, and trust that even when I feel unsteady, You are not. Amen.*

SATURDAY

Be the Light or Grab the Light

> *"You are the light of the world. A city set on a hill cannot be hidden... In the same way, let your light shine before others..."*
> Matthew 5:14,16 (ESV)

Some days, you are the light. On other days, you need to turn toward it. There's a beautiful rhythm in God's family—we lift each other.

SATURDAY: *Be the Light or Grab the Light*

Ecclesiastes 4 reminds us, "If either of them falls, one can help the other up." It's simple, but profound. We were never meant to walk this road alone. Some days you'll be the encourager. Other days, you'll need encouragement.

Let's be open to both. Give light when you can. And when your light flickers, don't be afraid to reach out for someone else's flame.

Prayer:
Father, thank You for the people who have carried me when I couldn't walk alone. And thank You for the strength to carry others in their time of need. Help me shine and share Your light. Amen.

SUNDAY

The Power of Gathering

"And let us consider how to encourage one another in love and good deeds, not abandoning our own meeting together, as is the habit of some, but encouraging one another." Hebrews 10:24-25 (NASB)

Sunday is a sacred invitation to pause, to gather, and to worship.

As you prepare your heart today, remember the importance of coming together with other believers. There's something beautiful about lifting your voice in worship alongside others, sitting under the Word, and letting God refresh your spirit through fellowship. Church is not just a building; it's a body. And you are a vital part of it.

So, find your place, settle in, and be present in God's house.

Prayer:
Lord, thank You for the gift of the church, a place to grow, to serve, and to be renewed. Help me enter Your presence with gratitude and expectation. Amen.

WEEK 2

MONDAY

Leave the Thinking to the Conductor

> *"You will keep him in perfect peace, whose mind is stayed on You, because he trusts in You." Isaiah 26:3 (NASB)*

I once read that overthinking kills our happiness. Let's be honest, overthinking is practically a sport for many women! 😊 It breeds anxiety, fear of the unknown, and a thousand imaginary worries.

But God gives us a better way.

In Isaiah 26:3, we're reminded that peace comes when our minds are stayed on Him. Psalm 73:23 comforts us with this truth: "I am continually with You; You hold my right hand." And of course, Matthew 6:34 echoes loudly: "Do not be anxious about tomorrow, for tomorrow will be anxious for itself. Sufficient for the day is its own trouble."

Are you restless about something today? Are you giving your worry wings? Clip them.

Overthinking and peace cannot co-exist. Whatever it is, leave it in the hands of the One who conducts the symphony of our lives. Follow His hand signals, and let His perfect music flow through you.

Look unto Jesus, the Author and Finisher of your faith. Trust Him with the score, and just play your part.

Prayer:
Lord, You know how often I let my thoughts spiral and my heart race with worry. Help me to release the need for control and trust the rhythm You've already written for my life. Teach me to rest in Your timing, to listen for Your lead, and to walk in step with Your peace. Today, I choose trust over tension. In Jesus' name, Amen.

Tuesday

Spiritual Snaccident

> *"Finally, brothers and sisters, whatever is true, whatever is honorable, whatever is just, whatever is pure, whatever is lovely, whatever is commendable—if there is any excellence, if there is anything worthy of praise—think about these things." Philippians 4:8 (ESV)*

"Snaccident" — the act of mindlessly eating an entire box or bag of junk food without realizing it. I saw that sign on my pantry door this morning and immediately thought about my spiritual intake.

In our home, mindless eating is practically a tradition: eating when bored, eating when stressed, eating because the food is there. No real hunger; just habit. There's not much room for the word "refrain." Even when health conditions, like diabetes, high blood pressure, etc., demand restraint, snacking still happens.

Why am I saying all this? Because spiritually, we often do the same thing.

We consume mindlessly. We scroll, watch, read, and take in messages and influences without ever pausing to ask: Is this good for my soul? Just because it looks good doesn't mean it carries God's approval. The world presents endless options, glittering behind every screen and doorway. But not everything we see is worthy of our spirit.

We need spiritual discernment, not just for the big decisions, but for our everyday intake. What we feed our hearts, minds, and souls will shape our lives. Junk in, junk out. But when we intentionally choose what is true, noble, pure, and lovely, as Philippians 4:8 reminds us, we nourish our spirit the right way. So today, let's ask God to help us be mindful of our intake, not just in the pantry, but in our hearts.

Prayer:
Lord, help me to stop consuming without thinking. Show me what is good for my soul and give me the wisdom to walk away from what isn't. Renew my appetite for things that are excellent, pure, and honoring to You. I don't want to live on spiritual junk food. Fill me with what truly satisfies — Your Word, Your truth, and Your presence. In Jesus' name, Amen.

WEDNESDAY

Invest Eternally

"Whoever has ears, let them hear." Matthew 13:9 (NIV)

Invest is the word of the day. We invest in so many things—our time, our energy, our money, our love. We pour ourselves into people, projects, ministries, and dreams. And often, we do it without seeing immediate results.

I've been sharing my faith with friends at every opportunity I get. They're close to my heart, and I long to see them surrender to Christ. Yet after all these years, the soil still seems dry. Some days I wonder, Is this seed even growing? But then the Lord gently reminds me that kingdom investments are rarely instant. They are deep, unseen, and often slow. But they are never wasted.

Jesus often spoke of seeds and soil—how the Word is sown and how only some ground bears fruit. He told us in Matthew 13:9, "Whoever has ears, let them hear." That reminds me: I am only the sower. God brings the growth. My role is obedience, not results.

Are you investing in something eternal today?

Maybe you're praying for a loved one who hasn't yet turned to Christ.

Maybe you're serving in a quiet place where no one notices.

Maybe you're raising children, discipling a friend, or walking with someone through a hard season.

Don't stop. Don't measure the harvest too soon. Heaven counts differently than we do. Start by investing your time in His presence. Let Him fill you with what you need to pour into others. Sow kindness, truth, grace, prayer, and trust that every seed counts, even the ones that seem buried in silence.

Prayer:
Lord, give me the patience and obedience to invest in what matters most. Help me not to chase instant results but to trust Your timing. Remind me that every act of faith, every word of truth, every prayer whispered is seen by You. May my seeds be sown with eternity in mind. In Jesus' name, Amen.

THURSDAY

Let It Go

"Cast all your anxiety on Him, because He cares for you." 1 Peter 5:7 (NASB)

Sometimes my heart feels like there's a traffic jam inside, with so many burdens trying to merge at once. Worry about the future, regret from the past, and pressure in the present. It's bumper-to-bumper stress. Why? Because I try to handle everything myself.

We say we believe in Christ, but do we behave like it?

Faith isn't just a statement; it's a posture. A heart that leans back into His arms instead of forward into self-reliance. When we trust Him, there's an ease to the heart. A release. A letting go.

God doesn't just ask us to cast our burdens; He invites us. It's not a cold command. It's a tender plea: "Cast your burden upon the Lord and He will sustain you" (Psalm 55:22). He's not annoyed by our mess. He's moved by our pain. And He offers a divine exchange: your anxiety for His peace.

What are you gripping tightly today? What thoughts keep circling your mind like cars on a roundabout?

Let it go.

Let go of the striving.

Let go of the illusion of control.

Let go of the weight you were never meant to carry.

And let God step in.

Prayer:
Lord, I release this tension, this fear, this striving. I trust You to hold what I cannot. Calm the traffic inside my heart. Clear the road of worry and lead me beside still waters. Remind me that You care deeply about every burden, every tear, every unspoken ache. In Jesus' name, Amen.

FRIDAY

ReSet. ReAdjust. ReStart. ReFocus.

"Commit your way to the Lord; trust also in Him, and He will do it." Psalm 37:5 (NASB).

These four "Re" words grabbed my attention this morning—Reset. Readjust. Restart. Refocus. They reminded me how easy it is to drift. Life happens. Distractions creep in. Emotions flare. Before we know it, we've veered off-center; slightly at first, but enough to need a course correction. Just like an airplane requires inspection before every takeoff, our hearts need daily recalibration. Not once a month. Not once a crisis hits. But daily. Moment by moment.

Even our GPS doesn't hesitate to recalculate when we take a wrong turn. Shouldn't we be just as willing to recenter when the Holy Spirit prompts us? Our pastor once said, "Sanctification is a daily surrender, not a one-time decision." That truth sticks with me. Every day is a new opportunity to bring my heart back to the Lord, to realign my thoughts, my choices, my attitude.

So this morning, what "Re" do you need to do?
Recenter?
Repent?
Recommit?
Reignite?
Refocus?

God is not waiting to condemn you for drifting. He's ready to guide you home.

Prayer:
Lord, help me recalibrate my heart to You. Reveal where I've drifted. Whether it's in my thoughts, my pace, or my priorities—gently realign me with Your purpose. Today, I recommit my way to You and trust that You will lead me forward. In Jesus' name, Amen.

Saturday: *Unsinkable?*

SATURDAY

Unsinkable?

> *"Behold, I am the Lord, the God of all flesh: is there anything too hard for Me?" Jeremiah 32:27 (NASB)*

The Titanic—the most famous ship in history. It was made of steel, a marvel of engineering and luxury, and its creators proudly declared it unsinkable.

To quote: "We place absolute confidence in the Titanic. We believe that the boat is unsinkable." — Philip Franklin, Vice-President of White Star Line, owners of Titanic.

Yet, within just three hours of its maiden voyage on April 15, 1912, the mighty Titanic sank into the depths of the Atlantic.

Now contrast that with Noah's Ark, a wooden vessel built not by engineers or shipwrights, but by a man who simply obeyed God's voice. It floated safely through a worldwide flood that covered the earth for forty days and forty nights. It never cracked, never broke, and never sank.

The Titanic had human pride. The Ark had God's presence.

One was designed with grandeur, the other with obedience. One carried the confidence of man, the other carried the covenant of God.

So, whose vessel are you trusting today? One that boasts its own strength? Or the one that anchors in God's promises?

In life, we may look strong on the outside, "unsinkable," even. But without God, we are always one iceberg away from disaster. If you're feeling overwhelmed, under pressure, or unsure of what's ahead, anchor yourself in the One who never fails. His sustaining power is not in the size of your ship but in the strength of His hand.

Prayer:
Lord, I don't want to trust in what I can build or boast about what I can carry. Help me to place my confidence in You, the One who commands the storm and calms the sea. Anchor me in Your strength, and let my life be a vessel that brings You glory. Amen.

SUNDAY

A Day to Refocus

"This is the day that the Lord has made; Let us rejoice and be glad in it." Psalm 118:24 (NASB)

Sunday is more than just the end of the week; it's the beginning of your next chapter. It's a reset. A divine pit stop to fuel your spirit before life picks up again on Monday.

Gather with fellow believers. Soak in the Word. Sing out your praise. Be still in His presence.

Let today be your reminder that no matter what last week held, God is giving you a fresh page. So go to church, be encouraged, and carry His peace into the week ahead.

Prayer:
Father, thank You for Sundays. Thank You for quiet moments, joyful songs, and the blessing of community. Let today mark the start of a week filled with Your purpose. Amen.

WEEK 3

MONDAY

Anchored Faith

> *"And He said to them, 'Because of your meager faith; for truly I say to you, if you have faith the size of a mustard seed, you will say to this mountain, 'Move from here to there,' and it will move; and nothing will be impossible for you." Matthew 17:20 (NASB)*

As children, this verse from Hebrews 11 was drilled into us: "Now faith is the substance of things hoped for, the evidence of things not seen." We memorized it like a mantra but never took it to heart. Even as adults, when our hearts are disturbed or our boat rocks, what's the first thing we do? We hop into the anxiety boat instead of the well-anchored faith boat.

Now read that verse again...with faith comes blessing. It's so hard to explain faith, but perhaps the best way to understand it is that it's a settled feeling. When we are settled, our minds are calm, and our hearts beat normally. Does it not?

I pray that all of us will be in an anchored boat of faith.

Prayer:
Lord, help me stay in the boat of faith today. Calm my heart and steady my mind, so that when life's winds blow, I will still know You are my anchor. Amen.

TUESDAY

Pleasing the One Who Called You

> *"For am I now seeking the favor of men, or of God? Or am I striving to please men? If I were still trying to please men, I would not be a bond-servant of Christ." Galatians 1:10 (NASB)*

> *"But just as we have been approved by God to be entrusted with the gospel, so we speak, not as pleasing men, but God who examines our hearts." 1 Thessalonians 2:4 (NASB)*

Our primary goal is to please God through our deeds. Sometimes work can be stressful—dealing with personalities, unreasonable deadlines, and more. But when we hand those challenges to God and believe in our hearts that we report to God, the task is no longer daunting. God brings an unbelievable calmness to our mindset.

So today, approach your tasks at work or at home with this mindset: I am here to please God.

> **Prayer:**
> *Father, help me to work as if I report to You. Let my words, attitude, and responses reflect the grace of the One I serve. Amen.*

WEDNESDAY

The Holy Habit

> *"My soul thirsts for You, my flesh yearns for You... I meditate on You in the night watches." Psalm 63:1,6 (NASB)*

WEDNESDAY: *The Holy Habit*

What kind of habits are you forming?

I've shared before how I started drinking coffee; it began with a simple sip and slowly became a daily ritual. Now it's automatic. I don't question it, I just reach for that cup. The same goes for brushing our teeth or showing up to work. We do these things out of routine, not emotion.

But here's the deeper question: What spiritual habits are forming in your life?

Are we as consistent in giving thanks?

Do we meditate on His Word as faithfully as we check our phones?

Are praise and prayer part of our daily rhythm, or only occasional responses to crisis?

Spiritual habits often begin with small, intentional steps. A morning whisper of gratitude. A verse repeated in the car. A commitment to encourage someone today. These things don't always feel profound in the moment, but over time, they form spiritual muscle memory. And just like with coffee, we find we crave His presence more and more.

Psalm 63 paints a beautiful picture of longing for God, not just with the soul, but with the body. A yearning that says, "I need You more than anything else." That kind of thirst is cultivated through habit—through seeking Him daily, not sporadically.

So, ask yourself today:

What habits have I already formed?

What new ones do I need to intentionally build?

What distractions need to be replaced with devotion?

> **Prayer:**
> *Lord, may my habits reflect a heart that seeks You daily. Let me thirst for Your presence and never grow weary of drawing near. Form in me a rhythm of gratitude, praise, prayer, and reflection—so natural that it becomes the default setting of my day. In Jesus' name, Amen.*

THURSDAY

Grace for Every Step

> *"And you will seek Me and find Me when you search for Me with all your heart. I will let Myself be found by you,' declares the Lord."* Jeremiah 29:13-14 (NASB)

> *"Make me know Your ways, Lord; Teach me Your paths. Lead me in Your truth and teach me, For You are the God of my salvation; For You I wait all day."* Psalm 25:4-5 (NASB)

Where do I begin?

Some days, that's the honest question of the heart. When life feels uncertain or overwhelming, it's hard to know the next right step. But here's the good news: I can begin right here.

He redeemed me.

He made me His child.

He gave me unlimited access to His throne of grace.

And when I fall, because I will, His grace lifts me up again and sets my feet on solid ground.

I need His grace not just for the big, life-altering decisions, but for the ordinary steps too. The hard conversations. The quiet obedience. The mundane tasks. Without His grace, I'm like a traveler without a compass, wandering, striving, but never arriving.

He is my GPS.

His Word is my map.

His Spirit is my guide.

And His grace? It's the fuel that keeps me going.

Sometimes, all I can whisper is:

I need Thee, oh I need Thee. Every hour I need Thee.

That hymn isn't just a song; it's a lifeline.

So today, whatever path you're on, know this: God delights in being found. He promises to guide those who seek Him wholeheartedly. You don't have to figure it all out; you just have to follow Him, step by step.

Friday: *He Walks With Me*

> **Prayer:**
> *Father, I need Your grace for every step today. Without You, I am directionless. With You, I can walk in peace. Lead me by Your truth, and let Your grace carry me where my strength cannot. In Jesus' name, Amen.*

Friday

He Walks With Me

"The Lord is my light and my salvation; Whom should I fear? The Lord is the defense of my life; Whom should I dread?" Psalm 27:1-2 (NASB)

The same God who asked Peter to step out of the boat and walk on water…

The same God who stood with Shadrach, Meshach, and Abednego in the fire…

The same God who journeyed with the Israelites in the wilderness…

The same God who parted the Red Sea…

That same God is walking with you.

Your journey may not include blazing fires or seas splitting in two. Maybe you've never seen walls fall or manna fall from the sky. But that doesn't mean He's not near.

Sometimes, His presence comes in quiet, steady ways—in the stillness of your car, in the hush of a troubled moment, in the silent strength that gets you through a hard day.

I remember one morning, I was driving to work carrying a heavy, almost suffocating burden. Tears welled in my eyes. But as I drove, a peace came over me, soft, yet undeniable. It was as if invisible arms wrapped around me and whispered, "You're not alone." I couldn't see Him, but I felt Him. I knew that was God.

You may not always feel fire or thunder. But He is always there. Always steady. Always holding you close.

> **Prayer:**
> Lord, thank You for walking with me, even when I don't see it. Thank You for the miracles and for the quiet moments of grace. Help me be ever aware of Your nearness. When my heart is overwhelmed, let me lean into Your embrace and rest in the safety of Your presence. In Jesus' name, Amen.

SATURDAY

The Divine Assignment

> *"Then the Lord came and stood, and called as at the other times: 'Samuel! Samuel!' And Samuel said, 'Speak, for Your servant is listening.'"* 1 Samuel 3:10 (NASB)

> *"Then I heard the voice of the Lord, saying, 'Whom shall I send, and who will go for Us?' Then I said, 'Here am I. Send me!'"* Isaiah 6:8 (NASB)

When God puts a thought in your heart—a name, a need, a prompting—He's not just suggesting something. He's entrusting you with an assignment.

Too often, we hesitate.

Was that really from God?

I'm not qualified.

What if I get it wrong?

But here's the truth: If He placed it in you, He will equip you. He's not looking for perfection. He's looking for obedience.

Think of God as our Divine VP, entrusting His trusted team with critical tasks. Every assignment matters. Whether it's speaking a word of encouragement, helping someone financially, writing a note, interceding in prayer, or showing up for someone, don't ignore His nudge.

We are His hands, His voice, His ambassadors on earth. Heaven's agenda flows through willing hearts.

BROKEN HEARTS HELD BY GOD: Week 3

SATURDAY: *The Divine Assignment*

Have you quieted yourself enough to hear Him today?
Can you feel that little tug?
That gentle whisper?
That thump in your heart with a name attached to it?
Don't push it aside. Respond like Samuel: "Speak, Lord, for Your servant is listening."
Or like Isaiah: "Here I am. Send me."

Prayer:
Lord, I am listening. Help me not to shrug off Your promptings or underestimate my role in Your mission. Give me the courage to respond with obedience and humility. Today, I say yes to whatever assignment You entrust to me. In Jesus' name, Amen.

 SUNDAY

Worship and Community

"Not giving up meeting together, as some are in the habit of doing, but encouraging one another—and all the more as you see the Day approaching." Hebrews 10:25 (NIV)

Sundays are sacred pauses in the rhythm of our week. Whether you gather in a large church or a small group, this day reminds us that we're not meant to walk alone. Worship anchors us. Fellowship strengthens us. And rest restores us.

We were created for communion, not only with God but with one another. Prioritize this day. Show up. Be present. Encourage someone. And let your soul breathe.

Prayer:
Lord, thank You for the gift of community and the power of gathered worship. Help me honor this day, not just as a tradition, but as a sacred appointment to be with You and Your people. Amen.

WEEK 4

MONDAY

When God Brings Someone to Mind

"Therefore, confess your sins to one another, and pray for one another so that you may be healed. A prayer of a righteous person, when it is brought about, can accomplish much." James 5:16 (NASB)

Have you ever had a name or face suddenly pop into your mind, seemingly out of nowhere? Don't brush it off. I truly believe those moments are the Holy Spirit's gentle whisper, inviting us to intercede. Take just 10 seconds to pray. That simple act may mean more than you'll ever know.

I remember a night I couldn't sleep. My mind was restless, and then, without warning, one of my manager's names surfaced in my thoughts. She wasn't someone I interacted with often, but I felt a tug. So I prayed. A quiet, short prayer. Later that week, I mentioned it to her. Her response stunned me:

"Please keep praying. My husband is cheating on me."

In that moment, I realized that God had used me, a broken and ordinary vessel, to stand in the gap for someone walking through heartbreak.

Another time, God woke me at exactly 1:30 a.m. with a young man on my heart. No explanation. Just his name and an urgency. I prayed. Days later, his mother told me he had been going through something intense, right around that same time.

This isn't about me. It's about God's prompting and our obedience.

We don't need the full backstory to pray. We need a willing heart.

So when that name comes, when that face flashes before you, pause. Pray. God may be inviting you into a divine appointment, one whispered nudge at a time.

TUESDAY: *More Valuable Than Sparrows*

> **Prayer:**
> *Father, help me to be sensitive to Your whispers. Let me not ignore those nudges, but respond in faith and prayer. Thank You for the privilege of partnering with You in the quiet work of intercession. In Jesus' name, Amen.*

TUESDAY

More Valuable Than Sparrows

> *"Look at the birds of the sky, that they do not sow, nor reap, nor gather crops into barns, and yet your heavenly Father feeds them. Are you not much more important than they?" Matthew 6:26 (NASB)*

Something is calming about watching the sparrows gather at my feeder. Tiny and fragile, they brave the winds, endure the cold, and greet each morning with song. They have no paycheck, no pantry, no plan, but they are fed.

Who takes care of them? Our Heavenly Father does.

Then comes the gentle question from Jesus: "Are you not of more value than they?"

If God tends to the needs of the sparrows, how much more attentive is He to your needs—your fears, your struggles, your unspoken prayers?

So today, if anxiety grips your heart or you feel invisible in a crowd, let the birds outside your window be a living sermon. You are seen. You are known. You are deeply valued.

> **Prayer:**
> *Lord, thank You for the sparrows that remind me of Your faithfulness. When I feel small or forgotten, I lift my eyes to the sky and let creation remind me: I matter to You. Amen.*

WEDNESDAY

Keep It Real

> *"Finally, brothers and sisters, whatever is true, whatever is honorable, whatever is right, whatever is pure, whatever is lovely, whatever is commendable... think about these things." Philippians 4:8 (NASB)*

This is my pet peeve: Society has trained us to be overly diplomatic and politically correct. But in doing so, we lose the authenticity of who we are.

Why can't we be real? Why do we filter our every word? My kids say, "No mincing words with my mom!" I take no offense. I'd rather be truthful than pretend behind a smoky mirror.

If we're constantly walking on eggshells, how can we think about what's true and honorable? Let's keep it real—with kindness, with love, and with truth.

Prayer:
Father, help me walk in truth. Strip away the fear of offense, and let my words be honest and seasoned with grace. Amen.

THURSDAY

But for Him

> *"In everything give thanks; for this is God's will for you in Christ Jesus." 1 Thessalonians 5:18 (NASB)*

THURSDAY: *But for Him*

This morning, my heart is overwhelmed with gratitude. A recent getaway reminded me just how deeply God surrounds our lives with provision, protection, and peace, often in ways we miss in the busyness of our routines.

When gratitude takes hold of our hearts, even the simplest moments feel sacred. I often find myself whispering, But for Him. It's not just a phrase; it's a lens through which I see everything.

But for Him, I have breath.

But for Him, I have peace in the storm.

But for Him, I have strength for today and hope for tomorrow.

Let that be your anthem today. Not a whisper of worry, but a declaration of dependence and thanksgiving.

> **Prayer:**
> *Lord, thank You for the countless ways You carry me, seen and unseen. Help me pause often, reflect deeply, and live daily with a grateful heart that recognizes it's all because of You. Amen.*

FRIDAY

From Sip to Sacred

> *"My soul thirsts for You, my flesh yearns for You... When I remember You on my bed, I meditate on You in the night watches."*
> *Psalm 63:1,6 (NASB)*

It started with just one sip; that's how my love for coffee began.

Over time, that simple taste turned into a daily ritual. A rhythm I no longer had to think about.

Some things in life become automatic. We don't question brushing our teeth or heading to work. We just do it. Why? Because habit has taken root.

What if our walk with God became that natural?

What if gratitude flowed before our feet even hit the floor?

What if Scripture wasn't just a checkbox, but a craving?

What if meditating on His promises and serving others became as instinctive as breathing?

Spiritual habits don't form overnight. But they do begin with a sip—a small, intentional moment with God. A whispered prayer. A verse on the mirror. A song lifted from a weary heart.

When those moments are pursued daily, the sip becomes sacred.

So, what are you sipping on today?

What sacred rhythms is God inviting you to build?

> **Prayer:**
> Lord, stir up in me a thirst that only You can quench. Help me cultivate habits that keep me close to Your heart. Let my day begin and end with You. Teach me to crave Your presence more than anything else. In Jesus' name, Amen.

SATURDAY

Assignment from Above

> *"And God spoke to Israel in visions of the night and said, 'Jacob, Jacob.' And he said, 'Here I am.'" Genesis 46:2 (NASB)*

> *"Then I heard the voice of the Lord, saying, 'Whom shall I send, and who will go for Us?' Then I said, 'Here am I. Send me!'" Isaiah 6:8 (NASB)*

When God places a thought or burden on your heart, it's never random; it's a divine assignment. He's not simply making a suggestion; He's entrusting you with something sacred.

Yet how often do we hesitate? We question whether we're good enough, ready enough, or strong enough. But if God has called you, He

SATURDAY: *Assignment from Above*

will also equip you. Your job is not to have it all figured out; it's to say, "Here am I."

Picture God as your Divine Vice President, assigning missions from the heavenly boardroom. He doesn't pick randomly; He chooses intentionally. The right person for the right task.

Be the one who answers, not with excuses, but with readiness.

> **Prayer:**
> *Lord, I'm listening. If there's something You want to entrust to me today, I say yes. Give me the courage to obey, the strength to carry it through, and the faith to trust Your plan. Amen.*

 SUNDAY

The Power of Gathering

> *"And let us consider how to encourage one another in love and good deeds, not abandoning our own meeting together, as is the habit of some, but encouraging one another."* Hebrews 10:24–25 (NASB)

Sunday is a sacred invitation to pause, to gather, and to worship.

As you prepare your heart today, remember the importance of coming together with other believers. There's something beautiful about lifting your voice in worship alongside others, sitting under the Word, and letting God refresh your spirit through fellowship. Church is not just a building; it's a body. And you are a vital part of it.

So find your place, settle in, and be present in God's house.

> **Prayer:**
> *Lord, thank You for the gift of the church — a place to grow, to serve, and to be renewed. Help me enter Your presence with gratitude and expectation. Amen.*

WEEK 5

Monday

Addinction

> *"All things are permitted for me, but not all things are of benefit. All things are permitted for me, but I will not be mastered by anything."*
> 1 Corinthians 6:12 (NASB)

God taught me a valuable lesson on addiction this week, and it all started with coffee.

During the pandemic, I picked up a new habit: drinking coffee. What began as an occasional sip became half a cup, then one cup, then two… and eventually three!

One Wednesday, our daughter unknowingly ran the Keurig without water. Since no coffee came out, she tried again. Twice. The poor Keurig had had enough and gave up its ghost.

Realizing what happened, she ran out and got me coffee from Starbucks (bless her heart) and also ordered a new Keurig to arrive by Friday. But that meant no coffee for two whole days.

What followed surprised me:

A pounding headache.

Zero energy.

Foggy thinking.

It was like having a hangover without the party.

In that moment, I had a wave of empathy for those fighting deeper addictions. I understood, even if just a fraction, how quickly dependence can form and how hard it is to break.

Addiction rarely starts as an addiction. It starts as "just once," "just a taste," "just a way to unwind." Before long, what we thought we could control begins to control us.

Monday: *Addiction*

Whether it's social drinking, smoking, gambling, shopping, or mindless scrolling, every habit begins with a taste. If it's not beneficial, it can become bondage.

Don't wait for the chains to tighten. Run. Don't reason with temptation; flee from it. Don't even taste it.

> **Prayer:**
> *Lord, help me recognize the small steps that can lead to bondage. Give me discernment and self-control. I want to walk in the freedom You offer, not be mastered by anything but Your love. In Jesus' name, Amen.*

Tuesday

Confidence in the Creator

"The Lord is my strength and my shield; My heart trusts in Him, and I am helped; Therefore my heart triumphs, And with my song I shall thank Him." Psalm 28:7 (NASB)

Have you ever watched a bird perched high at the top of a tree? It doesn't wobble or panic, even when the wind sways the branch. The bird isn't placing its confidence in the stability of the branch; it's trusting its own wings. What a picture of faith!

That bird knows that even if the branch gives way, it can still soar. Likewise, we are called to place our confidence, not in our jobs, relationships, finances, or even our talents, but in the One who created us. Branches break. Circumstances shift. Plans fail. But God remains faithful. He is our strength and our shield, and when we trust Him, we are helped. Our confidence shouldn't rest in what we stand on, but in who holds us up.

So today, if something you've leaned on feels unsteady, remember: your wings were made for higher ground.

> **Prayer:**
> Lord, help me shift my confidence away from the temporary things of this world and lean fully on You—my strength, my shield, and my sustainer. When the ground beneath me shakes, remind me that You are unshakable. In Jesus' name. Amen.

WEDNESDAY

Be the Bear

> *"Let love of the brothers and sisters continue. Do not neglect hospitality to strangers, for by this some have entertained angels without knowing it."* Hebrews 13:1–2 (NASB)

A bear wandered through the jungle and spotted a baby bear hanging from a tree branch, crying for help. The little one was stuck, dangling in fear. The big bear could've kept walking; it wasn't his cub, after all. But instead, he stood tall on his hind legs and told the baby bear to let go and drop onto his head.

That's sacrifice.

That's compassion.

That's love in action.

To be the bear means putting aside convenience and choosing compassion. It means showing up for someone when it's not our responsibility. It means stepping into a situation simply because someone needs us to.

God didn't create us to live in isolation. We're wired for connection. For the community. For caring. Hebrews 13 tells us to let brotherly love continue, and not to forget to show hospitality, even to strangers. Why? Because sometimes, we're doing far more than we realize. We may even be entertaining angels.

In a world where it's easy to walk away or scroll past someone else's struggle, God invites us to be the one who stays. The one who notices. The one who helps, even when it's not "our problem."

THURSDAY: *Be the Gardener of Grace*

> **Prayer:**
> *Father, open my eyes to see where I can step in. Make me willing to help with a generous and humble heart. Use me to carry the burdens of others, just as You carry mine. In Jesus' name, Amen.*

THURSDAY

Be the Gardener of Grace

"A generous person will be prosperous, And one who gives others plenty of water will himself be given plenty." Proverbs 11:25 (NASB)

When we're walking through storms, it's natural to turn inward. Pain has a way of narrowing our focus, making us feel isolated, tired, and even numb. I've felt that. Burdened, distracted, hurt when someone enters the room needing encouragement, and I wonder, Do I have anything left to give?

But even in those weary moments, God gives us strength to bless others, not from our own well, but from His overflowing grace.

You may be in the middle of your own struggle, yet God still wants to use you. Why? Because life-giving water flows best through cracked vessels. Sometimes, the most meaningful encouragement comes from someone who understands what it means to be empty, yet chooses to pour anyway.

Don't wait until everything is perfect to be a blessing.

Speak anyway. Serve anyway. Love anyway.

The words of Christ are never limited by our pain, unless we silence them ourselves. So pour into others. Water their hearts. Be the gardener of grace, even while God tends to your own.

> **Prayer:**
> Lord, use me today as a vessel of refreshment for others. Even when my heart is weary, may I speak words that uplift. Let Your living water flow through me, renewing both the giver and the receiver. In Jesus' name. Amen.

FRIDAY

Don't Lose Your Joy

> *"Trust in the Lord with all your heart And do not lean on your own understanding. In all your ways acknowledge Him, And He will make your paths straight." Proverbs 3:5–6 (NASB)*

Sometimes we lose our joy not because of what happened, but because of the questions that linger.

We take a "Why, God?" stance.

Why did this happen?

Why didn't You show up sooner?

Why them? Why now?

Slowly, almost quietly, our joy begins to fade, replaced by disappointment, frustration, and sometimes even desperation.

Mary and Martha knew that pain. When their brother Lazarus died, they said to Jesus, "Lord, if You had been here…" It was their way of saying, "This didn't have to happen."

But Jesus wasn't late. He was right on time for a greater purpose. He showed them the end of the story, one that would bring glory to God and deepen their faith beyond the grave.

Sometimes, we're in the middle chapters of a story that's not finished yet. That's when joy is most vulnerable—when we don't understand the plot twist and can't see the resolution.

But trust is the bridge that carries us from confusion to peace, trusting in His character, trusting in His wisdom and trusting in the unseen hand that is still writing our story.

SATURDAY: *Focus on the Rose*

> **Prayer:**
> *Lord, in the mystery of unanswered prayers and the ache of "not yet," help me not lose my joy. Remind me that You are still working, still moving, and still faithful. I choose to trust in Your perfect plan, even when I don't understand it. In Jesus' name, Amen.*

SATURDAY

Focus on the Rose

> *"And we know that God causes all things to work together for good to those who love God, to those who are called according to His purpose." Romans 8:28 (NASB)*

We live in an imperfect world, one full of ruffles, waves, bumps, and unexpected detours. Trouble is part of the journey, but how we respond to it determines whether we carry peace or lose it.

Every bump threatens to shake our joy. Every thorn tries to shift our focus to the pain.

But we have a choice: focus on the thorns or the rose.

Even among the sharpness and discomfort of life, there is beauty. There is purpose. There is grace. When we fix our eyes on the rose—on the goodness of God, His promises, His presence—we are reminded that He is still at work. Still faithful. Still weaving all things together for good.

Yes, the thorns are real. But so is the bloom.

So today, choose your focus. Let your eyes rest on what is lovely, not just what is hard.

> **Prayer:**
> *Lord, help me keep my eyes on Your goodness amidst the trials. Let me see the beauty even when surrounded by thorns. Remind me that You are working all things together for my good and Your glory. In Jesus' name, Amen.*

SUNDAY

A Day to Refocus

"This is the day that the Lord has made; Let us rejoice and be glad in it." Psalm 118:24 (NASB)

Sunday is more than just the end of the week; it's the beginning of your next chapter. It's a reset. A divine pit stop to fuel your spirit before life picks up again on Monday.

Gather with fellow believers. Soak in the Word. Sing out your praise. Be still in His presence.

Let today be your reminder that no matter what last week held, God is giving you a fresh page. So go to church, be encouraged, and carry His peace into the week ahead.

Prayer:
Father, thank You for Sundays. Thank You for quiet moments, joyful songs, and the blessing of community. Let today mark the start of a week filled with Your purpose. Amen.

WEEK 6

Monday

When Relationships Break

"If possible, so far as it depends on you, be at peace with all people." Romans 12:18 (NASB)

Relationships are complicated. They bring joy, connection, and purpose, but they can also wound deeply. Sometimes it's a friend who suddenly goes silent, a family member whose words cut too sharply, or a spouse whose love feels distant. The ache of relational brokenness is one of the heaviest burdens we carry.

As believers, we are called to be peacemakers. But the truth is, not all relationships can be mended on our timeline. Paul's words in Romans 12:18 offer both challenge and comfort. "If possible... as far as it depends on you..." This means we do our part. We forgive, reach out, speak truth in love, and let go of pride. But we also release the outcome to God.

You can't force healing. You can't make someone apologize. But you can choose to obey God in your response. Sometimes peace looks like reconciliation. Other times, it looks like boundaries, surrender, and ongoing prayer.

Has someone hurt you recently? Is there a relationship that weighs heavily on your heart?

Let God be the healer of your heart, and theirs. He sees the full picture, and even in the silence or distance, He is working behind the scenes.

Prayer:
Lord, You know the relationships that have fractured in my life. I surrender the pain, the misunderstandings, and even the unanswered questions to You.

Show me how to respond with grace and give me the courage to forgive, even if reconciliation doesn't come. I trust You to bring beauty out of brokenness. Heal what only You can heal. In Jesus' name, Amen.

TUESDAY

Only God Can Glue It Back Together

"He heals the brokenhearted and binds up their wounds." Psalm 147:3 (NASB)

There are some wounds that no human touch can reach. When a heart is shattered by betrayal, loss, rejection, or the weight of life's disappointments, no advice, no distraction, no time can fully restore it. People might say, "Just move on," but they don't see the deep cracks inside.

Only God can reach that deep.

Only He knows how your heart broke, where it splintered, and how to gently piece it back together. He doesn't use quick fixes or emotional bandages. He binds, He mends, He heals. Not with force, but with tenderness. Not by ignoring the pain, but by entering it.

Sometimes we try to glue ourselves back together with busyness, numbing, or forced smiles. But true healing can't come from the outside. It begins when we bring the pieces to the Father and say, "Here. I don't even know how to hold this anymore."

God is not overwhelmed by your brokenness. His specialty is restoration. Where you see ruins, He sees rebuilding. Where you feel unfixable, He sees a masterpiece in progress.

Prayer:
Lord, my heart is aching in places no one sees. The pain is sharp, and I feel scattered in pieces. But I trust that You see it all. You are the Healer of the brokenhearted. I bring every fragment to You—every silent cry, every disappointment. Please do what only You can do. Bind me up. Heal me deeply. And remind me that in Your hands, nothing is ever too broken. Amen.

WEDNESDAY

When It Was Never Meant to Be

> *"For the mountains may be removed and the hills may shake, but My favor will not be removed from you, nor will My covenant of peace be shaken," says the Lord who has compassion on you. Isaiah 54:10 (NASB)*

Some relationships were never meant to be.

You can pour your heart into it, give sacrificially, overlook flaws, and fight to keep it alive. But when the other person does not value the depth of your love, when they discard your presence, ignore your worth, or walk away without a second thought, it's not a reflection of your failure. It's a revelation of the truth.

Love is not one-sided. God never intended for us to beg for affection, chase after scraps of attention, or feel disposable in someone's life. Real relationships, whether friendship, family, or romance, are built on mutual honor, respect, and a shared commitment.

If someone could throw you away like a rag, the relationship was never rooted in love to begin with. Love doesn't discard. Love sees, stays, and speaks truth, even when it's hard.

And when human connection fails, God's nearness becomes undeniable. In that space, His arms wrap tighter. He whispers, "You are still chosen. Still valuable. Still deeply loved." He doesn't just tolerate you; He treasures you.

So let go of what was never meant to be and lean into the One who will never let go of you.

Prayer:
Father, thank You for loving me with a love that never fails or fades. You see the ache in my heart when human relationships fall apart. Help me stop chasing people who were never meant to stay. Teach me to rest in Your acceptance and remind me that I am never discarded or unwanted in Your eyes. Heal the rejection and replace it with holy confidence. In Jesus' name, Amen.

THURSDAY

Shake the Dust and Keep Moving

> *"Do not fear, for I am with you; Do not be afraid, for I am your God. I will strengthen you, I will also help you, I will also uphold you with My righteous right hand." Isaiah 41:10 (NASB)*

When you go through relationship hurts, whether from betrayal, neglect, or quiet abandonment, God often steps into the silence with a whisper: "Child, I am all you need."

People come and go. Some ride with you only for a season. Like passengers on a train, they get off when their station arrives. And that's okay. The final destination isn't about who stayed with you; it's about who never left. God is still on board. He's not getting off.

The ache of being dismissed or devalued can leave us gasping for closure. We replay conversations. We question our worth. But God says, "Don't chase what's walking away. Shake the dust off and keep moving. Your identity is not tied to those who couldn't see your value."

When someone treats your presence as optional, don't keep offering your heart as if it's disposable. You were never meant to beg for love. You were created to walk with the One who calls you chosen, beloved, and His.

You and God make it to the end of the line together.

Prayer:
Lord, thank You for being the constant in a world full of broken goodbyes. Help me release the people You never meant to stay. Remind me that my worth isn't defined by who leaves, but by the One who remains. I choose to shake the dust, lift my eyes, and walk on in Your strength. In Jesus' name, Amen.

FRIDAY

Frayed Edges and Faithful Friends

"I have called you friends, because all things that I have heard from My Father I have made known to you." John 15:15 (NASB)

Over time, we begin to evaluate the people who have walked through our lives. Some came for a season, and when they left, we tried to pull them back in, thinking maybe we could pick up where we left off.

But here's the truth: once a puzzle piece leaves and comes back altered, it rarely fits the same. The edges have frayed. The shape has changed. You may try your hardest to make it fit again, but it's often futile.

As I've gotten older, I can see the handful of people who have smooth edges, those whose presence still fits seamlessly into my life. They don't force their way in, nor do they slip away at the first sign of trouble. They remain. Oh, what a gift that is.

That's the kind of relationship we should have with God, only His is even greater. In the heavenly realm, despite our frayed edges, He makes us fit perfectly into His grand design. He doesn't discard us. He doesn't say, "You're too broken to be used." He accepts us with our flaws, imperfections, and all.

When you have a friend like that, One who stays, covers you in grace, and calls you friend, do you need another?

Still, I thank God for the few He's placed in my life. I remember going to a friend, sobbing uncontrollably, and she didn't try to fix it. She just wrapped me in her arms and prayed, with tears in her own eyes. I remember another friend showing up at my door, seeing my tear-streaked face, and saying nothing, just being there.

That's authentic friendship. That's the "in it with you" kind of love.

So, dear friend, be prayerfully selective about who walks into your life. Let God show you who is meant to stay. Trust Him to remove those whose time is done gently. Only He can give the discernment to know the difference.

> **Prayer:**
> Lord, thank You for the gift of Your friendship—steady, forgiving, unchanging. Thank You also for the few You've allowed to walk with me through seasons of brokenness. Teach me to value what is real and release what no longer belongs. Help me discern the relationships You have ordained and recognize those You are calling me to let go of. Surround me with people who reflect Your heart, and make me that kind of friend to others. In Jesus' name, Amen.

SATURDAY

Held in His Palms

> *"Behold, I have inscribed you on the palms of My hands; Your walls are continually before Me." Isaiah 49:16 (NASB)*

As this week comes to a close, I want to remind you of something beautiful and true: God's palms are wide enough to hold all the broken pieces of your heart.

Every shattered moment. Every disappointment. Every quiet ache you've carried behind a strong front; He sees it all, and He holds it tenderly.

Give it all to Jesus.

Your hope isn't in circumstances, relationships, or recognition. Those things can be blessings, yes, but they are also temporary. The only unshakable hope is found in Him.

Don't get me wrong, form healthy relationships. Love well. Build community. But don't let those become your "be all." They were never meant to carry the weight of your soul.

Only One can do that.

Your Heavenly Father knows how to hold what others have dropped. He sees what no one else can. While the healing might not come overnight, His hands are steady. His touch is gentle. He knows how to piece you back together, one sacred fragment at a time.

So rest tonight in the truth that you are not forgotten, and you are never too broken for His hands.

SUNDAY: *Coming to Your House*

> **Prayer:**
> *Lord, I surrender the broken pieces of my heart into Your open, nail-scarred hands. Thank You for holding what the world couldn't handle. Teach me to build relationships without placing my hope in them. Help me rest in the knowledge that Your love never fails, and that You are quietly, patiently, piecing me back together. In Jesus' name, Amen.*

 SUNDAY

Coming to Your House

> *"I was glad when they said to me, 'Let's go to the house of the Lord.'"*
> *Psalm 122:1 (NASB)*

Today is Sunday. Lord, I come to Your House, not out of habit, not out of duty, but because my soul needs it.

I come to find peace in Your presence.

I come to be reminded that I'm not alone.

I come to lay down the week behind me and lift up the name that carried me through it—Your name.

This week may have left some marks. Maybe it brought moments of weariness, confusion, or tears. But here I am, standing in Your courts, reminded that no matter how shaky my week felt, Your presence is steady. Your truth is still firm. Your love still surrounds me.

In Your house, I find refuge.

In Your house, I find renewal.

In Your house, I am reminded of who I am and whose I am.

So I come, just as I am. With praise on my lips and hope in my heart.

> **Prayer:**
> *Lord, thank You for the gift of Your presence and the privilege of gathering in Your house today. Meet me here. Speak to my heart. Quiet every distraction and lift my spirit. I need You more than anything this world can offer. Refresh me, restore me, and fill me anew for the week ahead. In Jesus' name, Amen.*

WEEK 7

MONDAY

You Are Not Alone

> *"Be strong and courageous. Do not be afraid or terrified because of them, for the Lord your God goes with you; He will never leave you nor forsake you." Deuteronomy 31:6 (NIV)*

Several things were weighing heavily on me, and sleep didn't come easily. I tossed and turned, waking up often, heart heavy with worry. But when morning finally came, God met me most unexpectedly through a song by Casting Crowns. The first lyrics I heard as I started my day were:

Oh, my soul, oh how you worry
Oh, how you're weary from fearing you lost control…
One more day, He will make a way.
Let Him show you how, you can lay this down
'Cause you're not alone.

Those words landed like a balm on my soul.

God has so many ways of reaching us. That day, He used music, right on time, right where I needed it. I had tasted His love before. I knew His promises. But sometimes, circumstances can cloud what we know to be true.

In those moments, we need gentle reminders:
We are not alone.
We are not forgotten.
We are not unseen.

God is always near. He steps into our situations, sometimes through a verse, a friend's text, a sunrise, or even a lyric on the radio. He knows exactly how to reach our tired, anxious hearts.

MONDAY: *You Are Not Alone*

So if you're feeling alone today, pause and listen. His presence may already be whispering comfort in ways you didn't expect.

> **Prayer:**
> *Lord, thank You for reminding me that I am never alone. Even when sleep escapes me and fear creeps in, You are with me. Help me recognize Your presence in the small moments and receive Your peace. In Jesus' name, Amen.*

TUESDAY

Red Lights and Stop Signs

"He has made everything beautiful in its time." Ecclesiastes 3:11 (NKJV)

Everyone has dreams. Some are big and bold, others are quiet longings we carry deep in our hearts. But the problem is, dreams don't always materialize right away. We live in a world of instant gratification, and when God seems slow to move, we grow anxious, discouraged... maybe even frustrated.

Along the journey to fulfillment, God often allows red lights and stop signs—delays, closed doors, detours, and unexpected setbacks.

Have you been seeing red lights everywhere?

Does it feel like every step forward is met with another stop?

Just wait.

That red light isn't rejection; it's redirection. That stop sign isn't punishment, it's protection. God's timing is never random. It's always intentional, even when it's invisible to us.

Ecclesiastes 3:11 reminds us of a powerful truth: "He makes everything beautiful in its time." Not in our time. In His.

So don't rush. Don't force. Don't abandon your hope just because it's taking longer than expected. In the hands of the Master Planner, even waiting has purpose.

> **Prayer:**
> Lord, give me the patience to wait on Your perfect timing. Help me not to rush ahead of You or interpret delays as denials. Let me trust that You are making all things beautiful—even in the waiting. In Jesus' name, Amen.

WEDNESDAY

Don't Withhold Good

> *"And do not neglect doing good and sharing, for with such sacrifices God is pleased."* Hebrews 13:16 (NASB)

At home, I often say, "God hasn't given you this intelligence so you can keep it tucked away." Whether in the office or the kitchen, I've noticed how people sometimes withhold knowledge, not out of malice, but out of insecurity or pride.

In the workplace, it's: "What if they get the credit instead of me?"

In the kitchen, it's: "What if she takes the glory for my recipe?"

But here's the truth: If you remember the Source of your gifts, you won't withhold.

Everything we have—our skills, knowledge, talents, and creativity—comes from God. He didn't bless you just so you could keep it all to yourself. He blesses us so we can be a blessing.

Sharing what you know doesn't diminish your value; it multiplies your impact.

Don't let fear or pride keep you from encouraging others. Teach someone. Share freely. Lift others up. Let generosity flow not just from your wallet, but from your wisdom, your time, and your words, because God sees the unseen sacrifices, and He is pleased.

> **Prayer:**
> Father, help me to freely share the gifts You've given me, knowing that every good thing comes from You. Remove any pride or insecurity that tempts me to

> *withhold. Let me be generous with what I know and intentional in building others up. In Jesus' name, Amen.*

THURSDAY

When God Closes the Door

"Rest in the Lord and wait patiently for Him…" Psalm 37:7 (NASB)

"For My thoughts are not your thoughts, nor are your ways My ways," declares the Lord. "For as the heavens are higher than the earth, so are My ways higher than your ways." Isaiah 55:8-9 (NASB)

Children and adults alike, we want things now. We're programmed for instant results. One-click purchases. Instant downloads. Microwave timelines.

But sometimes, God closes a door we were sure would swing open.

A job we wanted. A relationship we hoped for. A dream that seemed just within reach. And instead of an open door, we get silence… or a slammed one.

Our first instinct? Try to force it. Push harder. Make it happen. But when we bang on closed doors, we reveal something deeper: a heart that struggles to yield.

God isn't punishing us with closed doors; He's redirecting us, protecting us, and preparing us.

Isaiah reminds us that His ways are higher than ours. That means His "no" or "not yet" is rooted in a wisdom far beyond what we can see.

So today, if you're standing in front of a closed door, pause. Breathe. Let go. Trust that He sees the full blueprint, and you don't have to pry your way into His plan.

> **Prayer:**
> Lord, help me to stop banging on closed doors and trust Your divine detours. I surrender my timeline, my expectations, and my need for control. Lead me according to Your perfect will. In Jesus' name, Amen.

FRIDAY

Give the Day Back

> *"Commit your works to the Lord, and your plans will be established."*
> *Proverbs 16:3 (NASB)*

Many of us wake up and say, "Thank You, Lord, for a new day."

But how often do we go a step further to give that day back to Him?

It's one thing to acknowledge the gift of a new day. It's another to surrender it.

What would it look like if, before checking our calendars or to-do lists, we paused and said,

"Lord, here is my day. You steer it. If I take control, I'll make wrong turns. But if You navigate, I'll walk in Your shadow—under Your protection, peace, and provision."

Giving the day back is about giving Him full authority over our schedule, our thoughts, our plans, and even our interruptions. It's acknowledging that His way is always better, even when it reroutes ours. We're truly blessed to be called His children. Like a good Father, He wants to guide us, not just in life's major decisions, but in the ordinary steps of today.

> **Prayer:**
> Lord, I give this day to You. Take the lead. Let my every step align with Your will and purpose. May my plans be established by Your hand, not mine. In Jesus' name, Amen.

SATURDAY

Extraordinary in the Ordinary

"Be kind to one another, compassionate, forgiving each other, just as God in Christ also has forgiven you." Ephesians 4:32 (NASB)

Elder David A. Bednar once said,

> "Ordinary people who faithfully, diligently, and consistently do simple things that are right before God will bring forth extraordinary results."

We often long for big moments—platforms, recognition, visible impact. But God often works through what seems small: a kind word, a quiet prayer, an unnoticed act of service.

The world may never applaud these things, but heaven does.

Glory fades. Awards gather dust. Recognition is fleeting.

But the eyes of our Heavenly Father never miss a single good deed.

He sees you when you choose kindness over criticism.

He sees the compassion you show behind closed doors.

He sees when you forgive quietly and love unconditionally.

These things may seem ordinary, but they echo in eternity.

So keep going. Keep sowing seeds of grace. Keep being faithful in the simple, sacred things.

Prayer:
Father, remind me that what I do in secret, You reward openly. Help me to remain faithful in the small things, knowing they matter deeply to You. In Jesus' name, Amen.

SUNDAY

Rest and Worship

"Let us not give up meeting together, as some are in the habit of doing, but encouraging one another…" Hebrews 10:25 (NIV)

Sundays are a gift. A holy pause in our busy lives.

Go to church. Be in community. Worship. Recharge.

There is something powerful about being with other believers—hearing the Word, singing praises, and fellowshipping with people who can pray with you and for you. Don't miss it.

Prayer:
Lord, thank You for setting apart a day for rest and worship. Help me not neglect the joy of being with fellow believers. Amen.

WEEK 8

Monday

Prompted to pray

> *"Therefore, confess your sins to one another, and pray for one another so that you may be healed. A prayer of a righteous person, when it is brought about, can accomplish much." James 5:16 (NASB)*

Who is in your mind today? When someone's face or name pops into your head, take a few seconds to pray for that individual. I really feel that it is the Holy Spirit bringing that name to your attention. Just one example, one night I was so restless and my colleague's name popped into my head, and her marriage. By then, she was married to this person for 25 years. I prayed and went to work. Long story short, I stopped by her office and casually mentioned to her about my restlessness. She said, "Please continue to pray. My husband is cheating on me."

Another time, God knocked on the door of my heart around 1:30 a.m. and told me to pray for this young man. I didn't know what specific prayers I was praying for. But I prayed. In the morning, I called the mother and told her about praying for her son, and she said, "Please continue to pray. My son is struggling." I'm like, wow, God. You used this broken vessel to pray for someone with such deep need.

Not bragging at all, I just wanted to give you an example. When someone's name pops into your head, take a moment to pray. You may not know the need, just pray.

Prayer:
Lord, help me be sensitive to the prompting of Your Spirit. May I be quick to intercede, even when I don't understand the need. Use me as a vessel for Your mercy. Amen.

TUESDAY

But for Him

> *"So that you will walk in a manner worthy of the Lord, to please Him in all respects, bearing fruit in every good work and increasing in the knowledge of God; strengthened with all power, according to His glorious might, for the attaining of all perseverance and patience; joyously giving thanks to the Father, who has qualified us to share in the inheritance of the saints in light." Colossians 1:10-12 (NASB)*

We just returned from a mini vacation, and my heart was filled with gratitude.

Gratitude for the ability to get away.
Gratitude for the provisions to make it possible.
Gratitude for safety, health, rest, and all the little joys along the way.
As I reflected on the trip, one phrase kept rising to the surface:
But for Him.
But for Him, we wouldn't have had the strength to go.
But for Him, we wouldn't have the means to enjoy a break.
But for Him, we wouldn't have the peace we so often take for granted.

That simple phrase, "But for Him," became a theme for my heart. And truly, it can be the refrain of every believer's life. We can apply it to every blessing, every trial we've survived, every breakthrough, every moment of grace.

But for Him… we wouldn't be here.

When we live with that perspective, everything changes. Gratitude fills our hearts. Peace anchors us. Joy bubbles up in even the most ordinary moments.

So today, let your word be: But for Him.

Let those three words shape your thoughts, your praise, and your perspective.

WEDNESDAY: *Keep It Real*

> **Prayer:**
> Lord, every good and perfect gift comes from You. Thank You for Your covering, Your provision, and Your unshakable peace. May my heart overflow with gratitude, not just for the big things, but for every moment made possible by You. In Jesus' name, Amen.

WEDNESDAY

Keep It Real

> *"And the peace of God, which surpasses all comprehension, will guard your hearts and minds in Christ Jesus. Finally, brothers and sisters, whatever is true, whatever is honorable, whatever is right, whatever is pure, whatever is lovely, whatever is commendable—if there is any excellence and if anything worthy of praise, think about these things." Philippians 4:7-8 (NASB)*

One of my pet peeves? The way society trains us to be overly diplomatic and politically correct, sometimes to the point of losing our authenticity.

We smile politely, give filtered answers, and tiptoe around the truth to avoid discomfort. In doing so, we risk becoming mirrors covered in smoke, reflecting nothing.

Why can't we just be real?

My kids often say, "There's no mincing words with my mom." I laugh, but it's true. I believe in being straightforward with love, yes, but without pretending. Because when we're honest, transparent, and real, trust is built. More importantly, we reflect Christ, who is truth itself.

Paul challenges us to think on what is true and honorable. That includes how we speak and live. Being "real" doesn't mean being harsh; it means aligning our words and actions with what is true, even when it's hard.

Let's keep it real in our conversations, our confessions, our faith, and our witness. The world doesn't need more polished perfection. It needs truth wrapped in grace.

> **Prayer:**
> *Father, help me walk in truth—with You, with others, and with myself. Teach me to speak the truth in love and reflect the sincerity of Christ. May my words be honest, my heart authentic, and my life aligned with Your truth. In Jesus' name, Amen.*

THURSDAY

Eternity Is Long

"For what does it benefit a person to gain the whole world, and forfeit his soul?" Mark 8:36 (NASB)

We say it all the time: Life is short, better enjoy it.
But what if we shifted our mindset to this:
"Eternity is long; better prepare for it."
That quote stopped me in my tracks. Because it's true. Life on earth is a blink compared to eternity. Yet, how often do we share the gospel with our loved ones who don't know Jesus?
We want our relationship to last forever. But the hard truth is, without Christ, they won't.
We may love deeply, but love alone doesn't save; Jesus does.
Think of two people in your life who don't yet know Christ. What if you are the one God has placed in their path to plant the seed, to water it, or to help bring the harvest?
Let's carry the baton with love and boldness. Let's speak when God opens the door and live in such a way that our lives make people curious about the hope we carry.
Because eternity is long.
And nothing—nothing—matters more than where a soul will spend it.

> **Prayer:**
> Lord, break my heart for those who don't know You. Give me the courage to speak the truth and the wisdom to live out the gospel with grace. Use me to reflect Your love and extend the invitation of salvation. In Jesus' name, Amen.

Friday

Let Go of the Branch

> *"But those who wait for the Lord will gain new strength; They will mount up with wings like eagles, they will run, not get tired, They will walk and not become weary." Isaiah 40:31 (NASB)*

A bird doesn't learn to soar by clinging to the branch. As long as it stays perched, it may feel safe, but it will never fly.

Sometimes God asks us to release our grip on what's familiar. He calls us out of our comfort zones so we can experience the lift of His Spirit. It feels risky. Unstable. But faith often begins where comfort ends.

You weren't created to cling. You were created to soar.

Is there a branch you're holding onto? A place where fear has kept you grounded? Trust that God's wind will carry you when you take that leap of obedience.

> **Prayer:**
> Lord, give me the courage to let go of what's holding me back and the faith to believe You'll catch me. Help me trade security for surrender, and comfort for calling. In Your strength, I will rise. Amen.

SATURDAY

Decluttered Vision

> *"...fixing our eyes on Jesus, the author and perfecter of faith..."*
> *Hebrews 12:2 (NASB)*

Have you ever opened too many apps on your phone and noticed how slow it gets? That's what happens to our minds when we're juggling too many thoughts, distractions, and anxieties. Focus becomes fuzzy. Peace slips away. Priorities blur.

Sometimes it's not about adding more Scripture, more prayer time, or more spiritual "to-dos"—it's about removing the distractions that compete for our attention.

What's crowding your spiritual focus right now? What apps need closing in your heart? When we clear the background noise, we can lock our gaze fully on Jesus and walk with clarity and purpose.

Prayer:
Lord, help me fix my eyes on You. Quiet the noise around me and within me. Clear away the distractions so I can hear Your voice and follow You without hesitation. Amen.

SUNDAY

A Day to Refocus

> *"This is the day that the Lord has made; Let us rejoice and be glad in it."* *Psalm 118:24 (NASB)*

Broken Hearts Held by God: Week 8

Sunday: *A Day to Refocus*

Sunday is more than just the end of the week; it's the beginning of your next chapter. It's a reset. A divine pit stop to fuel your spirit before life picks up again on Monday.

Gather with fellow believers. Soak in the Word. Sing out your praise. Be still in His presence.

Let today be your reminder that no matter what last week held, God is giving you a fresh page. So go to church, be encouraged, and carry His peace into the week ahead.

> **Prayer:**
> *Father, thank You for Sundays. Thank You for quiet moments, joyful songs, and the blessing of community. Let today mark the start of a week filled with Your purpose. Amen.*

WEEK 9

MONDAY

Insulated by Christ

"I am not asking You to take them out of the world, but to keep them away from the evil one." John 17:15 (NASB)

When a hurricane is on the way, people prepare their homes with urgency, boarding up windows, sealing doors, and reinforcing weak spots. The goal? Protection. They know the storm is coming, but they also know preparation can make all the difference.

In the same way, insulation keeps a home secure against external temperatures, keeping what's inside stable, regardless of what's raging outside.

That's the image we're leaning into today. Insulation.

Jesus, in His high priestly prayer, doesn't ask the Father to remove us from the world. He knew we'd have to walk through storms, face trials, and confront evil. Instead, He asked that we be protected, not from life, but from the enemy's grip. That's divine insulation.

In a world filled with noise, chaos, temptation, and pressure, we are not left exposed. Christ Himself wraps around us like spiritual insulation, guarding our minds, steadying our hearts, and sealing us in His peace.

This doesn't mean we won't feel the wind or hear the roar of the storm—but it means we won't be destroyed by it. Because we're not just surrounded by circumstances; we're insulated by Christ.

So today, no matter what pressure comes your way, remember who surrounds you. He is your covering, your strength, and your safety. You are not fragile. You are fortified.

TUESDAY: *Check Your Signal*

> **Prayer:**
> Lord, thank You for being my insulation against the storms of life. While I may be in the world, I am not of it, and I am not alone. Keep me steady, protected, and wrapped in Your presence. In You, I am safe. Amen.

TUESDAY

Check Your Signal

> *"Arise, shine; for your light has come, and the glory of the Lord has risen upon you." Isaiah 60:1 (NASB)*

We've all experienced that moment of frustration—standing in a remote area, phone in hand, searching for a stronger signal. The battery is full, but the bar at the top barely registers one tiny line. We move around, hold the phone higher, step outside, all in an effort to reconnect.

Signal loss reminds us that even the best man-made systems are limited. They rely on towers, networks, and external factors that can fail at any time.

But here's the good news: our connection with Christ is not like that. His signal never weakens. His line is never busy. His presence is never out of range.

And yet, even though His signal is constant, we can become disconnected. Not because He moves, but because we do. We get distracted. We drift. We forget to check in.

Isaiah 60:1 tells us to "Arise, shine; for your light has come." The Light has already come—Christ is here, and the glory of the Lord is available to shine through us. But to shine, we must stay connected to the Source.

Before you rush into the demands of your day, pause and check your spiritual signal. Are you drawing strength from Him? Is your heart tuned to His voice? Are you intentionally connecting through prayer, worship, and time in His Word?

Unlike a cell tower, God's presence doesn't fade in remote places. In fact, it often grows strongest in the quiet, the isolated, the still moments. But it requires us to pause, reach up, and reconnect.

Don't start your day with a weak signal. You were meant to shine.

> **Prayer:**
> *Jesus, thank You that Your presence never fades. Help me begin each day by connecting to You, through prayer, worship, and Your Word. Keep my heart attuned to Your voice and my life aligned with Your will. Let me carry Your light into every place I go. Amen.*

WEDNESDAY

Stay Close to the Shepherd

> *"Know that the Lord Himself is God; it is He who has made us, and not we ourselves; we are His people and the sheep of His pasture."*
> Psalm 100:3 (NASB)

Do you remember the Disney movie where Simba and Nala wander away from the protected territory, despite their father's warning? They were curious. Adventurous. But outside the boundaries of safety, danger came quickly—ravenous hyenas waiting to pounce. What looked like harmless fun turned into a brush with disaster.

We're not so different, are we?

Sometimes we wander from the Shepherd's voice, not always out of rebellion, but distraction. We follow what looks exciting, what feels freeing, what seems harmless... until we find ourselves in unfamiliar territory. Vulnerable. Exposed.

But we have a Shepherd who doesn't just warn us; He rescues us. He leads us beside still waters. He calls us by name. He reminds us that true freedom is not found outside the fold, but within His care.

Wednesday: *Stay Close to the Shepherd*

He is our fortress, deliverer, rock, shield, and safe refuge. Let's know our place in the pen, not as prisoners, but as beloved sheep under the watchful care of the Good Shepherd.

> **Prayer:**
> Shepherd of my soul, keep me close to You. When I wander, call me back. When I'm tempted to stray, remind me of Your goodness. May I never leave the safety of Your arms. Amen.

THURSDAY

Walk in His Strength

> *"Do not be anxious about anything, but in everything by prayer and pleading with thanksgiving let your requests be made known to God. And the peace of God, which surpasses all comprehension, will guard your hearts and minds in Christ Jesus." Philippians 4:6-7 (NASB)*

Have you ever felt like a deflated balloon, drained, weary, stretched too thin? You wake up already exhausted, and before the day has truly begun, you're wondering how you'll make it through.

Life has a way of pressing in. Unexpected news. Demands that pile up. Worry that whispers in the background. On days like that, your strength may feel like it's running on fumes. But that's exactly where God meets us, not in our perfection or performance, but in our need.

Philippians 4 invites us to bring everything to God. Not just the big things. Everything. Through prayer and thanksgiving, we are invited to offload our anxiety, our fears, and our burdens. And in exchange? He gives us peace—a peace that goes beyond our understanding. A peace that guards not just our hearts, but also our minds.

You weren't meant to carry the weight of the world on your shoulders. You were meant to walk in His strength.

So if today feels like too much, pause and breathe. Whisper your worries to the One who can handle them. Invite Him to walk with you into every room, every meeting, every moment. Let His peace do the guarding, and His power do the lifting.

> **Prayer:**
> *God, You know the weight I'm carrying today. I bring it all to You—my fears, my fatigue, my frustrations. Fill my heart with Your peace and renew my strength. Help me walk forward not in my own ability, but in Your unfailing power. Amen.*

FRIDAY

Be Persistent

> *"But as for me, I will be on the watch for the Lord; I will wait for the God of my salvation. My God will hear me." Micah 7:7 (NASB)*

Is your heart weighed down with failed dreams, closed doors, or quiet prayers that seem to echo into nothingness? We've all been there watching and waiting, wondering if God hears, if He sees, if He's forgotten.

But Micah's declaration is powerful: "My God will hear me."

This is not the voice of someone who has seen the answer; it's the voice of someone who has chosen to believe anyway. That's what real faith looks like.

God's silence is never apathy. He is not idle or indifferent. Like a master artist behind the curtain, He is orchestrating something beautiful in the unseen. He doesn't always give us the timeline, but He always gives us His presence.

Remember the persistent widow in Luke 18? She didn't stop knocking. And Jesus praised her tenacity, not because God is like the unjust judge, but because our persistence is an act of trust. We knock because we know someone's on the other side of the door.

FRIDAY: *Be Persistent*

So keep praying. Keep believing. Keep showing up, even when heaven feels quiet.

> **Prayer:**
> *Father, strengthen me to wait patiently and persistently. When I don't see the answers and when Your voice feels far, remind me that You are near. My hope is in You, and I trust that You hear me. Amen.*

SATURDAY

You Are Valued

> *"Are five sparrows not sold for two assaria? And yet not one of them has gone unnoticed... even the hairs of your head are all counted. Do not fear; you are more valuable than a great number of sparrows."*
> Luke 12:6–7 (NASB)

How deeply known are you?

Not casually. Not occasionally. But intimately—intentionally.

So much so that God has numbered every strand of hair on your head. Not one sparrow falls to the ground without His notice. And yet, Jesus says, you are worth far more.

In a world that often measures worth by productivity, popularity, or perfection, God's scale is entirely different. He values you not because of what you do but because of who you are—His.

You are not overlooked. You are not forgotten. You are loved by the One who created galaxies and still chooses to count your every detail.

So when insecurity whispers, when rejection stings, when comparison steals your joy, remember: You are seen. You are known. You are cherished. Just as you are.

> **Prayer:**
> Lord, thank You that I am seen, known, and valued by You. When the world makes me question my worth, let Your truth anchor my soul and remind me who I am in You. Amen.

SUNDAY

The Power of Gathering

> *"And let us consider how to encourage one another in love and good deeds, not abandoning our own meeting together, as is the habit of some, but encouraging one another." Hebrews 10:24-25 (NASB)*

Sunday is a sacred invitation to pause, to gather, and to worship.

As you prepare your heart today, remember the importance of coming together with other believers. There's something beautiful about lifting your voice in worship alongside others, sitting under the Word, and letting God refresh your spirit through fellowship. Church is not just a building; it's a body. And you are a vital part of it.

So find your place, settle in, and be present in God's house.

> **Prayer:**
> Lord, thank You for the gift of the church, a place to grow, to serve, and to be renewed. Help me enter Your presence with gratitude and expectation. Amen

WEEK 10

Monday

Clear Your Heart's Cache

> *"I have set the Lord continually before me; Because He is at my right hand, I will not be shaken. Therefore my heart is glad and my glory rejoices; My flesh also will dwell securely." Psalm 16:8-9 (NASB)*

Let's talk tech for a moment. You know how your phone slows down when the storage is full? The apps freeze, the battery drains fast, and even opening your camera feels like a chore. What do we do? We clear the cache. We delete old photos, close unused apps, and give it a reset.

Our hearts are no different. Unpleasant memories, spiritual distractions, lingering guilt, bitterness, or even busyness, we carry more emotional and spiritual clutter than we realize. And when our hearts are full of all that, it clogs our connection with God.

Today, take a moment to ask: What do I need to delete from my heart's memory bank? Maybe it's fear. Maybe it's a comparison. Maybe it's yesterday's pain. Set the Lord continually before you, as the Psalm says. Make space for His presence.

Prayer:
Lord, help me clear the clutter from my heart today—emotional baggage, spiritual distractions, anything that blocks my connection with You. I want my heart to be light, my soul to rejoice, and my spirit to dwell securely in You. Amen.

TUESDAY

Insulated by Grace

> *"And do not be conformed to this world, but be transformed by the renewing of your mind..." Romans 12:2 (NASB)*

When a storm approaches, homeowners rush to prepare—boarding up windows, securing objects, checking insulation. Why? Because insulation protects. It keeps the home from being overtaken by the elements.

In the same way, grace is our spiritual insulation. We may not avoid the storm, but we can remain safe in it. The winds of culture may blow, the pressure of life may rage, but when our hearts are wrapped in Christ, we remain secure.

Don't be conformed, don't let the storm outside define what's going on inside. Let God renew your mind and insulate your spirit today with His truth, love, and peace.

Prayer:
Jesus, thank You for being my covering, my safe place, and my strength. When the pressures of the world close in, help me remain steadfast in You. Keep me anchored in Your Word and insulated by Your grace. Amen.

WEDNESDAY

Strengthening the Signal

> *"In the morning, Lord, You will hear my voice..." Psalm 5:3 (NASB)*

BROKEN HEARTS HELD BY GOD: Week 10

WEDNESDAY: *Strengthening the Signal*

> *"Man shall not live on bread alone, but on every word that comes out of the mouth of God." Matthew 4:4 (NASB)*

Have you ever been in a place where your phone signal was weak? Calls drop, texts don't go through, and your connection to the world feels interrupted. Sometimes, our spiritual lives feel like that too - patchy, disconnected, inconsistent.

A strong connection requires intentional alignment. It means starting the day by checking in with the One who gives us strength. Before breakfast, before emails, before scrolling, let God hear your voice.

Feed your spirit just like you feed your body. Without it, you're operating on empty.

Make space for that early morning connection, and your entire day will shift. His voice will guide, His Word will sustain, and His Spirit will strengthen you.

Prayer:
Lord, let my signal to You be strong and unwavering today. Tune my ears to Your voice. Feed my soul with Your Word and empower me to walk in Your strength. Amen.

THURSDAY

The Crushing That Refines

> *"I will bring the third part through the fire, refine them as silver is refined, and test them as gold is tested..." Zechariah 13:9 (NASB)*

During a trip to Bethany, I watched olives being crushed to release their oil, grapes crushed to yield wine, and gold being passed through fire to be purified. What struck me was that nothing precious comes without pressure.

THURSDAY: *The Crushing That Refines*

We don't like the crushing. We avoid the fire. But in God's hands, these moments are sacred. He doesn't crush to destroy; He crushes to refine. He doesn't burn to punish - He burns away what doesn't belong.

If you're in a season of pressure, pain, or pruning, take heart. God is producing something beautiful. The oil, the wine, the purity - it all comes through the process.

> **Prayer:**
> *Refining God, I may not understand this season, but I trust that You are working through it. Shape me, purify me, and use me for Your glory. Help me embrace the crushing, knowing it leads to something far greater. Amen.*

FRIDAY

Mindful of Me

> *"What is man that You are mindful of him?"* Psalm 8:4 (NKJV)

I woke up this morning with a heart full of praise. Not because something extraordinary happened, but simply because I was struck by this truth: God is mindful of me.

Pause and let that sink in.

The Creator of the universe, the One who holds galaxies in His hands, thinks of you. He sees you. He knows you. He remembers your name, your burdens, your dreams.

You are not overlooked. You are not forgotten. You are loved with an everlasting love that doesn't shift based on your performance. Just like the Psalmist, we too can stand in awe—Who am I, Lord, that You would be so mindful of me?

SATURDAY: *Quiet Time with God*

> **Prayer:**
> *Lord, thank You that I am always on Your mind. Your love is steady, personal, and never-ending. May I live today fully aware of how deeply I am known and loved by You. Amen.*

SATURDAY

Quiet Time with God

"A time to be silent and a time to speak." Ecclesiastes 3:7 (NASB)

Our days are filled with noise—notifications, conversations, decisions, responsibilities. But God often speaks the loudest in the quiet.

My favorite moments are early mornings with a cup of coffee in hand, the world still asleep, and my Bible open. No rush. No to-do list. Just me and God. In those moments, my heart breathes again.

Stillness is not a waste of time; it's a sacred invitation. Silence is not empty; it's filled with His presence.

Find your quiet today. Let it restore your soul. God still whispers, Be still and know that I am God.

> **Prayer:**
> *God, meet me in the quiet today. Let Your peace fill the silence and Your presence calm my spirit. Teach me to cherish the stillness where You speak. Amen.*

SUNDAY

Worship and Fellowship

> *"I was glad when they said to me, 'Let's go to the house of the Lord.'"*
> *Psalm 122:1 (NASB)*

There's something sacred about Sunday mornings — the intentional pause, the gathering of God's people, the lifting of voices in praise, the Word going forth, and the reminder that we're not walking this journey alone.

Scripture encourages us not to forsake assembling together (Hebrews 10:25), and there's a reason for that. In a world that constantly pulls us in every direction, corporate worship centers us. It realigns our priorities, refreshes our spirit, and reminds us of the bigger picture — God is on the throne, and we are part of His body.

Church isn't just a building; it's a lifeline. It's where iron sharpens iron, where burdens are shared, where joy is multiplied, and where we get a glimpse of heaven on earth.

This morning, don't let sleep, schedules, or excuses rob you of what God wants to deposit in your spirit. Go to His house, not just out of habit, but with expectation. The pew you sit in today might be the place God chooses to speak directly to your heart.

Prayer:
Lord, thank You for the gift of Sunday, for fellowship, for worship, and for the church. Help me not to treat it casually but to value it deeply. I come with an open heart today, ready to meet with You.

WEEK 11

MONDAY

The Gift Found in Stillness

"Stop striving and know that I am God." Psalm 46:10a (NASB)

Brokenness isn't something we seek—but it often becomes the place where God speaks the loudest. When life cracks open our strength, and striving comes to a halt, we're finally quiet enough to hear Him. No more performing. No more pretending. Just stillness… and surrender.

It's in those moments—where we have nothing left to offer but our honesty—that His presence becomes undeniable.

God doesn't scold us in our weakness. He doesn't meet us with frustration or disappointment. Instead, He enters softly, with healing in His hands and compassion in His voice. He reminds us: You don't have to hold it all together. I'm here. I've got you.

The stillness isn't empty. It's full of grace.

When we stop striving, we start receiving. And in the quietness of surrender, we discover a truth that changes everything: His love has never depended on our strength—only on His mercy.

Prayer:
Lord, in my brokenness, meet me with Your grip of love. Quiet my heart, still my soul, and help me rest in the truth that You are God. Let me feel Your nearness and trust Your promises again. Amen.

TUESDAY

When Cracks Invite His Strength

"But the Lord stood with me and strengthened me." 2 Timothy 4:17 (NASB)

Are there cracks in your heart—those quiet places where pain seeps in like water through a fracture? Sometimes it doesn't take much. A word spoken in anger. A closed door. A disappointment that lingers. All it takes is a sliver—and left unchecked, those cracks can grow. Slowly. Silently. Making room for fear, discouragement, or bitterness to settle in.

But here's the hope: You are not abandoned to your brokenness.

Paul, writing from prison, said, "The Lord stood with me and strengthened me." Not when things were easy—but in isolation. In need. In weakness.

That's our God. He doesn't walk away when we fracture. He steps in. He fills the gaps with grace. He doesn't just bind the wound—He becomes the strength we lack.

You don't have to patch yourself back together alone. The world may see cracks, but God sees an opportunity to pour in His power.

Prayer:
Lord, seal the cracks in my heart with Your peace. Let not the world seep in, but Your love overflow in me. When I am weak, be my strength. When I am broken, be my healer. Amen.

WEDNESDAY

You Are Wonderfully Made

> *"I will give thanks to You, because I am awesomely and wonderfully made; Wonderful are Your works, And my soul knows it very well."*
> *Psalm 139:14 (NASB)*

Some mornings begin with stillness—no rushing, no chaos, just a warm cup of coffee and a moment to breathe. But even on the calmest days, there's often a quiet current of self-doubt: Am I doing enough? Am I making a difference? Am I enough?

Psalm 139 quiets that swirl of insecurity with a bold, sacred truth: You are fearfully and wonderfully made.

You were crafted with care—knit together by the very hands that hung the stars. Every detail, every thread of your being, was intentionally designed by God. Even when the world's standards shout that you need to do more or be more, your identity remains unshaken. You are His. That's enough.

So lift your head—not in pride, but in confidence. You are the child of the King. Walk in the truth of who you already are.

Prayer:
Father, thank You for creating me with purpose. When self-doubt creeps in, remind me whose daughter I am. Help me walk in the strength and beauty You've placed within me. Amen.

THURSDAY

A Covenant That Cannot Be Shaken

> *"For the mountains may be removed and the hills may shake,*
> *But My favor will not be removed from you,*
> *Nor will My covenant of peace be shaken,"*
> *Says the Lord who has compassion on you."* Isaiah 54:10 (NASB)

Lately, our church has been immersed in teachings about covenant and commitment—what it truly means to be unwavering in our word, especially before God. And it's challenged me deeply.

Because life? It's anything but steady.

Mountains move. Hills shake. People shift. Promises are broken. Plans unravel.

But not with God. His covenant is anchored in His nature—not in our performance, not in our emotions, not in our ability to hold it all together. His peace remains, even when everything else feels uncertain. His favor stays, even when we feel undeserving.

That's the beauty of covenant. It's not a contract that can be canceled—it's a commitment rooted in compassion and faithfulness.

And as He is faithful, He calls us to reflect that faithfulness. To let our "yes" before Him carry weight. To treat our promises not as casual agreements, but as sacred declarations before a holy God.

So today, whether you're clinging to one of God's promises or reflecting on your own vows before Him—remember, He is the covenant-keeper. And He's calling us to mirror that steadfastness in return.

Prayer:
God, help me to be faithful to the covenants I make before You. Let my word be holy, my promises sincere, and my heart anchored in Your unshakable peace. Amen.

FRIDAY

Keepers of the Covenant

> *"But the mercy of the Lord is from everlasting to everlasting for those who fear Him, And His justice to the children's children, To those who keep His covenant And remember His precepts, so as to do them."*
> *Psalm 103:17–18 (NASB)*

Maybe I didn't fully grasp the seriousness of keeping a covenant.

Maybe, like many of us, I thought I could coast on good intentions.

But God, in His mercy, gave me a chance to learn—not to punish, but to remind.

Covenants matter to Him. They always have.

God doesn't forget His promises. And He calls us to mirror that faithfulness—not just in word, but in action. He honors those who keep His covenant and remember His precepts so as to do them. Not just to memorize them, quote them, or nod along on Sundays—but to live them out.

His mercy, thankfully, is from everlasting to everlasting. He doesn't write us off when we fall short. But He does call us to rise higher—to take our commitments seriously, especially those made in His name.

So today, if you've made a vow to the Lord—spoken or silent—ask yourself: Am I living it? And if not, ask Him for the grace to start again.

Prayer:
Lord, forgive my forgetfulness. Remind me of every promise I've made before You. Help me honor every vow, living each day in full-hearted commitment. Amen.

Saturday

Commit and be Established

"Commit your works to the Lord, And your plans will be established." Proverbs 16:3 (NASB)

As I came down this morning, the aroma of coffee filled the air—and so did a quiet reminder from God's Word. Just one simple verse caught my eye: "Commit your works to the Lord…" And suddenly, I was fully awake—spiritually and physically.

How often do we charge into the day with our own plans, mapping out every detail, trying to steer the ship of our lives with precision? But today's verse invites us to a better way: to place our efforts in God's hands first, not last.

When we commit our works to Him, it's not about abandoning our responsibilities—it's about surrendering control. It's about acknowledging that no matter how detailed our calendar is, only God can establish what truly matters.

So before the to-do list takes over, take a moment to commit it all to the One who sees the full picture. Let Him steer. Let Him establish.

Prayer:
God, today I place my plans in Your hands. Steer the boat of my life, and I will rest in Your direction. Amen.

Sunday: *The Power of Gathering*

 SUNDAY

The Power of Gathering

> *"And let us consider how to encourage one another in love and good deeds, not abandoning our own meeting together, as is the habit of some, but encouraging one another." — Hebrews 10:24–25 (NASB)*

Sunday is a sacred invitation — to pause, to gather, to worship.

As you prepare your heart today, remember the importance of coming together with other believers. There's something beautiful about lifting your voice in worship alongside others, sitting under the Word, and letting God refresh your spirit through fellowship. Church is not just a building — it's a body. And you are a vital part of it.

So find your place, settle in, and be present in God's house.

Prayer:
Lord, thank You for the gift of the church — a place to grow, to serve, and to be renewed. Help me enter Your presence with gratitude and expectation. Amen.

WEEK 12

Monday

Undivided Attention

> *"For the word of God is living and active, sharper than any two-edged sword, piercing as far as the division of soul and spirit... and able to judge the thoughts and intentions of the heart." — Hebrews 4:12 (NASB)*

I was experimenting with caramelization for one of my steamed pudding recipes, trying to get the sugar just right. The process requires constant attention. One moment too long, and the sugar burns; not long enough, and it doesn't transform. It reminded me how certain things — delicate, important things — demand our full, undivided focus.

So does the Word of God.

Hebrews 4:12 tells us that God's Word is "living and active" — sharper than any two-edged sword, able to pierce deep into the heart and soul. That's not something we can skim through while multitasking or distracted. If we truly want the Word to transform us — to separate soul from spirit, to sift our motives — we must be fully present.

Distraction dulls transformation.

God doesn't compete for our attention. He waits. But when we quiet the noise and give Him our full focus, something beautiful happens. Just like sugar slowly turning into caramel, our hearts begin to soften, deepen, and change under the steady heat of His presence.

Prayer:
Lord, help us give You our full attention when we sit with Your Word. May our hearts not be distracted but devoted. Amen.

TUESDAY

Your 24/7 Father

> *"I will never desert you, nor will I ever abandon you."* — Hebrews 13:5 (NASB)

I've been thinking about this topic for quite some time.

We honor and celebrate our earthly fathers—those who provided, protected, and prayed for us. But today, I'm also reminded of the One who never clocks out. The Father who doesn't sleep, doesn't leave, and doesn't fail. While earthly fathers do their best, they are human—limited by time, energy, and life itself. But our heavenly Father is on duty 24/7. He's not bound by earthly constraints or emotional burnout. He doesn't forget to show up. His love doesn't shift with seasons or struggles.

Hebrews 13:5 reminds us of His promise: "I will never desert you, nor will I ever abandon you." There's such strength and tenderness in those words. In a world of fleeting relationships and uncertain support, God stands unmovable—our ever-present Father.

So today, whether your earthly father is near or gone, strong or struggling, present or absent—celebrate your 24/7 Father too. The One who holds your life in His hands and never lets go.

Prayer:
Thank You, Father, for being constant and always near. Help us rest in the assurance of Your never-ending presence. Amen.

WEDNESDAY

Is Your Soul Parched?

"My soul weeps because of grief; Strengthen me according to Your word." Psalm 119:28 (NASB)

I neglected watering my outdoor plants for just two days. The sun had been merciless, and when I finally went out to check, the once-thriving leaves were limp, curling at the edges. Their thirst was evident. What they needed wasn't a gentle sprinkle—it was a deep, soul-refreshing soak.

And just like that, I felt the Spirit whisper: "What about your soul?"

We may not always realize it, but our hearts can become just as parched—dried out by grief, stress, worry, or even spiritual neglect. A busy week, a few skipped quiet times, a heart weighed down by unspoken burdens... and before we know it, our soul is gasping for life-giving water.

David understood this well when he wrote, "As the deer pants for the water brooks, so my soul pants for You, God." (Psalm 42:1, NASB). That imagery isn't poetic fluff—it's desperation. A soul crying out for its Source.

A quick verse or short devotional might help us stay upright, but deep restoration only comes when we linger—soaking in His Word, meditating on His promises, and letting His Spirit minister to our hidden places.

Jesus Himself invited us to this rest when He said, "If anyone is thirsty, let him come to Me and drink." (John 7:37, NASB). He wasn't offering a sip. He was offering streams of living water—abundant, endless, and soul-quenching.

So today, ask yourself: Are you merely sprinkling, or are you truly soaking?

THURSDAY: *Refueling Like Jesus*

> **Prayer:**
> *Water my weary soul, Lord, and strengthen me with Your Word today. Let me soak in Your presence. Revive the places I've allowed to dry up. In You alone, I find my refreshment. Amen.*

THURSDAY

Refueling Like Jesus

I'm sitting in the doctor's office, mindlessly scrolling through my phone data, when I had an Aha moment—one of those quiet realizations that sneaks up on you.

I noticed how much data I had used, how many apps were constantly running, and how much energy my phone was consuming... even when it wasn't in use. And suddenly, it hit me—I'm not all that different. Always running. Always "on." Always pouring out.

But even Jesus didn't run on empty.

Scripture tells us in Luke 5:16 (NASB), "But Jesus Himself would often slip away to the wilderness and pray." He didn't wait until burnout hit. He prioritized rest, retreat, and communion with the Father—even in the midst of miracles, ministry, and multitudes pressing in.

Another verse reminds us: "Come to Me, all who are weary and burdened, and I will give you rest." (Matthew 11:28, NASB). It's not just an invitation—it's a rescue. Jesus is calling us to step away from the rush and come back to what refuels us: His presence.

So here I am, sitting in a waiting room, realizing I don't need to keep running until I crash. Neither do you. Shall we follow His footsteps and take the time to refuel our tank?

Your soul doesn't need more scrolling, more striving, or more doing. It needs stillness. Silence. Sabbath. Jesus modeled it—not out of weakness, but out of wisdom.

> **Prayer:**
> Jesus, teach me to follow Your example and rest when needed. Let me not run on empty. Help me carve out quiet spaces to be refueled in Your presence. Amen.

FRIDAY

Blooming in Due Time

"I planted, Apollos watered, but God was causing the growth." 1 Corinthians 3:6 (NASB)

Yesterday evening I was watering my garden and admiring the blooms. Some flowers had opened wide and vibrant, others were still tightly closed, and a few patches were just beginning to show signs of green. But one thing was clear—everything was growing at its own pace.

As I stood there with the hose in hand, I felt a gentle reminder from the Lord: "You didn't make any of this grow—you just showed up and did your part."

It's so easy to grow weary when we don't see immediate results—especially in people. We pour into others, pray for them, encourage them, mentor them, correct them... and sometimes it feels like nothing is changing. But that's when 1 Corinthians 3:6 comforts and humbles us: "I planted, Apollos watered, but God was causing the growth."

Whether you're a parent sowing into a child, a friend watering someone in a rough season, or a teacher speaking truth over seemingly hardened hearts—don't give up. God sees your consistency. He honors your faithfulness. Growth is His business; obedience is ours.

Galatians 6:9 echoes this: "Let us not become discouraged in doing good, for in due time we will reap, if we do not become weary." Not if we see instant fruit, but if we do not give up.

FRIDAY: *Blooming in Due Time*

So keep planting. Keep watering. Even if someone else reaps the bloom, you were part of the process. And someday, you'll rejoice when the seeds you've nurtured burst into life.

> **Prayer:**
> Lord, help me to be faithful—whether sowing, watering, or simply watching You bring the growth. Remind me that the yield is in Your hands, and my role is not in vain. Amen.

SATURDAY

Eternal Investments

> *"Thus I hated all the fruit of my labor for which I had labored under the sun, for I would have to leave it to the man who will come after me... So I began to give myself over to despair."* Ecclesiastes 2:18–20 (NASB)

Ecclesiastes 2:18–23 is a sobering passage. Solomon, one of the wisest and wealthiest men who ever lived, reflects on all his accomplishments and declares, essentially: "I hated all of it."

Why? Because it didn't last.

Solomon's frustration is relatable. We pour so much time, energy, and emotion into careers, savings, possessions, and status—only to realize that none of it follows us when we're gone. We can't take the house, the title, or the bank account into eternity.

But Jesus offers a better way.

He said, "Do not store up for yourselves treasures on earth... but store up for yourselves treasures in heaven... for where your treasure is, there your heart will be also." (Matthew 6:19–21, NASB)

Unlike worldly investment, eternal investment finds a home in heaven. Every act of kindness, every soul we lead to Christ, every prayer whispered in the quiet, every moment we choose faith over fear—those things endure.

There's nothing wrong with work or possessions. But if that becomes the entirety of our legacy, we've missed the point. The only work that outlives us is the work done in and for the Lord.

Let your life count for more than just what can be counted.

> **Prayer:**
> *Help me, Lord, to invest in what truly matters—souls and eternity. Let my legacy be one that lasts forever in You. Amen.*

 SUNDAY

Reflection & Renewal

Take this Sunday to rest in God's promises and reflect on His goodness.

Whether you're in a season of sowing seeds, faithfully watering what others have planted, or simply learning to rest and trust—God sees you. Every quiet sacrifice, every hidden act of service, every moment you choose faith over weariness—it matters.

> *"For God is not unjust so as to forget your work and the love which you have shown toward His name, by having served and by still serving the saints." — Hebrews 6:10 (NASB)*

Sometimes it feels like the work we do—especially the spiritual kind—goes unnoticed. But God doesn't miss a thing. He keeps record of every gesture of love offered in His name, even when no one else claps or congratulates.

So breathe today. Worship freely. Reflect on where He has brought you and trust Him for what's ahead. Your labor is not in vain, and your rest is not wasted either. Take joy in simply being His.

> **Prayer:**
> *Lord, I rest today in Your love and in the assurance that nothing done for You is ever wasted. Amen.*

WEEK 13

Monday

Wait for the Walk Sign

> "This is what the Lord says:
> 'Stand by the ways and see and ask for the ancient paths,
> Where the good way is, and walk in it;
> Then you will find a resting place for your souls.'" Jeremiah 6:16 (NASB)

When COVID hit, my perspective on day-to-day living shifted. God brought a sense of awareness into my life—an awareness that was totally God-centered. In my younger days, I would often jump into situations, only to fumble and then call on God to rescue me. But over time, and through many life experiences, I learned to pause before stepping forward.

Think of a crosswalk. We wait until the 'WALK' sign lights up before crossing. Why? For safety. In the same way, life will often bring us to crossroads. Every decision, every step, every signature—we need to pause and wait for the Lord's signal.

Proverbs 4:12 says, 'When you walk, your steps will not be impeded.' When you wait on God, your steps will be sure-footed.

Prayer:
Lord, teach me to pause before I act. Help me wait for Your direction rather than rush ahead. Let my steps be guided by Your wisdom, not my impulse. Thank You for being my signal and my safe path. Amen.

TUESDAY

Sighing at God's Requests

> *"If anyone is willing to do His will, he will know of the teaching, whether it is of God or whether I speak from Myself."* John 7:17 (NASB)

When I ask my kids to do something they'd rather not do, I'm often met with a sigh—a big, dramatic, exaggerated sigh. That sigh? It's louder than words. It signals reluctance, even resistance. And to me, it changes the whole moment.

Then I wondered: When God asks me to do something, do I sigh too?

Do I frown internally? Stall? Complain under my breath?

Do I treat His calling like a burden instead of a privilege?

Reluctance doesn't just delay obedience—it drains the joy out of it. But something beautiful happens when we shift our posture. When children do their chores with cheerfulness, it changes the atmosphere. Likewise, when we respond to God with joy and eagerness, it changes us.

God delights in willing hearts—not just obedient ones, but joyfully obedient ones. Today's challenge: swap your "have to" for a "get to." Replace reluctance with readiness. Let your obedience be wrapped in joy.

> **Prayer:**
> Lord, I want to do Your will—and do it cheerfully. Help me respond with joy and readiness when You call. Let my attitude reflect a heart that's willing, not weary. Amen.

WEDNESDAY

The Power of a Parent's Tear

"You have taken account of my wanderings; Put my tears in Your bottle. Are they not in Your book?" Psalm 56:8 (NASB)

This morning, as I looked around my quiet home, memories of parenting overwhelmed me—the struggles of raising kids, understanding teenagers, and watching adult children face their own battles.

The tears of a parent are sacred. They are pure, filled with love and burden, and they are never wasted. Some bear fruit quickly; others take time—but every tear matters.

In the Civil War, women were said to collect tears in bottles for their husbands to see how deeply they were loved. Our God does even more—He records them. Tears are prayers when words fail.

Prayer:
Father, thank You for hearing my tears as prayers. For every tear I've cried as a parent, thank You for giving them meaning. May they water the seeds of faith, healing, and growth. Amen.

THURSDAY

Seeing Clearly

"This is what the Lord says: 'Stand by the ways and see and ask for the ancient paths, Where the good way is, and walk in it." Jeremiah 6:16 (NASB)

THURSDAY: *Seeing Clearly*

Driving home recently, I saw a majestic sky—crisp, colorful, breathtaking. Then I looked ahead at man-made headlights: harsh, blurry, blinding. What a contrast.

God's design is always clearer. His light is always more precise.

When we fix our eyes on Christ, the world fades into the background. It becomes strangely dim. Like the blind man in the Bible who said, 'I see people, but they look like trees walking,' we need another touch from Jesus to see clearly.

Let's put on our 'God glasses' today—and see life through His lens.

> **Prayer:**
> *Jesus, open my eyes to Your beauty and truth. Let me see past the artificial distractions of this world and focus on Your light. Help me walk in clarity, not confusion. Amen.*

FRIDAY

Don't Discard the Pot

> *"But God, being rich in mercy... even when we were dead in our trespasses, made us alive together with Christ." Ephesians 2:4–5 (NASB)*

We nearly discarded an old pot—dry stems, weeds, lifeless. But days later, a tiny bud appeared. It was a dwarf sunflower.

How many people do we discard because we don't see value? How often do we pass judgment or refuse second chances?

Remember Susan Boyle's first appearance on 'Britain's Got Talent'? Judged by her appearance—but she stunned everyone.

God doesn't discard us. He sees beyond appearances. He keeps giving grace—and expects us to do the same.

SATURDAY: *ASAP — Always Say a Prayer*

> **Prayer:**
> Lord, help me see others through Your eyes. Teach me to extend grace and withhold judgment. Thank You for not discarding me in my lifeless state. Help me honor others with that same mercy. Amen.

SATURDAY

ASAP — Always Say a Prayer

> *"Commit your works to the Lord, And your plans will be established."* Proverbs 16:3 (NASB)

Cleaning through a drawer, I found a bracelet engraved with ASAP: Always Say a Prayer. That moment changed how I viewed this common phrase.

We often feel limited—health issues, distance, emotional fatigue. But prayer is never limited.

There's a girl in my radio station's Facebook group. Severely disabled, in a wheelchair, deformed bones—and the brightest spirit. Her message is always the same: 'How may I pray for you?'

That's power. That's purpose. No matter your limitations—ASAP.

> **Prayer:**
> Father, help me remember the power of prayer. When I can't *do*, I can *pray*. Let me be quick to say a prayer, even in silence. May my limitations never limit Your work through me. Amen.

Sunday

A Day to Refocus

"This is the day that the Lord has made; Let us rejoice and be glad in it." Psalm 118:24 (NASB)

Sunday is more than the end of the week—it's a divine reset. A day to pause, recharge, and gather strength for what's ahead.

Let today be your reminder that God is handing you a fresh page. Be still in His presence. Gather with His people. Soak in His Word. And let your spirit rest in His grace.

> **Prayer:**
> *Father, thank You for Sundays. Thank You for quiet moments, joyful songs, and the blessing of community. Let today mark the start of a week filled with Your peace and purpose. Amen.*

WEEK 14

Monday

God's Joy, My Strength

> *"Do not be grieved, for the joy of the Lord is your refuge." Nehemiah 8:10 (NASB)*

No one can steal our joy. The joy that comes from God is not an item with shape or form; it rests within our hearts. It shows in our words, actions, and attitude. Happiness fades; joy endures.

We recently had some bathroom tile work done. It made me happy, sure. But over time, that happiness faded; it became just another thing. Joy, on the other hand, overflows. It's seen in our eyes, heard in our voices, and felt in our presence. Joy is like a faithful friend who stands with you through thick and thin.

I used to greet the receptionist at work every day, smiling as I passed. One day, she muttered, "What is there to smile about?" Her question didn't take away my joy; that smile was anchored in Christ. Don't let others be your killjoy. Trust God with your baggage and keep your eyes on Him.

The joy of the Lord is our strength. Not our circumstances, not our possessions; our joy is in Him.

Prayer:
Lord, help me live from a place of joy today. Let nothing steal what You have placed within me. Even when life is messy, let my joy in You shine through. Amen.

Tuesday

Soul Doctors

> *"And Jesus answered them, 'It is not those who are healthy who need a physician, but those who are sick.'" Luke 5:31 (NASB)*

Are you a physician? Maybe not, but spiritually speaking, yes; you are a Soul Doctor.

When Jesus spoke these words, He was making a profound statement: He came for the broken, the burdened, the sin-sick and weary. But here's the twist—once He heals us, we are called to step into His work and minister to others.

You may not wear a white coat, but if you belong to Christ, you've been entrusted with a spiritual specialty. Some of us are:

Dr. Embrace – offering warmth through hugs and presence.

Dr. Comfort – with listening ears that make others feel seen and safe.

Dr. Humor – bringing healing through laughter in hard places.

Dr. Mentor – offering wise counsel and guidance to those who feel lost.

You may be one of these, or something unique. The key is to recognize that your past pain, your personality, and your spiritual gifts are not random. They were all shaped to serve.

God doesn't call perfect people; He calls the healed to help heal. You were restored not just to feel better, but to pass it on. That friend who's weeping in silence? That coworker who's discouraged? That young person looking for direction? They may need your kind of care.

Ask God today: What kind of soul doctor am I? Then lean into that calling. You carry a message someone desperately needs to hear: "You're going to be okay. Let me walk with you until you believe it again."

> **Prayer:**
> Lord, reveal my spiritual specialty. Whether it's listening, encouraging, serving, or simply being present, help me use it to comfort, uplift, and minister to the hurting. Let me be a faithful soul doctor for Your kingdom. Amen.

WEDNESDAY

My Trustworthy Father

> *"Blessed is the one who trusts in the Lord, whose confidence is in Him." — Jeremiah 17:7 (NIV)*

In the quiet hours of the night, I was stirred awake with the words of a simple Hindi worship song translated in my spirit: "My trustworthy Father, I will praise You always." Isn't that the truest response to a God who has never failed? Even in our sleep, our souls can still sing to the One who holds us steady.

He is worthy of our praise—not just for what He has done, but for who He is. Every breath we take, every grace we receive, every unseen danger we're protected from—it all flows from the hands of a Father who can be trusted without question. Let's reflect on some of His unshakable attributes:

His forgiving heart — He welcomes us back every time we stumble.

His steady presence — We are never truly alone, even when the world feels silent.

His comforting arms — Like a child wrapped in a parent's embrace, we find rest.

His unchanging nature — Trends shift and people change, but He remains the same.

His generous provision — Even when resources run low, His storehouse never empties.

His faithful promises — Not one has ever been broken.

The list could go on endlessly—and maybe it should. Spend a few moments today meditating on who your Father is. Not just what He's done for you, but what He is to you. Then ask yourself a sincere question:

Who have I entrusted myself to?

If your answer is anyone or anything other than the Trustworthy Father, it's time to release that grip and return to His steady hands.

> **Prayer:**
> Father, You are so trustworthy, so good, and so steady. Forgive me for the times I put my confidence in temporary things or fragile people. Today I come back into Your arms—arms that never close, never grow weary, and never drop what You hold. Thank You for being my safe place, my anchor, and my comfort. I will praise You always, for You alone are worthy. In Jesus' name, Amen

THURSDAY

Rest, Refuel, Rejuvenate

> *"And He said to them, 'Come away by yourselves to a secluded place and rest a little while.'" Mark 6:31 (NASB)*

> *"Rest in the Lord and wait patiently for Him." Psalm 37:7 (NASB)*

Do you crave rest?

Jesus did too. Even He called His disciples to step away from the crowds, the noise, the demands, because He knew what our bodies and souls sometimes forget: we can't pour from an empty vessel.

Rest has nearly vanished from our culture. We glorify hustle and badge busyness like honor. But in God's economy, rest isn't laziness; it's obedience. A sacred rhythm.

Like a quiet river that flows regardless of who's watching, God's presence is always available, inviting us to come, sit, breathe, and be restored. His house, His Word, His presence... all beckon us weekly, daily, moment by moment.

But are we responding? Or are we just walking past the river?

Rest isn't a luxury. It's a divine invitation to refuel what's depleted, to rejuvenate what's weary, and to remind us that our worth isn't measured by output, but by being with Him.

Friday: *Choose to Refuel*

> **Prayer:**
> Lord, thank You for inviting me to rest. Help me say yes to Your rhythm of renewal. Let me find peace in Your presence today, and strength to carry what You've assigned me to do. Amen.

Friday

Choose to Refuel

> *"Cast your burden upon the Lord and He will sustain you; He will never allow the righteous to be shaken."* Psalm 55:22 (NASB)

Are you running on fumes today? Emotionally drained? Spiritually dry? Depleted from the duties of yesterday, or the burdens of tomorrow?

This is your reminder: today is for rest. For refueling. For being reminded of the Source who never runs out.

God invites us to cast our burdens on Him, not carry them around like a badge of endurance. He offers strength for the weary and sustenance for the soul. But here's the catch: we have to choose it.

You can operate on an empty tank, or you can refill.

You can press on in your strength or pause and receive His.

One leads to burnout. The other leads to renewal.

What will you choose today?

> **Prayer:**
> Lord, I bring my exhaustion to You. I cast my burdens at Your feet. Fill me with Your strength, renew my spirit, and remind me that You are my sustaining power. Amen.

SATURDAY

In the Waiting Room

> *"For My thoughts are not your thoughts, nor are your ways My ways,' declares the Lord. 'As the heavens are higher than the earth, so are My ways higher than your ways and My thoughts than your thoughts".* Isaiah 55:8-9 (NASB)

Are you pounding on God's door this morning? Praying hard, hoping faster, asking louder, desperate for something to change?

Waiting can feel unbearable. Especially when you're in the "ICU" season of life—when what's at stake is personal, urgent, and painful.

But think about the real ICU waiting room. You don't barge into the operating room or question every move the surgeon makes. You sit. You wait. You trust that the one behind the doors knows what they're doing, even if you don't understand it in the moment.

In the same way, life's waiting rooms are sacred spaces. They're not signs of divine silence, but divine precision. The Chief Physician is on call. He's not pacing. He's not panicking. He's working—carefully, perfectly, lovingly.

You don't have to understand to trust. And you don't have to feel peace to choose it.

So while you wait, worship. Be still. And remind your heart: His ways are higher.

> **Prayer:**
> Lord, help me surrender what I can't control. In the waiting, teach me to trust Your plan and lean on Your perfect timing. I choose faith over frustration and worship over worry. Amen.

SUNDAY: *A Day to Refocus*

 SUNDAY

A Day to Refocus

"This is the day that the Lord has made; Let us rejoice and be glad in it." Psalm 118:24 (NASB)

Sunday is more than just the end of the week; it's a divine reset.

Take this day to pause, gather with other believers, soak in the Word, and be refreshed in His presence. Let go of last week and enter the new one with renewed focus and purpose.

Go to church, worship with joy, and let today realign your soul.

Prayer:
"Father, thank You for Sundays. For stillness, songs, and Your people. Let today be a holy beginning to a week filled with Your grace and purpose. Amen."

WEEK 15

MONDAY

Never Alone

> "Make sure that your character is free from the love of money, being content with what you have; for He Himself has said, 'I will never desert you, nor will I ever abandon you.'" Hebrews 13:5 (NASB)

Separation is part of life. Sometimes it comes through loss. Sometimes through distance. A child leaves for college. A relationship shifts. A loved one passes. Even joyful visits can end with tearful goodbyes.

Leaving my 87-year-old parents was one of those moments. The longing in their eyes. Their slow steps. Their fragile helplessness. It choked me. Nothing dramatic had happened, just life unfolding as it does. But it still hurt.

And yet, in every goodbye, God whispers a truth we need to hear again and again: "I will never leave you. I will never abandon you."

He is the only constant in a world full of change. The only presence we never have to release. No matter where life takes us, or whom we have to leave behind, He remains. He goes before us. Stays beside us. Carries us through.

No, never alone.
He promised never to leave me.
No, never alone.

Prayer:
Lord, thank You that in every goodbye, You remain. You are my constant, my comfort, and my forever Companion. In the ache of separation, anchor me in the assurance of Your presence. Amen.

TUESDAY

Milk or Meat?

> *"For everyone who partakes only of milk is unacquainted with the word of righteousness, for he is an infant. But solid food is for the mature..." Hebrews 5:13-14 (NASB)*

Last night, I watched a video of my grandkids bubbling with excitement about school—their curiosity, their eagerness to learn, their wide-eyed wonder. It stirred something in me. I remembered that same spark from the early days of my walk with Christ.

Back then, we devoured the Word. We lingered in our Bibles, underlined with purpose, and wrestled with deep truths. But slowly, that hunger can fade. Routines sneak in. Life gets busy. What was once a feast becomes a nibble, just a verse on a calendar or a quick devotional while multitasking. But just like in school, when you stop learning, you stop growing.

God didn't call us to stay on a spiritual formula. Growth in Christ requires more than surface sips; it requires solid food. Truth that stretches us. Conviction that challenges us. Wisdom that shapes our walk. Are you still drinking milk? Or are you hungry for more?

The mature are those who keep pressing in. Who wants not just comfort, but transformation. Who say, "Lord, teach me," even when it's hard.

Prayer:
Lord, renew my hunger for Your Word. Help me move beyond the basics and grow in maturity—rooted in truth, equipped for every good work, and hungry for more of You. Amen.

WEDNESDAY

The Years Will Be Restored

> *"Then I will compensate you for the years that the swarming locust has eaten…" Joel 2:25 (NASB)*

There are days when regret creeps in quietly, reminding us of missed opportunities, broken relationships, or seasons that feel wasted. Maybe today is one of those days for you.

Early this morning, thanks to jet lag, I found myself reflecting on my 62 years of life. It was like a roller coaster ride of memories: joyful highs, painful lows, and everything in between. Some of those seasons I'd gladly relive. Others, I wish I could rewrite.

But as I ended my prayer time, this verse from Joel came to mind: "I will restore the years the locusts have eaten."

God doesn't just comfort us; He restores. He doesn't ignore what's been lost; He redeems it. Nothing is beyond His reach. Not the broken years. Not the wilderness seasons. Not even the moments we wish had never happened. Restoration isn't a wishful thought. It's a divine promise.

Our God is not a silent observer. He's not distant from your past. He is a Redeemer who takes what was devoured and turns it into testimony. The locusts may have eaten, but God still reigns.

Prayer:
Lord, thank You that no season is beyond Your reach. Restore the years I've lost. Heal the places I mourn. And turn my memories into testimonies of grace, hope, and Your redeeming love. Amen.

THURSDAY

Don't Linger at Closed Doors

> *"I will lead those who are blind by a way they have not known... I will turn darkness into light before them." Isaiah 42:16 (NASB)*

Helen Keller once said, "When one door of happiness closes, another opens; but often we look so long at the closed door that we do not see the one which has been opened for us."

We've all lingered at closed doors.

The job we didn't get.

The relationship that ended.

The dream that didn't unfold the way we hoped.

And the longer we stare, the blurrier the open doors become.

Disappointments are real. But they don't have to define us. Peace begins when we stop demanding explanations and start surrendering the outcome to God's will.

Early in life, I used to say things like, "I did it" or "I failed." But looking back, I see clearly: it was always God's hand guiding, redirecting, opening, closing. His sovereignty was at work, even when I couldn't see it.

Even athletes lose games. But they don't stay on the bench. They review, reset, and get back in the game. We must do the same—shift from disappointment to determination, knowing that God is coaching us forward toward something greater than what we left behind.

So don't linger. Let go of what was. Step into what is, and trust the One who opens doors no one can shut.

Prayer:
Lord, help me let go of what You've closed. Give me eyes to see the new doors You're opening and the courage to walk through them with faith. Amen.

FRIDAY

Are You Living or Just Surviving?

> *"So then, be careful how you walk, not as unwise people but as wise, making the most of your time, because the days are evil."* Ephesians 5:15-16 (NASB)

A day isn't lost because you didn't complete your to-do list.
It's only lost if you didn't love well.
If you didn't pause to notice beauty.
If you forgot that breath itself is a gift.
Every morning now, I whisper, "Lord, thank You for this breath."
The older I get, the more that simple truth humbles me—each day is precious, fleeting, and full of purpose. What we do with today shapes our eternity.
We often respond to others, "I'm surviving." And sometimes, yes, that's real. Life can be heavy. But what if we reminded each other: You're not just surviving; you're alive. You have breath. God gave you this day. Live it with purpose.
We are carriers of hope in a weary world.
Let's not just endure the day. Let's inhabit it.
Let's notice the sacred in the ordinary.
Let's live the abundant life Christ died to give us.

Prayer:
Lord, thank You for the gift of this day. Don't let me miss it by going through the motions. Help me to live, not merely survive. Use me to bring hope to those who've forgotten how to live. Amen.

SATURDAY

The Beauty Around You

"The heavens tell of the glory of God; and their expanse declares the work of His hands." Psalm 19:1 (NASB)

Autumn has arrived, and with it, God's palette is on full display. The trees blaze with yellow, orange, and crimson. Every window in my home becomes a frame for a new masterpiece, each view whispering, "Look what God has done."

We move so fast. We carry so much. And sometimes, the weight of life makes us forget to simply look up. But the heavens are declaring something if we'll just pause long enough to listen.

God didn't just create the earth; He designed it to reflect His glory. The rustle of leaves, the softness of light, the vivid skies… they're not just scenery. They're signs. Evidence of a Creator who sees beauty as essential, not optional.

Then comes the most tender truth: we, too, are part of that beauty.

No fingerprint alike.

No soul duplicated.

We are fearfully and wonderfully made, another masterpiece of the same Artist who painted the sunset.

So today, step outside. Breathe deep. Marvel. And remember: the same God who crafted the world crafted you.

Prayer:
Lord, thank You for the beauty that surrounds me—in creation, in others, and in myself. Slow me down today. Help me pause, reflect, and worship You through the wonder of Your handiwork. Amen.

 ## SUNDAY

Worship and Renewal

> *"Come to Me, all who are weary and burdened, and I will give you rest." Matthew 11:28 (NASB)*

Today is your invitation to pause, reflect, and renew.

Let His presence be your peace. Let worship stir your heart. Let rest become a holy rhythm.

Whatever this past week held, victories or valleys, today is sacred ground.

Prayer:
Lord, thank You for this day of rest. Quiet my mind, steady my heart, and prepare me for the week to come. Amen

WEEK 16

MONDAY

Soaring in the Shadow

> *"But those who hope in the LORD will renew their strength. They will soar on wings like eagles; they will run and not grow weary, they will walk and not be faint." Isaiah 40:31 (NASB)*

This morning, a powerful image caught my attention—an eagle, wings outstretched, sheltering its eaglets beneath. It instantly brought to mind the song we're practicing for Sunday: "Shadow of Your Wings."

There's something deeply comforting about the image of God's wings—wide, strong, and unwavering. Not hurried. Not hesitant. Just steady and sure. Scripture tells us that those who hope in the Lord will soar like eagles. But before the soaring, there's shelter. The shadow of His wings is where we wait, where we rest, where we are renewed.

You are not outside His reach. You are not forgotten. You are not flying solo. God's strength lifts us when our own strength fails. His covering shelters us when life's winds howl. And under His shadow, we are not just protected; we're prepared to soar again.

Prayer:
Lord, help me rest beneath the shadow of Your wings. When I'm weary, lift me. When I'm anxious, cover me. Thank You for being my strength and my refuge. Teach me to soar in You. Amen.

TUESDAY

Hold On to the Lifeline

"Even if my father and mother abandon me, the Lord will hold me close." Psalm 27:10 (NASB)

Rejection hurts. Whether it's from family, a job, a friend, or even a spiritual community, it cuts deep. It's the kind of pain that doesn't always leave visible bruises, but it lingers in the heart.

Jesus knew this pain. He said, "A prophet is not without honor... except in his own house." Even the Savior of the world was dismissed, overlooked, and pushed aside by those closest to Him.

But here's the hope: God is the One who never walks away. Scripture is full of rejected people whom God redeemed—Joseph, betrayed by his brothers. Hannah, misunderstood in her pain. David, overlooked by his own father. Paul, abandoned by many but held by grace.

I'll never forget the day I fell out of a whitewater raft. I couldn't swim. The current was stronger than me, and panic rose fast. A lifeguard threw out a rope and shouted, "Hold on!" That rope became my lifeline, it felt like the hand of Jesus reaching into the chaos.

Jesus is your lifeline. He's the One who holds when everything else lets go. So don't release your grip. Even when the current is strong. Especially then.

Prayer:
Lord, thank You for never abandoning me. When others walk away, help me cling tightly to You—my constant, my anchor, my true and faithful Lifeline. Amen.

WEDNESDAY

Today's Assignment

Each morning holds new treasure, a divine assignments waiting to be discovered. Not always dramatic. Not always loud. Sometimes it's a gentle nudge to send a text, offer a prayer, encouragement, or simply listen well.

God's assignments aren't always grand in scale, but they're always sacred in purpose.

The challenge is that we often miss them. Yesterday's regrets can blur today's vision. Distractions, insecurities, or the comparison trap can pull us out of alignment. But God doesn't ask us to walk in someone else's calling; He's given us our own path to walk.

And here's a truth worth remembering:

If God wanted us to walk backward, He would've given us feet that point behind us. So press forward. Walk with purpose. Look for the treasure He's placed in your hands today. Your assignment may seem small, but in God's hands, it becomes eternal.

> **Prayer:**
> Lord, open my eyes to the treasure You've placed before me today. Don't let me miss my assignment. Help me walk faithfully, without distraction or comparison, in what You've called me to do. Amen.

THURSDAY

Permission to Rest

"Come to Me, all who are weary and burdened, and I will give you rest." Matthew 11:28 (NASB)

THURSDAY: *Permission to Rest*

As women, we wear many hats—mother, daughter, friend, leader, caregiver, counselor. Sometimes all at once. And before our feet even hit the floor, our minds are already running—lists forming, responsibilities weighing.

But no vessel can pour from empty. No heart can overflow if it's been running on fumes. Rest isn't weakness; it's wisdom. It's not selfish; it's sacred. Even Jesus, the Savior of the world, withdrew to rest. If He needed it, how much more do we?

Scripture speaks of rest over and over, not as a luxury, but as a rhythm. A gift. A command. God never asked us to be superhuman. He asks us to be still enough to remember that He is God.

So today, give yourself permission to rest. Not after everything is done. Not when everyone else is taken care of. Now.

Prayer:
Lord, I release the pressure to do it all. Quiet the noise in my heart. Teach me to rest—body, mind, and soul—and to trust that even in stillness, You are at work. Amen.

FRIDAY

Listen to the Voice

"Your ears will hear a word behind you, saying, 'This is the way, walk in it,' whenever you turn to the right or to the left." Isaiah 30:21 (NASB)

I lost an earring the other day, one of my favorites. As I was putting it on, I felt a small nudge: The backing is loose.

I brushed it off.

Hours later? Gone.

It may sound trivial, but it reminded me of something bigger. How often do we ignore the gentle voice of the Holy Spirit? That inner prompting? That quiet check in our spirit?

FRIDAY: *Listen to the Voice*

He warns. He guides. He leads. And still, we move forward on our own terms, assuming we'll be fine. But even small instructions carry divine intention. If we can't respond to the whisper, how will we respond to the storm?

God is always speaking, but we have to quiet ourselves to hear Him. It won't always be dramatic. Sometimes it's a nudge. A pause. A sense of hesitation. That's where obedience begins—in the stillness before the decision.

So today, find your spot of silence. Turn down the noise. Ask Him to speak, and when He does, listen.

> **Prayer:**
> *Lord, help me to hear Your voice and not brush it aside. Give me a heart that obeys, even when the instruction feels small or inconvenient. Speak, Lord, Your servant is listening. Amen.*

SATURDAY

The Test of Trials

> *"And we know that God causes all things to work together for good to those who love God." Romans 8:28 (NASB)*

Sometimes life feels like a never-ending exam. Just when one trial ends, another begins—harder, deeper, more exhausting than the last.

But Scripture reminds us: trials aren't signs of abandonment. They're often tools of refinement. God doesn't waste pain. He uses it to shape us, strengthen us, and draw us closer to Him.

Consider the lives of those who walked through fire before us:

Job lost everything, yet he worshipped.

Joseph was betrayed, yet he forgave.

Jeremiah was persecuted, yet he endured.

Paul suffered, yet he rejoiced.

Jesus carried the cross, yet He surrendered completely.

None of their journeys were easy. And ours won't be either. But they all trusted something greater than the trial: God's purpose. And so must we. One day, every tear, every struggle, every unanswered "why" will fade in the light of His words: "Well done, good and faithful servant."

That alone will make it all worth it.

> **Prayer:**
> *Lord, strengthen me through every test. Let me cling to You when things don't make sense. Refine me through trials, and help me trust that Your purpose will always prevail. Amen.*

--- SUNDAY ---

Worship and Reflection

"Remember the Sabbath day, to keep it holy." Exodus 20:8

Rest isn't about inactivity; it's about intentionality. Sunday is your reset, your realignment.

Worship. Reflect. Refocus. The week ahead may be uncertain, but today, you are invited to rest in God's unchanging presence.

Let Him refuel your soul and fill you with peace.

> **Prayer:**
> *Lord, I surrender this day to You. Let worship renew me and Your presence steady me for the week ahead. Amen.*

WEEK 17

Monday

Guided by His Eye

"I will instruct you and teach you in the way which you should go; I will advise you with My eye upon you." Psalm 32:8 (NASB)

At 3 a.m., half asleep, Psalm 32:8 kept whispering itself into my spirit.
It was so persistent that I finally got up, flipped on the light, and read the verse aloud.
God's Word met me in the stillness.
His eye sees what I can't. It sees past fear, past confusion, past detours and foggy crossroads. His vision isn't hindered by emotion, uncertainty, or limited perspective. While we guess, He knows. While we waver, He guides.
And He doesn't just give distant instructions; He watches with care. Like a parent watching a child take their first wobbly steps, His gaze is attentive, close, and full of compassion.
If you're at a crossroads today, unsure, weary, or overwhelmed, pause. He's not slow. He's strategic. He's guiding you not with pressure, but with purpose.
Trust His eye. Trust His timing. Trust that even if you can't see the full road ahead, He can.

Prayer:
Lord, thank You for seeing what I cannot. For staying near, even in my uncertainty. I trust You to guide me step by step, even when the way feels unclear. Direct my path, and steady my heart. Amen.

TUESDAY

When Trust Gets Tested

> *"So faith comes from hearing, and hearing by the word of Christ."*
> *Romans 10:17 (NASB)*

I remember watching my granddaughter leap fearlessly into her dad's arms. No hesitation. No second-guessing. Just pure, childlike trust.

As a grandmother, my heart skipped a beat.

But my son? He caught her with a confident smile and said, "Mom, I got her."

It made me wonder: How are we doing in the trust department? We say we trust God... but sometimes we add a few "backup" suggestions, just in case He needs help. We pray bold prayers, then tiptoe back into worry. We hand God our burdens, then pick them right back up.

But here's the truth: Doubt and trust don't coexist.

Where one grows, the other shrinks.

And when doubt creeps in, Satan sees an open door to whisper lies like, "God's forgotten you... This won't work out... You're on your own."

That's why we must read the Word, speak the Word, and arm ourselves with the truth. Faith doesn't grow in silence; it grows when we stay rooted in what God has said.

So today, choose trust. Real trust. No conditions. No backup plans.

> **Prayer:**
> *Lord, I choose to trust You fully. Help me shut out the lies and lean completely into Your faithfulness. You've never dropped me, and You never will. Amen.*

WEDNESDAY

Running on Empty

"My flesh and my heart may fail, but God is the strength of my heart and my portion forever." Psalm 73:26 (NASB)

Have you ever had one of those days where your energy, inspiration, and drive just vanish?

That was me this morning. Even after coffee and a banana, I felt stuck—emotionally sluggish, spiritually foggy, like my engine just wouldn't turn over.

But God isn't waiting for us to power through. He's waiting for us to pause and plug in. In moments like these, it's okay to whisper, "Jesus, take the wheel." Let Him take over. Let Him carry what you can't. He is not only your strength; He is your portion - Your enough.

So if you feel depleted today, don't fake it. Don't force it. Surrender it.

Prayer:
Lord, I'm tired. I feel depleted. Be the strength I don't have. Recharge my soul, restore my joy, and help me walk in Your power today. I surrender it all to You. Amen.

THURSDAY

Wisdom in the Wrinkles

"Wisdom is with the aged, and with long life comes understanding." Job 12:12 (NASB)

Lord, I'm tired. I feel depleted. Be the strength I don't have. Recharge my soul, restore my joy, and help me walk in Your power today. I surrender it all to You. Amen.

Today's generation moves fast. Answers are just a click away. Information is instant. But wisdom? That's not downloaded; it's developed.

Our elders carry stories written through seasons of scarcity, endurance, and faith. Their wisdom isn't outdated; it's hard-won. Lived and proven through trial and grace.

Think of Mordecai, guiding Esther in a moment that changed history. Or Paul, mentoring Timothy as he led the early church. Their words weren't flashy; they were faithful. And they still echo with relevance today.

Then there's Rehoboam, who dismissed the counsel of the older men and chose the voices of his peers. That one decision? It split an entire kingdom. We'd be wise not to repeat his mistake.

Don't disregard wisdom that walks with a cane. Don't overlook the voice that speaks slower but with deeper weight. Seek it. Honor it. Learn from it.

> **Prayer:**
> *Lord, give me a teachable heart. Help me see the wisdom in those who've walked before me. Let me value their voice and cherish the counsel of the faithful. Amen.*

FRIDAY

Rejection Redefined

"If the world hates you, keep in mind that it hated Me first." John 15:18 (NASB)

Rejection stings. Whether it comes from family, friends, coworkers, or even fellow believers, it cuts deep. It makes us question our worth. Our

FRIDAY: *Rejection Redefined*

calling. Sometimes even our faith. But here's the truth: you're in good company.

Jesus was rejected by His own people.

Joseph was betrayed by his own brothers.

Paul was misunderstood, beaten, and imprisoned by the very ones he came to help.

So no, rejection doesn't define you. It refines you. It's not a stop sign; it's often a redirection. A holy reroute toward the people and purpose God has truly prepared for you.

Letting go of rejection isn't easy. It requires forgiveness, perspective, and time. But healing comes when we release the weight and remember: Jesus understands. He doesn't just sympathize; He empathizes. He's felt it firsthand.

So flip the script. Don't let rejection lead to dejection.

Let it fuel your mission. Let it drive you closer to the One who never casts you aside.

Prayer:
Lord, thank You for understanding my pain. Help me release rejection, forgive freely, and keep moving forward in grace and confidence. Amen.

SATURDAY

The Scar Healed

"He heals the brokenhearted and binds up their wounds." Psalm 147:3 (NASB)

A grinder accident left me with second-degree burns across my face, neck, and shoulder. The doctors were kind, but realistic. They said that the scars will last for years and there is no guarantee of the scars to completely disappear. But God had the final say. In just six months, the scars were gone.

SATURDAY: *The Scar Healed*

Physically, I was healed. But emotionally? That healing ran even deeper. I wept when a "memory photo" popped up, not from pain, but from gratitude. Not from fear, but from the awe of what my Savior had done.

God doesn't just heal bones and bodies. He heals memories. He heals fears. He heals hearts. And He cares about every scar, visible and invisible. Some of our scars no one else can see - Rejection. Trauma. Shame. Loss. But none of them are overlooked by the One who binds up wounds and restores what was broken.

Your scars may be different, but they're not meaningless. They can become testimonies in the hands of a healing God.

> **Prayer:**
> Lord, thank You for caring about every wound. Thank You for healing what others said couldn't be healed. I give You every scar, past and present, and I trust You to turn pain into praise. Amen.

SUNDAY

Worship and Rest

> "Come to Me, all who are weary and burdened, and I will give you rest." Matthew 11:28 (NASB)

Pause. Breathe. Reflect. Worship.

The week ahead will have its own demands, but today, let it be holy. Let your soul breathe in His goodness and exhale every burden.

Let worship renew you. Let rest restore you. Let His presence be your peace.

> **Prayer:**
> Lord, thank You for the Sabbath. Still my heart, quiet my spirit, and ready me for the journey ahead.

WEEK 18

MONDAY

God of Impossibilities

> *"But He said, 'The things that are impossible with people are possible with God.'" Luke 18:27 (NASB)*

Sometimes, it's not the big heartbreaks that overwhelm us; it's the small, quiet ones. A little sadness. A quiet disappointment. A hidden hurt. Like a tiny hole in the hull of a mighty ship, it may seem small, but left unattended, it slowly pulls us under.

Are you feeling burdened this morning?

Is your peace shaken?

Does your spirit feel a little heavier than usual?

Here's your reminder: God is near.

He's not just the God of miracles. He's the God of impossibilities.

He heals what feels unhealable. He restores what looks lost. He redeems what seems too far gone.

Whatever your circumstance today, don't let it drown your spirit.

Get up. Go worship. Go expecting.

Expect to hear from Him. Expect Him to meet you because He will.

Prayer:
Lord, thank You for being the God of the impossible. Speak to my heart today. Patch the quiet holes that sadness tried to slip through. Restore my joy. Rekindle my hope. Amen

Tuesday

He Hears Every Cry

> *"In my distress I called upon the Lord, and cried to my God for help; He heard my voice from His temple, and my cry for help before Him came into His ears." Psalm 18:6 (NASB)*

What a powerful image:

Your cry, not ignored, not delayed, not filtered, is going straight into the ears of Almighty God.

Psalm 56 takes it further, telling us that He collects every tear in His bottle. Not one drop escapes His notice. Not one ache is overlooked.

I thank God for the gift of tears. They express what words often fail to say.

They are holy. Healing. Human.

Tears connect us to each other, but more than that, they connect us to Him.

They bring a sacred kind of release.

A surrender that doesn't require explanation.

So don't hold back. Don't bottle it up. Whether you're grieving, aching, or quietly discouraged, pour it out. Your tears are not weakness. They are prayers. And none of them are wasted.

Prayer:
Lord, thank You for listening, not just to my words, but to my tears. Thank You for hearing what my heart can't always say aloud. Collect every cry and comfort me with Your nearness. Amen.

WEDNESDAY

Shine Anyway

> *"In the same way, let your light shine before others, that they may see your good deeds and glorify your Father in heaven."* Matthew 5:16 (NASB)

The moon doesn't wait for perfect conditions; it just shines.
Through clouds. Through storms. In silence. In darkness.
No spotlight. No stage. No applause.
It simply reflects what it was designed to reflect.

And we could learn a lot from that.
So often, we let our circumstances dim our light.
Discouragement whispers, What's the point?
Criticism says, You're not enough.
Exhaustion tempts us to hide instead of shine.
But God created us with a divine purpose, to reflect His light in a world that desperately needs it. Not because we're perfect. But because He is.

So shine.
Even if no one notices.
Even if the night is long.
Even if your surroundings are less than ideal
Your faithfulness still matters.

Prayer:
Lord, help me shine for You, no matter the season or setting. Let me reflect Your light in the quiet places, in the hard moments, and in the dark. May I walk boldly in the purpose You've given me, shining for Your glory alone. Amen.

Thursday

Addiction: — Mastered or Mindful?

> *"No temptation has overtaken you except something common to mankind... but with the temptation will provide the way of escape also, so that you will be able to endure it." 1 Corinthians 10:13 (NASB)*

The Keurig broke again. But this time?

No panic. No overnight shipping. No frantic search for a replacement. Just a deep breath and a silent chuckle.

Progress.

Addictions don't always come in dramatic forms. Sometimes, they're disguised in our daily routines—coffee, impulse shopping, mindless scrolling, sugar, or needing to be in control. They sneak in quietly and grow roots before we realize they've taken hold.

But here's the truth: there's a difference between enjoying something and being mastered by it.

And the difference begins with awareness.

God is gracious; He doesn't just reveal our dependencies to shame us. He reveals them to free us. Because He knows what true freedom feels like. And He offers a way out, not just from sin, but from anything that subtly replaces Him.

So today, ask yourself:

Is this habit helping me thrive?

Or is it holding me back?

Prayer:
Lord, reveal any area where I've become mastered by habit instead of surrendered to You. Give me the strength to walk in self-control and the wisdom to recognize when enough is enough. Amen.

Friday

Touch the Hem

> *"Yet those who wait for the Lord will gain new strength; they will mount up with wings like eagles, they will run and not get tired, they will walk and not become weary." Isaiah 40:31 (NASB)*

Are you barely holding on — by a thread?

Then make sure it's the hem of His garment.

Like the woman in Mark 5, don't let the noise of the crowd or the chaos of life distract you. She didn't need a full embrace, just a graze of His robe. That single, determined reach changed everything.

Sometimes we think we need grand gestures or perfect words. But Jesus responds to faith, even if it's weary, trembling, or tear-streaked. One touch can break cycles, heal wounds, and restore what was lost.

Don't wait for the storm to pass. Bow low. Reach out now. Even in your weakness, His power is available — steady, present, healing.

Let hope spark like a current through your soul. Let that thread of faith tether you to the One who never lets go.

Prayer:
Lord, when I'm weary, help me reach for You. Remind me that just one touch from You is enough. I wait on You — expectant, trusting, and ready to be renewed. Amen.

SATURDAY

God's Boot Camp

> *"But solid food is for the mature, who because of practice have their senses trained to distinguish between good and evil."* Hebrews 5:14 (NASB)

Life with God isn't a cushy classroom; it's more like boot camp. There's training, discipline, and spiritual sweat involved. Every hardship, every delay, every unexpected detour is part of a divine regimen designed to shape us into mature believers.

God doesn't waste pain. He uses it to stretch our faith, sharpen our discernment, and strengthen our spiritual muscles. Like soldiers in training, we don't get promoted without testing. The same way muscles grow under resistance, our faith grows through trials.

We can't survive on spiritual milk forever. Growth demands more. Maturity means welcoming the weight room of life—the challenges, the spiritual drills, the uncomfortable lessons—knowing they're forging endurance in us.

Don't fear the boot camp. Embrace it. God is preparing you for more than just survival; He's preparing you for service.

> **Prayer:**
> *Lord, help me pass each test with grace. When trials come, remind me they're part of Your training ground. Let me grow stronger, wiser, and more rooted in You each day. I don't want to stay where I am, build me into who You've called me to be.*

SUNDAY: *Renew and Be Restored*

 SUNDAY

Renew and Be Restored

> *"He restores my soul; He guides me in the paths of righteousness for the sake of His name."* Psalm 23:3 (NASB)

Today is a day for rest and restoration. Before the week rushes in, allow yourself to be still.

God's guidance comes more clearly when we stop striving. Let worship fill your heart. Let rest renew your soul.

Be intentional. Be quiet. Be with Him.

Prayer:
Lord, thank You for this sacred pause. Restore what's been worn down this week and ready me for what's ahead.

WEEK 19

Monday

Covenant of Love

> *"Then it shall come about, because you listen to these judgments and keep and do them, that the Lord your God will keep His covenant with you and His faithfulness which He swore to your forefathers."*
> *Deuteronomy 7:12 (NASB)*

While mentally arranging my week, I heard a whisper saying, Deuteronomy 7:12. As I paused to read it, I was struck by the beauty and weight of that promise: God keeps His covenant and His faithfulness; if we listen and obey.

God's covenant of love is not a casual contract or a one-sided blessing. It's a relationship. One rooted in devotion, trust, and obedience. We long for His faithfulness, but are we being faithful in return?

This isn't about legalism; it's about love. When we love someone deeply, we naturally respond with commitment and care. That's what God desires from us: not perfection, but pursuit.

Rededicate your heart daily. Yearn for more of Him. The covenant was never meant to be forgotten; it was meant to be lived.

Prayer:
Lord, I rededicate my heart to You today. Teach me to walk in faithfulness. Let my life reflect the love and devotion You've always shown me through Your covenant.

TUESDAY

Eternal Friends

"For God so loved the world, that He gave His only Son, so that everyone who believes in Him will not perish, but have eternal life." John 3:16 (NASB)

God's love sought me, bought me, and brought me into His fold. It wasn't because I was good, but because He is. His love isn't based on performance, pedigree, or perfection. It's rooted in sacrifice. It's eternal.

We live in a world where friendships often fade and love comes with conditions. But not with God. His love is steadfast — a covenant, not a contract. He doesn't ghost us when we fail. He doesn't walk away when we are weak. He came searching for us long before we ever turned to Him.

Pause today and ask: Is my eternity secure? Human accolades may fill an obituary, but what truly matters is your relationship with Christ. Titles fade. Awards gather dust. But eternity is forever.

Let's shift our focus. Let's realign our hearts. Let's encourage one another to live not just for today, but for forever.

Prayer:
Lord, thank You for seeking and saving me. Teach me to live with eternity in view, and to share Your everlasting love with others. Amen.

WEDNESDAY

Gift Giving Like God

"For God so loved the world that He gave His only begotten Son..." John 3:16 (NASB)

God didn't give us leftovers or something convenient; He gave His only Son. That's the standard of true generosity: sacrificial, intentional, and rooted in love.

This season, let's ask ourselves: Am I giving like God?

Gift giving isn't about obligation or tradition. It's an opportunity to reflect the heart of the Father. That might mean blessing someone who doesn't expect it — the mail carrier, the trash collector, the elderly neighbor who lives alone. Sometimes the most meaningful gift isn't wrapped in paper, but in kindness — a handwritten note, a prayer, a listening ear, or your undivided attention.

Even in tight seasons, we all have something to give. The gift of presence, encouragement, or time can mean more than anything money can buy.

Let's give with thoughtfulness, not out of habit. Let's give with eternal purpose, not just seasonal cheer.

> **Prayer:**
> *Lord, help me to give as You gave, not out of convenience, but with intention, compassion, and joy. Let my giving reflect Your heart this season and always.*

THURSDAY

Let It Go

> *"Forget the former things; do not dwell on the past. See, I am doing a new thing!" Isaiah 43:18-19*

The year may be slipping away, but the baggage doesn't have to follow.

Let go of the pain. Let go of the disappointments. Let go of the heavy what ifs and if only. God's voice echoes through Isaiah like a gentle but firm whisper: Do not dwell on the past... I am doing a new thing.

THURSDAY: *Let It Go*

We often carry things God never asked us to — grudges, regrets, guilt, or grief. But His invitation is simple and powerful: Release it. The future He has prepared begins where surrender meets faith.

Pray honestly: Open my clenched fists, Lord. I release it all to You — every hurt, every memory, every failed plan.

Step into the new year with open hands and an open heart, ready to receive the fresh work God wants to do in you and through you.

> **Prayer:**
> *Lord, thank You for new beginnings. Help me let go of the past and walk forward with freedom, trusting in the beauty of what You are preparing. I surrender the old and welcome the new.*

FRIDAY

Anchored in Gratitude

> *"God is our refuge and strength, an ever-present help in trouble."*
> *Psalm 46:1 (NASB)*

On the last day of the year, I find myself in my "Jesus recliner," heart full and eyes teary. I reflect on the highs and lows, the victories and valleys, the laughter and losses.

In all 34,000 emotions I've felt this year, He walked beside me.

Gratitude has a way of shifting our perspective. It doesn't erase the pain, but it reminds us that we were never alone. Even when the prayers weren't answered the way we hoped, His presence was still constant. His strength was our steadying force.

Gratitude lets us fall in love with the life we have, even when it hasn't looked the way we imagined. It allows us to say, "God, You are good," not just when things go right, but because You are right — always.

As we close the chapter on this year, let's remember His faithfulness. Let's reset our hearts, realign our focus, and anchor our souls in the One who has carried us through.

> **Prayer:**
> *Lord, thank You for walking with me through every season, every storm, and every silent moment. I release the year behind me and embrace the one ahead, anchored in the unshakable truth that You are with me. Always.*

SATURDAY

Calm Beneath the Waves

"My soul, wait in silence for God alone, for my hope is from Him."
Psalm 62:5 (NASB)

Storms will come. The waves may crash loudly against our plans, our peace, and our expectations. Life has a way of tossing us into turbulent waters — news we didn't expect, situations we didn't plan, feelings we didn't know how to process. But beneath all of that turmoil lies a stillness we can access, if our soul is anchored in God.

I once experienced this firsthand during a submarine ride in Grand Cayman. On the surface, the waters were choppy and unsettled, winds whipping against the boat. But as we descended into the depths, something incredible happened — silence. Calm. Below the surface, everything was undisturbed. Peace reigned, even while chaos churned above.

Isn't that just like the Christian walk? On the outside, the world may be noisy — financial burdens, family drama, health challenges. But when we are rooted in Christ, our spirit doesn't have to rise and fall with the tides. There's a deep, anchored peace that only God provides.

SATURDAY: *Calm Beneath the Waves*

We can't always calm the storm, but we can calm our souls in the storm. And sometimes, the loudest praise is the one whispered through tears — Lord, I trust You anyway.

Don't let the storm steal your praise. Worship anyway. Breathe. Wait. Trust. The calm you seek is already beneath the surface, waiting to hold you.

> **Prayer:**
> Lord, let my soul find rest in You, even when the waves of life surround me. When the noise is deafening, anchor me in Your peace. Teach me to wait quietly, to hope boldly, and to worship faithfully, even in the storm.

SUNDAY

Worship and Community

> *"Not giving up meeting together, as some are in the habit of doing, but encouraging one another..."* Hebrews 10:25 (NIV)

Sunday is a gift; a time to gather, reflect, and worship. There's something sacred about meeting together and lifting our voices in unity. It refocuses our hearts and reminds us we're not walking this journey alone.

Take time today to be in God's presence — in worship, in rest, in fellowship.

> **Prayer:**
> Lord, thank You for this day set apart. Help me to honor it and enter the week refreshed and encouraged.

WEEK 20

MONDAY

Foggy Drive

> *"Your word is a lamp to my feet and a light for my path." Psalm 119:105 (NASB)*

Have you ever driven through dense fog? The road disappears, the world feels muffled, and you can only see a few feet ahead. But somehow, you keep going because your headlights give just enough light for the next few steps.

That's how God often leads us, not with a floodlight showing the full journey, but with just enough illumination to take the next faithful step.

We crave certainty. We want the full itinerary, the GPS route with ETA included. But God says, "Trust Me." Proverbs 16:9 reminds us: "The heart of man plans his way, but the Lord establishes his steps."

If we trust a man-made headlight to guide us through the fog, can we not trust the Creator of the road itself?

Prayer:
Lord, help me to walk by faith, one step at a time. When the way ahead seems unclear, remind me that Your Word is enough to guide my feet, and Your presence is the light I need.

TUESDAY

The Power of 'I'

> *"I have been crucified with Christ; and it is no longer I who live, but Christ lives in me." Galatians 2:20 (NASB)*

The letter "I" is just one small stroke of the pen, yet it carries tremendous weight.
"I want."
"I need."
"I did this."
"I don't deserve that."
From childhood, we're trained to be independent, self-sufficient, and self-promoting. But in the Kingdom of God, the journey is about dying to self so that Christ can live through us. The gospel calls us to exchange the power of I for the power of Christ in me.

Paul didn't say, "I've improved with Christ." He said, "I no longer live." That's a full surrender — the ego dethroned so that Jesus can reign.

It's a radical shift:
From I did it → to He did it through me.
From I want this → to Lord, Your will be done.
From I deserve better → to I trust Your plan.

Teach your children to say, "Thank You, Jesus," not just "I did it!" Train your heart to say, "Not I, but Christ." Let today be a turning point from self-promotion to Savior-exaltation.

> **Prayer:**
> *Lord, strip me of pride. Let my life reflect not my achievements, but Your glory. Replace my "I" with "Christ in me" — every word, every deed, every breath.*

WEDNESDAY

Are You a Sower?

> *"And the one on whom seed was sown on the good soil, this is the one who hears the word and understands it, who indeed bears fruit."*
> *Matthew 13:23 (NASB)*

Lately, I've been waking up at 3:15 a.m. That quiet hour when the world is still and the Lord whispers. In those moments, a question keeps stirring: Are we still excited about Jesus?

The magi journeyed far, guided only by a star, driven by wonder and a hunger to find the King. Do we still follow like that? Or have we grown numb in a world filled with noise, distractions, and delayed outcomes?

We live in a results-driven culture. But the Kingdom of God doesn't work on spreadsheets or instant metrics. God calls us to sow, faithfully and generously, even when we don't see the harvest.

My father, in his late 80s, continues to share God's Word with quiet tenacity. He doesn't look for applause or count conversions. He sows. And the Lord, in His timing, brings fruit.

What about you? Are you bold in sowing seeds of truth, encouragement, and hope? Or are you waiting to see signs before you step out?

Don't measure the mission by visible growth. Sow because He asked you to. Sow because His Word never returns void. Sow and trust the soil to Him.

Prayer:
Lord, make me a faithful sower. Even in dry seasons, even when I can't see the fruit, help me plant Your Word with joy, confidence, and trust in Your timing.

THURSDAY

Simple Obedience, Great Reward

> *"But whoever listens to me will live securely and be at ease from the dread of evil." Proverbs 1:33 (NASB)*

The magi were filled with joy when they saw the star. They didn't overthink it. They didn't hesitate and ask, "But what if it leads nowhere?" They simply obeyed. They followed the light with anticipation in their hearts and gifts in their hands, not knowing where the journey would end, but trusting the One who sent the sign.

That's the kind of obedience God desires from us. Not delayed, reluctant obedience. Not conditional obedience that says, "If I do this, You'll bless me, right?" But joyful, trusting, wholehearted obedience — the kind that moves when He says go, even if we can't see the whole map.

Let's be honest: we often want guarantees before we act. We ask for signs, confirmations, and then more signs. But obedience isn't about certainty; it's about surrender. It's not a transaction; it's a trust walk.

God's Word says that whoever listens to Him, not just hears, but listens and acts, will live securely. That kind of obedience ushers in peace. It calms the dread that stalks our thoughts. It anchors us in the storm.

Sometimes, the greatest blessings are found not in grand gestures, but in small, simple acts of obedience. Like sending that text. Forgiving someone. Praying for a stranger. Saying "yes" to a God-nudge that doesn't make sense. Because on the other side of obedience, there's always purpose, even if it's not visible right away.

Return to that childlike excitement, like the wise men who followed the star. Get excited about following Jesus again. Not for what He gives, but for who He is.

Prayer:
Lord, I choose obedience over negotiation. Let me follow You with joy, even when the path is unclear. Train my heart to say yes without conditions. I trust that Your way leads to peace, protection, and deeper purpose.

FRIDAY

Should I or Should I Not?

"But seek first His kingdom and His righteousness, and all these things will be provided to you." Matthew 6:33 (NASB)

Indecisiveness shows up in the most ordinary ways — what to wear, what to cook, whether to speak or stay silent. And in bigger moments, it can feel paralyzing. But God has already given us a principle that simplifies everything: Seek Him first.

When we put Him at the center, not as an afterthought, but as the starting point, clarity follows. It doesn't mean every answer will come instantly, but it means we're no longer navigating in the dark. The One who sees the end from the beginning is now steering the ship.

So start the day with surrender. It's not weakness; it's wisdom. Let the One who designed your path also direct your steps.

Try it for two weeks. Bring every decision before Him, big or small, and watch peace replace pressure.

> **Prayer:**
> Lord, I surrender this day, and every decision, into Your hands. Be my compass and my calm. When I'm unsure, remind me that seeking You first is always the right answer.

SATURDAY

Anchored Calm

"My soul, wait in silence for God alone, for my hope is from Him." Psalm 62:5 (NASB)

SATURDAY: *Anchored Calm*

Storms may rage, winds may howl, and life may toss us around, but beneath it all, there can still be peace. I was once on a submarine ride where the surface waves were violent, crashing in every direction. But once we descended below, the water was calm, silent, still, undisturbed.

That's what it means to be anchored in God. The chaos above doesn't dictate the calm within.

Life won't always be smooth sailing, but our souls don't have to rise and fall with the waves. When we are deeply rooted in Him, worship becomes our anchor, and His presence becomes our peace. Even when we don't have the answers, we can have the assurance.

So today, if the storm is loud, go deeper. Quiet your soul. Wait on Him. He is the anchor that holds.

Prayer:
Lord, when the waves of life crash around me, draw my soul into Your stillness. Let my heart wait in silence, anchored in Your promises. May my worship rise above every storm.

SUNDAY

Renewal and Readiness

"Create in me a clean heart, O God, and renew a steadfast spirit within me." Psalm 51:10 (NIV)

Sunday is more than rest; it's renewal. Take time to realign with God's heart, reset your focus, and get fueled for the week ahead.

Come before Him with a surrendered heart, and ask for fresh strength, joy, and clarity.

Prayer:
Lord, as I enter this new week, renew my heart, restore my spirit, and fill me with Your presence.

WEEK 21

Monday

Welcome to Our Happy Mess

> *"With a strong hand and an outstretched arm, for His faithfulness is everlasting." Psalm 136:12 (NASB)*

Sometimes life is just a mess, not necessarily sad or tragic, just wonderfully chaotic. A little noisy, a little cluttered, a little wild. There's a pillow in my home that reads, "Welcome to our happy mess," and every time my grandkids turn the house upside down, it reminds me to smile, breathe, and embrace the beautiful imperfection.

God's outstretched arm is always there, not just for the cleaned-up, picture-perfect moments, but right in the middle of the mess. When we fall short, when the house is loud, when the to-do list is forgotten, He welcomes us with grace. His love doesn't flinch at the clutter of our lives. It enters and sits with us.

Think of the peace that floods a crying child when they collapse into their parent's arms. Now multiply that comfort infinitely — that's the power of our Savior's embrace.

Prayer:
Lord, thank You for loving me in the middle of my mess. When I stumble, remind me that Your arms are still open. I run into Your embrace today — joyfully, gratefully, and just as I am.

Tuesday

Customized Wisdom

> *"But if any of you lacks wisdom, let him ask of God, who gives to all generously and without reproach." James 1:5 (NASB)*

Wisdom is not reserved for the elite, the educated, or the spiritually mature. It's available to anyone who asks. That includes the overwhelmed mom, the uncertain leader, the anxious graduate, and the weary soul making yet another hard decision.

Proverbs 7:4 encourages us to treat wisdom like family: "Say to wisdom, 'You are my sister.'" That speaks of closeness, a trusted presence in your everyday walk. God doesn't hand out generic advice; He gives customized counsel for each moment, each heart, and each crossroad.

So why do we hesitate? Sometimes pride stops us. Other times, it's fear of looking foolish. But God isn't like man; He doesn't roll His eyes at our questions. He doesn't shame us for not knowing. Instead, He welcomes the ask and answers with grace.

Prayer:
Lord Jesus, I lack wisdom in more ways than I know. Please give me clarity where I feel confusion, direction where I'm uncertain, and courage where I hesitate. Thank You for being generous with Your guidance, and gentle with my doubts.

Wednesday

The Temptation of Warm Bread

> *"But he does not know that the dead are there, that her guests are in the depths of Sheol." Proverbs 9:18 (NASB)*

WEDNESDAY: *The Temptation of Warm Bread*

Temptation rarely shows up looking dangerous. It comes wrapped in warmth and comfort, like fresh bread out of the oven. Appealing. Harmless. Irresistible. But just like the woman described in Proverbs 9, what looks inviting can lead straight to destruction.

Satan doesn't bait us with obvious traps. He knows how to appeal to our cravings for approval, for comfort, and for control. And just like Eve in the garden, one small compromise can unleash far-reaching consequences.

Temptation promises satisfaction but delivers sorrow. That's why Paul reminds us in 2 Corinthians 12:9, "My grace is sufficient for you, for My power is made perfect in weakness." The antidote to temptation isn't more willpower; it's more surrender.

When the "warm bread" moment comes, pause. Pray. Remember what's at stake.

> **Prayer:**
> *Lord, help me recognize temptation for what it truly is — a counterfeit promise. When I'm weak, let me run to Your strength. Remind me that no momentary pleasure is worth the long-term pain. Your grace is enough.*

THURSDAY

White as Snow

> *"Though your sins are like scarlet, they shall be as white as snow."*
> Isaiah 1:18 (NASB)

One winter morning, I opened my front door to a breathtaking scene, a blanket of freshly fallen snow, untouched and pure. Not a single footprint, not a speck of dirt. Just white perfection covering everything in sight.

It reminded me of Isaiah 1:18, God's promise to make our sins white as snow. Not mostly clean. Not better than before. Completely cleansed.

THURSDAY: *White as Snow*

We carry stains from regret, failure, and brokenness. Sometimes we fear that we've gone too far or fallen too many times. But God's mercy doesn't just cover; it transforms. His forgiveness doesn't leave residue. When He washes us, He restores us fully.

Let that image settle in your soul: your past, erased by grace. Your heart, made new.

> **Prayer:**
> *Lord, thank You for the powerful cleansing of Your mercy. When I feel unworthy, remind me that Your grace makes me whole. Wash me again and make me truly white as snow.*

FRIDAY

Victim or Conqueror?

> *"Little children, you are from God and have overcome them, for He who is in you is greater than he who is in the world." 1 John 4:4 (NASB)*

Are you feeling afraid, helpless, lonely, weak, or discouraged? These emotions are real, but so is the power of God within you. Scripture is not just a comfort; it's a weapon. For every emotion, there is a verse to anchor you. For every lie of defeat, there is a truth that declares your victory.

We often fall into the trap of a victim mindset, rehearsing the pain, replaying the betrayal, magnifying the problem. But the Word says you are from God and have overcome. Not will overcome someday, but already have. Why? Because He who is in you is greater.

So today, peel off the mask of defeat. Cancel the pity party. Refuse the victim label. Instead, walk like the conqueror you are. Speak truth. Stand firm. You've already been equipped for victory.

> **Prayer:**
> Lord, I choose to live as a conqueror, not a victim. You are my strength in weakness, my hope in sorrow, and my victory in every battle. Thank You for living in me.

--- SATURDAY ---

Broken Pieces

> *"The LORD is close to the brokenhearted; He rescues those whose spirits are crushed."* Psalm 34:18 (NLT)

Broken dreams. Shattered relationships. Unanswered prayers. Life has a way of scattering pieces in every direction, leaving us numb, discouraged, and wondering if things can ever be whole again. But brokenness is not the end of the story, not with God.

When my niece was involved in a devastating train accident, doctors worked skillfully to piece together her crushed bones and reconstruct her arm. It took time, precision, and care, but healing came. And if a human surgeon can do that with physical bones, imagine what the Great Physician can do with a broken heart.

Maybe you're holding shattered pieces today — trust, hope, confidence, dreams. Don't hide them. Bring them to the One who specializes in restoration. He doesn't just patch things up; He makes all things new.

What the world discards, God redeems. What feels beyond repair is never beyond His reach.

> **Prayer:**
> Lord, I bring You every shattered piece of my life, seen and unseen. Thank You for being close to the brokenhearted. I believe You are restoring beauty, even in what feels beyond repair. Make me whole again in You.

 ## SUNDAY

Worship and Community

> *"Let us not give up meeting together, as some are in the habit of doing, but encouraging one another."* Hebrews 10:25

As you prepare for worship today, remember the strength found in community. God didn't design us to walk alone. Take time to gather, worship, and be refreshed in His presence.

Let this day reset your spirit and refill your soul.

Prayer:
Lord, thank You for the gift of fellowship. Help me value the body of Christ and enter this week renewed by worship.

WEEK 22

--- MONDAY ---

Flying Solo

> *"You adulterous people! Do you not know that friendship with the world is enmity with God? Therefore whoever wishes to be a friend of the world makes himself an enemy of God." James 4:4 (ESV)*

Pay attention to the phrase: "whoever wishes to be a friend of the world."

Have you ever felt like you're flying solo?

Flying solo — hmm... have I? Yes, we all have.

As a child, the other kids might say, "I don't want to play with you."

You are flying solo.

You go to a new school, and until someone warms up to you...

You are flying solo.

You speak up in a meeting at work and offer a suggestion no one supports...

You are flying solo.

You get married, and sometimes your spouse doesn't see things the same way...

You are flying solo.

You're raising children, and you and your partner disagree on how to do it...

You are flying solo.

Often, our Christian walk mirrors these moments — flying solo.

The world sees us differently because we are not meant to be part of its patterns.

We are in the world but not of the world.

Monday: *Flying Solo*

This world is full of intellects, scientists, philosophers, and skilled debaters, all of whom can easily pull you into their logic. But our omniscient God gave us a warning in His Word. What does He say in Colossians?

"See to it that no one takes you captive through hollow and deceptive philosophy..." (Colossians 2:8, paraphrased)

During my school days, all my friends were from different religions, and even the few Christians I knew were into partying and drinking. Have you ever noticed in foreign films how Christians are often portrayed? Drunkards. Partygoers. People with loose morals. Why?

This is how the world projects us.

In those days, I often had to fly solo. And believe me, it wasn't easy. But thank God for the solid foundation I had. That foundation helped me say no to certain activities. It's not about bragging on my discipline; it's to say that when your foundation is in Christ, He gives you the strength to fly solo.

Only by His strength can we face the world.

Day in and day out, our heart's cry should be: "Lord, I need You."

Prayer:
Lord, help me walk with courage when I feel alone. Strengthen me when I must fly solo for Your sake. Amen.

Tuesday

Enter by the Narrow Gate

"Enter by the narrow gate. For the gate is wide and the way is easy that leads to destruction, and those who enter by it are many." Matthew 7:13 (ESV)

As a little girl, I clearly remember a framed artwork that hung at the entrance of our home. It depicted two distinct gates — one wide, one narrow.

On the wide side of the gate, crowds of people were pouring in. The scene was filled with partying and entertainment, laughter and noise. But at the end of that path, there was a striking image of fire. Destruction.

On the other side of the painting stood the narrow gate. Very few chose that entrance. The path was difficult, filled with obstacles, trials, enemies, and temptation. Yet, those who persevered reached a glorious destination. By His grace alone, they were welcomed by the Master Himself.

"Blessed is the man who remains steadfast under trial, for when he has stood the test he will receive the crown of life, which God has promised to those who love him." James 1:12 (ESV)

Obtaining citizenship in a country typically requires living there for several years before you're even eligible to apply. But citizenship in heaven? That's granted not by years, but by how we live — daily walking the narrow path, making choices that reflect our love for God, enduring trials, resisting temptation, and keeping our eyes on the eternal prize.

Are we working toward our eternal citizenship?

"But our citizenship is in heaven, and from it we await a Savior, the Lord Jesus Christ." Philippians 3:20 (ESV)

> **Prayer:**
> Lord, keep me steadfast as I walk the narrow path. Help me live with eternity in view. Amen.

Wednesday

Blame Game

> *"If we confess our sins, He is faithful and righteous to forgive us our sins and to cleanse us from all unrighteousness." 1 John 1:9 (NASB)*

When Pharaoh saw Sarai, he remarked that she was a beautiful woman. And what was Abraham's instant response? "She is my sister."

Wednesday: *Flying Solo*

He had already plotted this with Sarai, asking her to say she was his sister so that his life would be spared.

What do you make of that statement?

It sounds incredibly selfish. To save his own neck, he was willing to sacrifice his wife. What if Pharaoh had taken her in and defiled her? This blame-shifting and self-preservation didn't start with Abraham. Go further back.

When God confronted Adam in the garden, what did Adam say? "The woman You gave me…" — he shifted the blame to Eve.

Then Eve? She blamed the serpent.

And Cain, after committing the most heinous crime? "Am I my brother's keeper?"

This pattern is as old as humanity.

Here's a real-life example: you ask a child if they took a cookie.

The first response? "No."

Followed by: "She took it!"

In our home, we had a rule: if you own up to your mistake, the punishment is lighter; sometimes grace even kicks in! 😊

Call it shifting blame, throwing someone under the bus, or pointing fingers, it's all the same. There's something in human nature that finds temporary relief in shifting blame just to avoid guilt.

But forget all that. Let's look at Jesus.

Blameless. Sinless. Yet falsely accused of blasphemy by the very religious leaders who were supposed to recognize Him.

He never shifted blame. He bore it for us.

Why do we shift the blame? Because we're trying to cover up our own faults.

But the Word of God is clear; we are accountable for our sins. Not someone else's. Ours.

And the good news? When we own up to our sins, God doesn't cast us away. He forgives.

Stop shifting. Start taking ownership!

That is the gospel. We have a faithful and merciful Father who is willing to forgive when we confess.

Prayer:
Father, give me the humility to own up to my mistakes and receive Your grace. Amen.

THURSDAY

Heart Check

> *"A tranquil heart is life to the body, But jealousy is rottenness to the bones." Proverbs 14:30 (NASB)*

Perhaps today is a day of rest for many who work during the week. So let me ask, how is your heart today?

Is it calm?

Free from the rush of a weekday morning?

Devoid of random to-do lists racing through your mind?

Check your blood pressure, it might be surprisingly normal.

When our minds race, our hearts often race too. Instead of being a calming factor, the heart becomes an accomplice, caught up in the chaos. Can you picture that?

Mind racing + heart racing = inner turmoil.

But look at Proverbs 14:30 again:

A tranquil heart is life to the body.

That's not just poetic; it's profoundly true.

Medically, a peaceful heart promotes physical well-being. But Scripture takes it even further.

"Guard your heart with all diligence, for from it flow the springs of life." Proverbs 4:23 (BSB)

Don't even let yourself get to the point of restlessness. The heart is one of the most powerful organs in the body. It literally screams life.

When someone passes away, what do we say? Their heartbeat stopped.

The heartbeat is the essence of living. It's not just physical; it carries emotional, hormonal, and even spiritual weight.

So how do we settle a racing, restless heart?

God, in His goodness, gives us the answer in His Word.

"Peace I leave with you; My peace I give to you. Not as the world gives do I give to you. Do not let your heart be troubled, nor let it be fearful." John 14:27

Let's do the math:

Thursday: *Heart Check*

Heart + Peace = Life
Heart + Restlessness = Loss of Life

Prayer:
Lord, settle my restless heart today. Fill me with Your peace so I can live and not just survive. Amen.

Friday

Monarch in a Storm

"When you pass through the deep, stormy sea, you can count on Me to be there with you... you will not drown." Isaiah 43:1-2 (paraphrased)

Have you ever watched a monarch butterfly? These delicate creatures have incredibly fragile wings, yet they exhibit a profound wisdom in times of trouble. When a storm hits, monarchs don't flap in panic or try to fight the wind; they enter a self-preservation mode and simply wait. When the storm passes, they rise and fly again, gracefully and unharmed.

We could learn something from them.

Many of us are walking through storms, some gentle, some harsh. And when we're in it, our first instinct is to react, to fix, to carry the burden ourselves.

But what if we didn't?

What if, like the monarch butterfly, we simply paused... and waited?

Our bodies weren't designed to carry the full weight of the storm. We were created to transfer that load to the One who can handle it.

Picture this: standing at the seashore as furious waves charge toward you. They crash, splash, and roar, but the moment they reach you, their force dies down. If you've dug your heels in, they may soak you, but they cannot shake you.

Remember Daniel's friends, they were thrown into the fire, yet they came out without even the smell of smoke. Sometimes our storms feel like that. Intense. Fiery. Overwhelming.

But we are never alone.

Let these promises wash over your soul:

"We are afflicted in every way, but not crushed; perplexed, but not despairing." 2 Corinthians 4:8 (ESV)

"When you pass through the waters, I will be with you." Isaiah 43:2 (ESV)

> **Prayer:**
> Lord, help me wait like the monarch and trust like the Hebrew boys. Let me be still and know that You are God. Amen.

SATURDAY

Which Clay Pot Are You?

"But the one sown on the good soil, this is the one who hears the word and understands it, who indeed bears fruit and produces..." Matthew 13:23 (NASB)

My cousin shared a picture that lingered in my heart all week. It showed several clay pots, each representing a different spiritual condition:

One pot stood upright but was leaking, like hearing the gospel but not retaining it.

Another lay on its side, completely immersed in the world.

One stood tall but remained empty, a life with no Word inside.

One was bubbling over, overflowing with the love of Christ.

And the last? Sealed tight with a lid, like a hardened heart that won't let God in.

If we're honest, we've all been in each of these pots at some point in life. But the question isn't who you were; it's who you are now.

SATURDAY: *Which Clay Pot Are You?*

Which pot are you today?

God doesn't just call us to hear His Word. He calls us to receive it deeply, to retain it, and to bear fruit. Not just to be filled, but to overflow.

And sometimes, it's not a sermon or a verse that changes a heart; it's a kind gesture. A listening ear. A small act of love. I know people who came to Christ because someone simply showed kindness when it wasn't deserved.

Today, stop making excuses. Stop waiting for a perfect opportunity or the "right words." Let your life preach. Let your actions pour out the love of Christ.

Prayer:
Lord, help me be the vessel that receives, retains, and reflects Your love. Make me overflow with the Gospel. Amen.

SUNDAY

A Day to Refocus

"This is the day that the Lord has made; Let us rejoice and be glad in it." Psalm 118:24 (NASB)

Sunday is more than just the end of the week; it's the beginning of your next chapter. It's a reset. A divine pit stop to fuel your spirit before life picks up again on Monday.

Gather with fellow believers. Soak in the Word. Sing out your praise. Be still in His presence.

Let today be your reminder that no matter what last week held, God is giving you a fresh page. So go to church, be encouraged, and carry His peace into the week ahead.

Prayer:
Father, thank You for Sundays. Thank You for quiet moments, joyful songs, and the blessing of community. Let today mark the start of a week filled with Your purpose. Amen.

WEEK 23

--- MONDAY ---

Inner Beauty Over Outward Appearance

> *"But the Lord said to Samuel, 'Do not look at his appearance or at the height of his stature, because I have rejected him; for God sees not as man sees, for man looks at the outward appearance, but the Lord looks at the heart.'" 1 Samuel 16:7 (NASB)*

This morning, I was reading from Genesis 24, where Abraham's servant sets out to find a wife for Isaac. His mission was serious, not just to find a woman who looked good on paper, but someone who was truly right for his master's son.

And what stood out? Not status. Not beauty. Not height.

What impressed him most was Rebekah's kindness.

She didn't just offer him water. She offered to draw water for all his camels, an exhausting, generous act. That wasn't staged. It was character.

Her inner beauty just burst through her actions.

For years, I had only seen this passage as a story about matchmaking. But now I realize, it's a powerful reminder that what God values is not what we often look for. He sees the heart. And so should we.

I'm reminded of my own union with my husband of 40 years. At our very first lunch together at his niece's wedding, he leaned over and told me he had a bank balance of just $400. Now, many girls might've walked away. But that was what impressed me most, his honesty and integrity. (And the running joke in our family? After 40 years, we still have only $400! ☻)

God sees what really matters.

May we, too, have the wisdom to see the inner beauty in those around us — to be captivated not by the shell, but by the soul.

> **Prayer:**
> Lord, teach me to look beyond appearances. Help me value integrity, kindness, and character in myself and others. Let me see people through Your eyes. Amen.

TUESDAY

Cleft of the Rock

> *"I will put you in a cleft of the rock and protectively cover you with My hand until I have passed by." Exodus 33:22 (paraphrased)*

Several times last night, my spirit kept whispering the words: "cleft of the rock."

I woke up praying, "Lord, please… let me hide myself in the cleft."

What does the cleft of the rock symbolize?

It's a place of safety.

A place of protection.

If you've ever seen a picture of a cleft, a narrow crevice in the rock, it often looks like a dark, dead-end space. Yet, it's surrounded on both sides by strong stone. It's as if two hands are shielding you from every direction. That's exactly what our God does; His hands are like those two rock walls, covering us and guarding us from danger.

We see this vividly in Exodus 33, where God tells Moses,

"I will put you in the cleft of the rock and cover you with My hand…"

Moses only saw the back of God as He passed by because God's protection was so personal, so intentional. Being hidden in the cleft was not a punishment; it was a privilege.

I remember being in high school during a time of war threats. We had brown paper covering our windows, and when the warning siren went off, we all rushed to hide, not in classrooms, but in ditches dug for protection. Oddly enough, the safety wasn't in the usual places.

TUESDAY: *Cleft of the Rock*

It was in the ditch.
And so it is with Christ.
He is our Rock. The cleft is where we are protected — hidden — shielded from the storm.

The challenges of life — grief, fear, pressure, loss — they can slam against you. But when you're in the cleft, the Rock absorbs the blow. To say, "Christ is my Rock" is more than a metaphor. It's truth. It's shelter. It's home.

There are many hymns inspired by this image, but one that always moves me to tears is:

"A Wonderful Savior Is Jesus, My Lord"
He hideth my soul in the cleft of the rock,
That shadows a dry, thirsty land.
He hideth my life in the depths of His love,
And covers me there with His hand,
And covers me there with His hand.

I pray today you find yourself in that cleft. And if not, search for it. God is always ready to receive you there.

> **Prayer:**
> *Father, thank You for being our refuge. Help us find safety and comfort in the cleft of the Rock, protected by Your hand. Shelter us from the storms of life. Amen.*

WEDNESDAY

The Chief Cupbearer Did Not Remember Joseph

"And the chief cupbearer did not remember Joseph, but forgot him."
Genesis 40:23 (paraphrased)

WEDNESDAY: *The Chief Cupbearer Did Not Remember Joseph*

Does that sound familiar?

How often, in our moments of desperation, do we reach out to someone for help? In the moment, they express gratitude — a thank-you, a nod of appreciation — and then... years pass. That moment, that kindness, that effort we made on their behalf is completely wiped from memory.

Joseph knew that sting.

He had interpreted the chief cupbearer's dream, asked for help in return, and yet, when the cupbearer was restored, he forgot. Not just briefly. For two years.

In contrast, I think of my father. In our conversations, he often reflects on people who helped him, in ways big and small, and always begins with the phrase, "I can never forget..."

Some of the stories sound so trivial, but there's a deep gratitude that pours out of those words. That is the kind of heart that honors God.

Scripture is clear about this kind of goodness and remembrance:

"And whoever gives one of these little ones just a cup of cold water to drink in the name of a disciple, truly I say to you, he shall by no means lose his reward."

Matthew 10:42 (NASB)

"God is not unjust so as to forget your work and the love which you have shown toward His name..."

Hebrews 6:10 (paraphrased)

Even if the world forgets, God does not forget.

Let's not be like the cupbearer in Joseph's story. Many have walked with us through grief, loss, disappointment, and uncertainty. Some were strangers. Some were angels in disguise. But all were sent by God.

Let your morning begin with gratitude oozing out of every fiber in your body.

Maybe today's the day to send a note, a call, or a message to someone who helped you in your hour of need.

Let gratitude be part of your DNA today.

Prayer:
Lord, help us to remember the kindness others have shown us. Teach us to be grateful and to express our appreciation. Let gratitude flow from our hearts each day. Amen.

Thursday

Writing on the Wall: Grateful

> *"Bless the Lord, my soul, And do not forget any of His benefits."*
> *Psalm 103:2 (NASB)*

We've been reflecting on the story of Joseph, particularly on **the** lack of gratitude shown by the chief cupbearer who forgot him.

Yesterday, something simple yet powerful happened to me. I had left the front door open and walked into my dining room. That's when I noticed a shadow of a plaque that was reflecting on the wall: "Grateful."

I had never seen that reflection before. It stopped me in my tracks.

There I stood, in a warm home on a cold day, sheltered by four walls, and all I could do was whisper gratitude.

Before I knew it, I was walking around my home, speaking thankfulness aloud, overwhelmed by God's goodness in the everyday.

In contrast, the cupbearer forgot Joseph just once. But what about us?

How often do we go through the motions of our day, consumed by tasks and responsibilities, and fail to pause and reflect on the blessings all around us?

Psalm 103 is a beautiful reminder to our forgetful souls.

"Bless the Lord, O my soul, and forget not all His benefits."

Let that be our anthem. Let gratitude live in our DNA, not as an occasional visitor, but as a constant companion.

Prayer:
Father, open our eyes to the blessings all around us. May we live each moment with a grateful heart and never take Your goodness for granted. Amen.

FRIDAY

Safety Net

> *"Whoever listens to me will live in safety and be at ease, without fear of harm."* Proverbs 1:33 (NASB)

This morning, one of my readings came from Proverbs. And I paused on this verse — safety and ease — in a world full of fear and uncertainty.

How often does the fear of the unknown consume us?

Our minds go on a "joy ride," imagining worst-case scenarios, spiraling in fear rather than resting in faith.

But then, I'm reminded of a beautiful Scripture we often sing as a benediction, words of deep comfort from Lamentations:

"The steadfast love of the Lord never ceases;
His mercies never come to an end;
They are new every morning;
Great is Your faithfulness."

Are you carrying something today?

A fear that is unsettling your peace — release it.

A worry that is gnawing at your mind — release it.

A broken relationship that has consumed your soul — release it.

Don't let fear, anxiety, or distraction pull you away from God's safety net.

This safety net is His presence. His promises. His protection.

It is His provision for His children.

Stay inside the net.

"God is our refuge and strength,
A very ready help in trouble." Psalm 46:1 (NASB)

Ask yourself:

Is God your safety net?

Let nothing and no one take His place.

> **Prayer:**
> Lord, You are our refuge and safety. Keep us steady and unafraid as we face the unknown. Thank You for Your faithful protection. Amen.

Saturday

No More Excuses

"For the Lord will be your confidence, And will keep your foot from being caught." Proverbs 3:26 (NASB)

I was reading Exodus 4 and found myself shaking my head at Moses' excuses. Despite witnessing God's miracles firsthand, Moses still said, "I have never been eloquent."

And God's response? So powerful.

"The LORD said to him, 'Who gave human beings their mouths? Who makes them deaf or mute? Who gives them sight or makes them blind? Is it not I, the Lord?'"

Exodus 4:11 (NIV)

God was saying, "I know your limitations. I made you. And I still chose you."

That truth still applies today. If God has called you to something, a task, a ministry, a conversation, a new step, don't hide behind excuses. Don't shrink back in fear or insecurity. God equips those He calls.

Let your response be like Samuel's:

"Here I am."

We often hold ourselves back, citing our weaknesses, our lack of skill, or our past failures. But our confidence isn't in ourselves; it's in the Lord.

So no more excuses.

> **Prayer:**
> *God, silence our doubts and strengthen our resolve. May we serve You with confidence, knowing You equip those You call. Amen.*

SUNDAY: *A Day of Worship and Renewal*

 SUNDAY

A Day of Worship and Renewal

As we enter into this day of rest, let's realign our hearts with the One who holds it all together. Use this day to worship, to breathe, to reset. Let your soul be refreshed in His presence. Whether you are attending church, gathering with family, or simply sitting in stillness, acknowledge Him.

Prepare for the week ahead not with worry, but with worship. For the same God who brought you through last week is the One who walks before you in the days to come.

"Yet those who wait for the Lord will gain new strength; They will mount up with wings like eagles,

They will run and not get tired, They will walk and not become weary." Isaiah 40:31 (NASB)

Prayer:
Lord, as we pause today, fill us with fresh strength and perspective. May our worship be pleasing to You, and our hearts realigned for the week ahead. Amen.

WEEK 24

MONDAY

Blessed Assurance, Jesus Is Mine

I woke up this morning with this hymn on my lips. Sometimes we sing songs just because we know the words. But today, I decided to prayerfully read through the lyrics. Fanny Crosby—what an amazing writer of hymns. Like Helen Keller, she was blind, yet her spiritual sight was so clear.

The very first line struck me with new depth: Blessed assurance, Jesus is mine.

It shouts certainty. Confidence. Identity. Jesus is mine.

And then that last verse; what a powerful ending:

Perfect submission, all is at rest
I in my Savior am happy and blest
Watching and waiting, looking above
Filled with His goodness, lost in His love

This hymn is all about looking up. Looking at the Savior. We find rest when we are in perfect submission to His will. And it ends with that beautiful line: lost in His love.

Can we truly be lost in His love? I believe we can. And when we are, the gossip, the disappointments, the discouragements, they slowly take a backseat. They don't hold the same power over us. Our peace comes when we rest in Him.

Try being lost in His love today. Your perspective will shift. Your priorities will change. Why? Because:

Blessed assurance, Jesus is mine.

Let me jog your memory; remember when you were courting or newly married? You were so in love. Nothing else seemed to matter. You

Monday: *Blessed Assurance, Jesus Is Mine*

held hands in public, smiled for no reason, and floated through your day. You were lost in love, and you didn't care who noticed.

If we could feel that way about an imperfect human partner, with all the flaws and stumbles that come with earthly love, how much more should we be swept up in love with our perfect, heavenly Father, whose love for us never fails?

We don't know what challenges or storms today will bring. But through it all, keep singing:

Blessed assurance, Jesus is mine.

> **Prayer:**
> *Lord, help us to be lost in Your love today. May Your unconditional love fill our hearts and shape our responses. Amen.*

TUESDAY

Writing on the Canvas – Only What's Done for Christ Will Last

"So we make it our goal to please Him, whether we are at home in the body or away from it." 2 Corinthians 5:9 (NIV)

A cousin of mine made a framed canvas for me that simply says: "Only what's done for Christ will last." Apt. Simple. And such a gentle reminder. I decided to hang it in my prayer/work room. Now, every time I go to make my coffee, those words stare right back at me, and immediately, they set the tone for my day.

The hustle and bustle of everyday life... the fun and laughter of the season... they can all quietly pull us away from our time with God. I'll be the first to confess—I just returned from a 6½-day whirlwind trip to India, and my quiet time with God suffered. It wasn't intentional. It just happened. Days were packed, and I got carried away.

But this taught me something: we must be intentional and cautious not to rob God of our time or deprive Him of our presence. As the old hymn goes, "A little talk with Jesus makes it right, all right."

We need Him every moment. That's where we draw strength, wisdom, encouragement, and direction. Don't let distractions take away what matters most. We don't want to lose sight of the mission God has given us.

Just like that framed reminder says:
Only what's done for CHRIST will last.
No substitution.

> **Prayer:**
> Father, remind us daily to put You first in everything. Let our lives reflect what truly lasts — a walk that pleases You. Amen.

WEDNESDAY

Representing the Savior Well

"Whatever happens, conduct yourselves in a manner worthy of the gospel of Christ." Philippians 1:27a (NIV)

Anything that has even the slightest reference to God thrills my heart. Today was one of those days. I was driving to work, and traffic was moving at a snail's pace. In the next lane, I spotted an 18-wheeler truck, and I was immediately drawn to it. Bold letters across the back caught my eye and put a smile on my face – Jesus is Lord.

Now, my husband always says: either go ahead of the truck or stay behind it, never drive side by side. But this time? I was so thrilled by what I saw that I secretly hoped traffic would stop! I even pulled out my phone to take pictures. That's how moved I was. It was refreshing to see someone boldly display their faith for all to read.

WEDNESDAY: *Representing the Savior Well*

And then it hit me—we are just like that truck, chugging along in life. But does our demeanor boldly declare, "I am God's child"?

Think of the different reactions people might have had when they saw that message on the truck:

Shaking their head
Muttering, "Ah, these Christians..."
Feeling thankful
Feeling convicted
Whispering a prayer
Or like me—absolutely thrilled

The message was bold. But here's the thing—it comes with a responsibility. That truck represents Christ now. People are watching:

Is the driver following the rules of the road?
Is he cutting someone off?
Is he getting irritated and honking?

It made me reflect on how we display our faith. Maybe we wear a cross necklace. Or a T-shirt that says "Jesus is Lord." But what does our behavior say?

Are we representing the Savior well?

Prayer:
Lord, help us live in a way that reflects Your character. May our words and actions boldly display our faith in You. Amen.

THURSDAY

Don't Forget Your Humble Beginnings

"Do not forget to do good and to share with others, for with such sacrifices God is pleased." Hebrews 13:16 (NIV)

I was watching a woodpecker yesterday, trying to reach into an undrained pot of stagnated water—diving in several times, unsuccessfully, just to

THURSDAY: *Don't Forget Your Humble Beginnings*

get a little sip. Eventually, the bird gave up and flew away. I thought to myself, I could've made it easier by simply placing some water in a shallow pan. And that simple thought led to this picture in my mind.

God wants us to care for others and meet their needs whenever we can. He blesses us so that we can be a blessing. Our resources aren't just for us; they're tools to help others.

That small act, putting out water for a bird, is just one example of being mindful. I have a bird feeder too, but some days I'm just too lazy to refill it. And when I see the birds perched on the fence waiting, I feel awful. That's a picture of how easy it is to slip into the "my needs are met, so who cares" mindset.

But we're called to more.

Be there for others.

Don't let anyone fall behind.

The blessings we receive must be passed around. Sometimes, it's about meeting a physical need. Other times, it's just offering a listening ear.

As I continue to grow in my walk with God, I've made it a practice to start each day with this simple commitment:

"Lord, use me in whatever capacity You want me to be used."

That intentional prayer has led me to cancel an exercise class just to give a coworker a ride home because they had too much to carry, and the subway wasn't a good option. It wasn't a big sacrifice. But sometimes, putting someone else's need before your own is exactly what being used by God looks like.

I don't share this to boast; it's just a reminder that our hearts must be open and yielded. Even the smallest acts matter. I remember when I was that person, catching a bus with a diaper bag in one hand, my office bag and lunch bag in the other, and a bundled-up toddler who didn't want to walk, trudging five blocks to the babysitter's house on a cold morning.

As I write this, tears of gratitude stream down my face.

Let's not forget our humble beginnings.

Let's be a blessing to someone today.

Prayer:
Lord, open our hearts and eyes to the needs of others. May we live generously and humbly, remembering how far You've brought us. Amen.

FRIDAY

Break Now the Bread of Life

At church, we sang this beautiful hymn:
Break now the bread of life, dear Lord, to me,
As once you broke the loaves beside the sea.
Beyond the sacred page I seek you, Lord;
My spirit waits for you, O living Word.

I grew up singing this as the communion hymn in our church. Hearing it again stirred something deep within me. Back then, I didn't fully grasp its meaning, but yesterday, it landed differently.

Are we breaking the Bread of Life every day?

Are we sharing that bread with others?

It's so important to ask God to break open His Word to us when we sit with Him, especially in those quiet morning hours. Our pastor preached from Psalm 119:105-120, and every verse spoke about the power and beauty of the Word.

"Your word is a lamp to my feet and a light to my path." Psalm 119:105 (NASB)

God's Word is our flashlight; it shows us where to step so we don't stumble.

It's our hiding place and our shield.

It nourishes our soul and steadies our spirit.

"Break now the Bread of Life" isn't just a hymn; it's a prayer. Just like the loaves by the sea, the Word must be broken so we can receive it. And unless we break it open and eat, we remain spiritually famished.

We eat physical food daily to stay strong, so why do we try to go days without spiritual food?

Make it a rhythm. A practice. A source of revival.

Break open the Word.

Hold His promises close.

Draw strength from them for the challenges that lie ahead.

Prayer:
Lord, break open Your Word to us daily. Let it nourish our souls and draw us closer to You. Revive us with Your truth. Amen.

Saturday

Giving Thanks in All Circumstances

"Give thanks in all circumstances; for this is God's will for you in Christ Jesus." 1 Thessalonians 5:18 (NIV)

Not getting what we've been hoping or praying for doesn't always mean God is displeased with us, or that we lack faith. Sometimes, it simply means God sees something we don't.

Let me share a real-life scenario.

Back in December 2022, my immediate boss retired, and I was asked to step into that role in an "acting" capacity. I came home and prayed a very specific prayer:

"Lord, if this role will hinder our ministry in any way, please let it not be offered to me."

I did the job for a year and four months. Double duty. The feedback was positive. Upper management made several attempts to place me officially in that position. But the chief of the department had a different idea; he brought in someone from another state, someone he knew well.

When I was called in to be told the final decision, I didn't shake. I wasn't angry or disappointed. I was at peace, completely calm.

Why?

Because I had already submitted the outcome to God.

My peace didn't come from the outcome. It came from surrender.

My prayer all along had been, "Lord, only give it to me if it won't hinder the Kingdom work." And He answered.

We often memorize verses like 1 Thessalonians 5:18 in Sunday School, but there's something different about living it out. I truly experienced what it meant to give thanks in all circumstances.

When we surrender our desires and opportunities to God, we exchange anxiety for peace. He sees the full picture. We only see what's right in front of us.

So here's the encouragement:

Surrender first.
Yield completely.
And let thanksgiving follow, even when the answer is no.

> **Prayer:**
> *Father, thank You that You see the full picture. Teach us to surrender and give thanks in every situation, trusting that Your way is best. Amen.*

Sunday

Reflection and Renewal

As another week draws to a close, pause and reflect on God's faithfulness. Think back to where you saw His hand move, in moments of peace, in answered prayers, or even in the quiet strength to get through a hard day.

This week reminded us to rest in the cleft of the rock, to show gratitude, to recognize God as our safety net, and to live surrendered to His will. Let us not lose sight of these truths as we prepare for a new week.

Worship today. Sit under the Word. Let the fellowship of believers stir your spirit. Ask God to refresh your heart for the assignments ahead. Take time to simply say: "Thank You, Lord."

"What shall I repay to the Lord
For all His benefits to me?" Psalm 116:12 (NASB)

> **Prayer:**
> *Lord, thank You for walking with us through each day of this week. Prepare our hearts for worship today, and renew us for what lies ahead. Amen.*

WEEK 25

Monday

Drifting

> *"For this reason we must pay much closer attention to what we have heard, so that we do not drift away from it."* Hebrews 2:1 (NASB)

There's a kind of drifting that happens so subtly we don't even notice it. Not out at sea, but in our faith. You don't wake up one day and declare, "I think I'll drift from God." It happens slowly. Silently.

Hebrews 2:1 warns us to pay much closer attention to what we've heard so that we don't drift away. Drifting doesn't require rebellion, just neglect. A missed quiet time. A skipped service. A prayer left unsaid. A lingering doubt unspoken. A slow, steady slide into numbness.

But here's the grace: drifting doesn't have to end in being lost. We have an anchor. His name is Jesus. And He's still where we left Him.

The remedy isn't panic; it's realignment. Open the Word. Whisper a prayer. Tell Him you miss Him. He's not far.

Prayer:
Lord, when my heart begins to drift, pull me back to You. Help me pay attention to what I've heard and hold fast to what is true. Amen.

Tuesday

Enlighten

> *"The unfolding of Your words gives light; it gives understanding to the simple."* Psalm 119:130 (NIV)

Lord, without Your enlightenment, Your Word can feel like just another storybook — read and quickly forgotten, offering momentary comfort but no lasting change. But when You illuminate Your truth, something eternal happens. Our hearts ignite. Our minds are renewed. The pages of Scripture come alive and speak directly to our need.

Today, enlighten us in a way that lingers, not a passing glow, but a deep, enduring radiance. May the light of Your Word burn within us so brightly that we, too, become a light in the darkness. Let us not merely be readers but reflectors. Let our lives echo the power of Your truth in such a way that others are drawn not to us, but to You.

Let this be the word of the day — enlighten — and let its effect be lasting.

> **Prayer:**
> Lord, let me not walk in borrowed light. Let me shine from what You reveal personally to me. Amen.

Wednesday

Detective

> *"Call to Me and I will answer you, and I will tell you great and mighty things, which you do not know."* Jeremiah 33:3 (NASB)

WEDNESDAY: *Detective*

I was thinking about my son and his job. I decided to take his job, dissect it, and see if I can relate it to our walk with Christ.

Being a detective comes with an element of suspense and thrill. There's curiosity, a search for truth, and a commitment to dig deeper—even when things don't make sense at first glance. A good detective doesn't settle for surface answers. They gather clues, pay attention to small details, and connect the dots patiently until the full picture comes into view.

What if we approached our Christian walk the same way?

Too often, we treat our faith like a casual glance rather than a careful investigation. We skim Scripture. We hear a sermon but don't meditate on it. We feel the Spirit prompting us, but we ignore the deeper message.

God has invited us into the ultimate mystery, not to keep us in the dark, but to lead us into truth. Jesus said, "Seek and you will find." But seeking requires effort. It means asking questions, listening, searching, and not giving up too soon.

Prayer:
Lord, give me the heart of a spiritual detective—curious, observant, persistent. Help me seek You with intention and joy. Amen.

THURSDAY

Love Like a Widow

"Shepherd the flock of God among you, exercising oversight, not under compulsion but voluntarily, according to the will of God; and not with greed but with eagerness;" 1 Peter 5:2 ()

"But if anyone does not provide for his own, and especially for those of his household, he has denied the faith and is worse than an unbeliever." 1 Timothy 5:8 (NASB)

THURSDAY: *Love Like a Widow*

Shepherd the flock of God among you... not with greed, but with eagerness.

And if anyone does not provide for his own... he has denied the faith.

Visiting my homeland reminded me how little we really need. There, simplicity reigns. I've witnessed the most profound expressions of love and hospitality from those who have very little.

One pastor, facing persecution, still arrived with sweets made by hand. Another, working among the Gonda tribe, joyfully shared the story of his newborn daughter. A boy from our local church brought chicken curry for us — a feast from the heart.

These gestures reminded me of the widow who gave her last meal to Elijah. They gave, not from abundance, but from love.

How is your love tank today? Are your spiritual eyes open to the needs around you, especially among those serving God?

> **Prayer:**
> Lord, thank You for reminding me what true generosity looks like. Help me see the needs of Your servants and respond with love, not leftovers. Amen.

FRIDAY

Choose Joy

"Rejoice in the Lord always; again I will say, rejoice!" Philippians 4:4 (NASB)

We often wait for joy to arrive like a guest, but Scripture commands us to choose it, right now, right where we are.

Joy isn't a denial of hardship; it's a declaration that God is still good in the middle of it. Paul wrote these words while in prison. He didn't say, "Rejoice when everything's perfect." He said, "Rejoice in the Lord always."

Choosing joy doesn't mean we ignore the pain. It means we anchor ourselves to the One who carries us through it.

> **Prayer:**
> Lord, today I choose joy. Not because everything is easy, but because You are with me in everything. Amen.

SATURDAY

When God Rewrites Your Story

> *"And we know that God causes all things to work together for good to those who love God, to those who are called according to His purpose."* Romans 8:28 (NASB)

Sometimes we hold the pen so tightly that we forget who the real Author is. We map out our lives with bullet points and timelines, thinking we've got it all figured out. Then something unexpected happens—a loss, a closed door, a disruption—and we panic.

But God is not editing your life. He's rewriting it with purpose.

Romans 8:28 reminds us that God causes "all things," not just the joyful, planned parts, to work together for good. Your detour isn't the end of the story. It may be the beginning of your most powerful chapter yet.

> **Prayer:**
> Lord, when life doesn't go the way I planned, help me trust the hand that writes with eternal ink. Amen.

 ## Sunday

Reflection & Renewal

"What shall I repay to the Lord For all His benefits to me?" Psalm 116:12 (NASB)

Take this Sunday to rest in God's promises and reflect on His goodness.

This week reminded us to investigate deeply, to respond generously, to return when drifting, and to trust the Author of our story.

Pause today. Worship with others. Sit under the Word. Let your soul be restored. You don't have to earn His love, just receive it.

> **Prayer:**
> *Lord, thank You for walking with us this week. May our hearts find rest in You today. Amen.*

WEEK 26

MONDAY

Lord, Plant My Feet on Higher Ground

> *"I press on toward the goal for the prize of the upward call of God in Christ Jesus."* Philippians 3:14 (NASB)

I woke up with this hymn in my heart:

"Lord, lift me up, and let me stand
By faith on Canaan's tableland;
A higher plane than I have found—
Lord, plant my feet on higher ground."

Isn't that the cry of every believer's heart? That we wouldn't become stagnant in our walk, but that God would plant us on higher ground—in character, in wisdom, in faith, and in spiritual maturity. Higher ground isn't about status. It's about surrender. It's about choosing obedience when excuses would be easier. It's about pressing forward when comfort would tell us to stay still.

Paul reminds us that there is a goal, a heavenly prize, and we must press on to attain it. That means stretching beyond what we've known. It means trusting God to lift us up even when we don't feel ready or worthy. Sometimes the higher ground feels unfamiliar, even lonely. But it's where God meets us and grows us.

Don't be content with flat land. Don't settle for spiritual plateaus. Ask the Lord today to elevate your thoughts, your conversations, and your purpose.

Monday: *Do Not*

> **Prayer:**
> *Lord, lift me beyond where I've been. Don't let me grow comfortable or complacent. Plant my feet on higher ground—in holiness, in love, in truth. Help me press on toward the goal You've set before me. Amen.*

Tuesday

Do Not

> *"Do not be anxious about anything, but in everything by prayer and pleading with thanksgiving let your requests be made known to God. And the peace of God, which surpasses all comprehension, will guard your hearts and minds in Christ Jesus." Philippians 4:6-7 (NASB)*

I was thinking about the phrase "Do not"—a phrase we're all familiar with. We say it to our children. It's posted on signs. It's used as a warning. But when God says "Do not," it carries something deeper than just prohibition; it comes wrapped in promise.

When He says, "Do not be anxious," He's not ignoring our reality. He knows the chaos around us. Yet He calls us into a higher truth—that in the middle of our mess, we can bring every care to Him in prayer.

This Scripture is a "Do Not" paired with a divine invitation: Don't worry, come talk to Me. Don't panic, present your requests with thanksgiving. Don't spiral, trust Me to guard your heart and your mind.

Sometimes we hear "Do not" and feel like God is withholding something. But in truth, He's protecting us. "Do not fear," "Do not be afraid," "Do not be anxious," each one is a lifeline from a loving Father saying, I've got this, and I've got you.

> **Prayer:**
> *Lord, help me to embrace every "Do Not" You have spoken, not as a restriction, but as a promise that You are near. Teach me to bring every concern to You, knowing that Your peace will guard my heart. Amen.*

WEDNESDAY

The King of Kings Calls Me His Own

> *"He came to His own, and His own people did not accept Him. But as many as received Him, to them He gave the right to become children of God, to those who believe in His name, who were born, not of blood, nor of the will of the flesh, nor of the will of a man, but of God." John 1:11–13 (NASB)*

My tears are just flowing.

To think that Jesus, the Son of God, left the splendor of heaven, laid aside His glory, and came down to this earth for me... To redeem me. To call me His own.

He was rejected by the very people He came to save. Yet, to those who receive Him, He gives the right to become children of God. Not just forgiven. Not just saved. But adopted, embraced, and called His own.

We live in a world where people search endlessly for identity and belonging. But we, as believers, already have the greatest title we could ever carry: child of the King. No matter how others see you, or fail to see you, Jesus saw you worth dying for. That changes everything.

Walk today with that truth wrapped around your heart. You belong. You are His.

Prayer:
Jesus, my Living Hope. Thank You for calling me Your own. Let me walk today with the confidence of one who belongs to the King of Kings. Amen

THURSDAY

Stay in His Presence

> *"The Lord is my rock and my fortress and my deliverer, My God, my rock, in whom I take refuge; My shield and the horn of my salvation, my stronghold." Psalm 18:2 (NASB)*

Don't leave His presence.

It's tempting to rush through the day, jumping from one task to the next. But when we stay in God's presence, when we remain aware of Him, we find strength we didn't know we had. We find peace in the middle of pressure. We find protection in the face of spiritual attack.

God is not just a momentary refuge. He is our rock, our fortress, and our deliverer. He doesn't just give strength; He is strength. His presence isn't a one-time encounter; it's where we are meant to live and move and have our being.

If you're feeling overwhelmed today, pause and remember: you're not alone. Don't drift. Don't disconnect. Stay in His presence, and you'll find yourself grounded even when everything around you is shifting.

Prayer:
Lord, keep me anchored in You today. Let me not drift from Your presence, for there I find strength and peace. Amen.

FRIDAY

You Are Not Forgotten

> *"Behold, I have inscribed you on the palms of My hands; Your walls are continually before Me." Isaiah 49:16 (NASB)*

FRIDAY: *You Are Not Forgotten*

My tears are just flowing, just to know that He left all His glory to come down to this earth for me.

He didn't come because I deserved it. He came because love moved Him. He came to redeem, restore, and write my name on His hands.

The world may forget your name. People may overlook you. But God never does. You are not forgotten. You are engraved, permanently marked, on the palms of the One who stretched out His hands on the cross.

When we feel invisible, this truth anchors us: God sees. God knows. And more than that, He remembers. Not in a passing thought, but with covenant love.

You are not just noticed by God, you are known, held, and treasured.

> **Prayer:**
> *Thank You, Lord, for such boundless grace. Let my life echo the joy of being called Your own. Amen.*

SATURDAY

I Will Not Be Shaken

> *"I have set the Lord continually before me;*
> *Because He is at my right hand, I will not be shaken.*
> *Therefore my heart is glad and my glory rejoices;*
> *My flesh also will dwell securely." Psalm 16:8-9 (NASB)*

Don't let anything weigh you down, especially unpleasant memories, regrets, or worries that try to linger in your mind. Those burdens have a way of stealing joy and distracting us from what matters most.

David reminds us of a powerful truth: when we keep our eyes on the Lord, we don't have to live shaken or overwhelmed. Our footing becomes secure, not because life is easy, but because God is near.

SATURDAY: *I Will Not Be Shaken*

Sometimes the shaking comes from within, unanswered questions, guilt, or fear. But even then, "with Him at my right hand, I will not be shaken." That's not denial; that's trust. That's choosing to focus on the unchanging One rather than the changing circumstances.

Today, fix your eyes on the Lord. Keep Him before you. Let His presence steady your steps and lift the weight off your heart.

Prayer:
God, help me to fix my eyes on You today. With You at my right hand, I will not be shaken. Amen.

— SUNDAY —

A Day of Worship, Rest, and Renewal

"Not abandoning our own meeting together, as is the habit of some people, but encouraging one another; and all the more as you see the day drawing near." Hebrews 10:25 (NASB)

Take this day to worship, rest, and recharge. If possible, gather with other believers in fellowship. There is something sacred about coming together, lifting our voices, sitting under the Word, and encouraging one another in love and faith.

Let today be a reset, not just physically, but spiritually. Step away from striving. Lay aside the distractions. Remember whose you are and where your strength comes from. **Sabbath is not about doing nothing**; it's about doing what matters most—being still, worshipping freely, and realigning your heart with the One who sustains you.

Prayer:
Lord, thank You for setting aside a day for rest and renewal. Refresh my soul and prepare me for the week ahead. Amen.

WEEK 27

Monday

Bloom Where You're Planted

> *"The plan of the Lord stands forever,*
> *The plans of His heart from generation to generation."* Psalm 33:11 (NASB)

I am reminded of the quote, "Learn to bloom where you are planted." It's easy to look around and be consumed by "I wish..." or "What if..." But these words often lead to envy, discontent, and despair.

God has a unique plan for each of us, tailored to our situation, our needs, and even our limitations. Yes, we've all had moments where we've looked at someone else and thought, "She has it all together."

More than once, I've been shocked to hear the real stories behind the polished smiles of colleagues who seemed so composed. Beneath the surface, they were fighting battles no one could see. Everyone carries hidden sorrow. Every smile masks a struggle.

So today, choose to trust God's placement. Make the most of where you are, even if it doesn't look like where you want to be. His plans are firm, steady, and eternal. One day, you'll have that "a-ha" moment when it all makes sense.

> **Prayer:**
> Lord, help me to trust Your plan, stay rooted where You have placed me, and flourish through faith. Amen.

Tuesday

Whiter Than Snow

*"Purify me with hyssop, and I will be clean;
Cleanse me, and I will be whiter than snow." Psalm 51:7 (NASB)*

God has been teaching me so much through the everyday moments of life.

Just this morning, I opened the front door to see what was outside, and was met with a breathtaking scene. It looked like God had rolled out a pure white blanket, completely spotless. No footprints. No marks. Just untouched, dazzling snow.

Immediately, Isaiah 1:18 came to mind: "Though your sins are like scarlet, they will be as white as snow."

Can you picture it? That clean, perfect whiteness? This is the visual God gives us of what His forgiveness looks like—complete, covering, transforming. How blessed we are to live in a place where we can see this verse come to life. Nature becomes a sermon, and the snow becomes a symbol of mercy.

Wow, Lord.

Prayer:
Lord, cleanse me and make me whiter than snow. Thank You for these glimpses of grace through Your creation. Amen.

WEDNESDAY

Decluttered by Grace

> *"But the eyes of the Lord are on those who fear Him,*
> *on those whose hope is in His unfailing love,*
> *to deliver them from death and keep them alive in famine.*
> *We wait in hope for the Lord; He is our help and our shield.*
> *In Him our hearts rejoice, for we trust in His holy name.*
> *May Your unfailing love be with us, Lord,*
> *even as we put our hope in You." Psalm 33:18–22 (NIV)*

Last night was one of those nights when thoughts cloud your mind, worries occupy your heart, and your brain feels like a traffic jam of noise and chaos. Should I credit that to the fallen state of man? Absolutely. Because God is anything BUT that.

(Yes, I know that may not be grammatically correct, but it is spiritually powerful.)

This morning, I knew I had to get my thoughts together—declutter my system so I could receive from the Lord. As I shuffled to make coffee and quietly whispered, "Lord, release me from whatever is going on in my head," I suddenly heard, "Look up Psalm 33."

I dropped everything and turned the pages. And just like that, God spoke peace.

Sometimes, we torment ourselves with burdens we were never meant to carry. We worry over things far beyond our control, and in doing so, we make ourselves miserable.

But Psalm 33 reminded me:

His eyes are on us.

His love never fails.

He is our help, our shield, our joy, and our hope.

So yes, this devotional started as a personal moment, a way to process my thoughts. But maybe, just maybe, you needed to hear it too.

Prayer:
Lord, thank You for knowing our anxious thoughts even before we speak them. Help us to let go and rest in Your unfailing love today. Amen.

THURSDAY

God's Love Bubbles Over!

> *"Also keep Your servant back from presumptuous sins;*
> *Let them not rule over me;*
> *Then I will be innocent,*
> *And I will be blameless of great wrongdoing."* Psalm 19:13 (NASB)

God didn't love us because Christ died for us—

Christ died for us because God already loved us.

Do you see the difference?

Such was the magnitude of His love. So what's holding you back from loving a God like that? He gave it all, even His only Son, to remove our scars. The blameless, unblemished One was crucified in our place.

Can you picture that sacrifice?

The anguish of the Father, watching His Son being nailed.

The pain of Jesus' family, seeing blood dripping from the crown of thorns.

The heartbreak of His loved ones, witnessing the lashes, the shame, the suffering.

We can't bear to see our children sick, let alone endure watching them suffer in a hospital. But this Father loved us so deeply that He allowed His Son to die for us.

This morning, pause and reflect. Think of the sins, known and unknown, that you've committed. And then picture the blood that dripped down for you and me. Every drop was priceless. The only way to respond is to love Him with all our hearts and live for Him until He calls us home.

Even as seasoned Christians, we stumble. We fall into the "sin trap" time and time again. But His grace is still available.

Prayer:
Father, thank You for the priceless sacrifice of Jesus. Cleanse our hearts today and draw us closer to Your love. Amen.

FRIDAY

Faith Wi-Fi

> *"Now faith is the certainty of things hoped for, a proof of things not seen." Hebrews 11:1 (NASB)*

We've read this verse many times, maybe even memorized it. But do we truly grasp what faith is?

Faith is unseen. Yet when we cling to it, we walk with confidence. We become sure-footed in an uncertain world.

The other day, I saw a T-shirt that said:

"Faith is like your Wi-Fi."

You don't see it, but when you're connected, everything changes. With that invisible signal, a whole new world opens up. It's the power of connection.

Faith in Christ works the same way.

It connects us to God's promises.

It filters what comes in and what goes out.

It keeps us grounded while unlocking the good things He has planned for us.

My grandchildren have iPads with parental controls—limits set to keep them safe. Faith is like that, too. When it's active in our lives, it becomes a spiritual safeguard, nudging us away from danger and guiding our steps.

So ask yourself today:

Have you activated your Faith Wi-Fi?

Unlike earthly networks, this connection never drops. Even in the darkest valleys, the signal is strong. Always on. Always available.

> **Prayer:**
> *Lord, help us reconnect with You through faith. Strengthen our signal so we never lose sight of Your presence and power. Amen.*

SATURDAY

Tears on the Pillow

> *"You turned my wailing into dancing;*
> *You removed my sackcloth and clothed me with joy,*
> *that my heart may sing your praises and not be silent.*
> *Lord my God, I will praise You forever."* Psalm 30:11–12 (NIV)

Parasomnia—a sleep disorder involving abnormal behaviors or emotions during sleep.

One pastor's wife once described it as the "wet pillow syndrome." The idea that bottled-up sorrows often surface during the night, leaving behind tear-stained pillows as silent witnesses to our pain.

Maybe your pillow isn't soaked, but it might bear the stains of weary prayers and muffled cries. The good news? God sees them. Every tear. Every sigh. Every ache of the heart.

The Word of God becomes our balm in those nighttime hours:

"I flood my bed with weeping..." (Psalm 6:6)
"My face is red with weeping..." (Job 16:16)
"My tears have been my food day and night..." (Psalm 42:3)
"You have collected all my tears in Your bottle..." (Psalm 56:8)
"I have heard your prayer; I have seen your tears." (2 Kings 20:5)
He knows.

He is in your sorrow, your sighing, and your storm.
He does not waste pain.
He is your life vest in deep waters, your calm in chaos, your healing after heartbreak.
And in time, He will turn your mourning into dancing.
Your silence into song.
Your sorrow into joy.

Prayer:
Lord, You know every tear and every silent cry. Thank You for being near to the brokenhearted and turning our mourning into joy. Amen.

Sunday

Renewal and Readiness

> *"Create in me a clean heart, O God, and renew a right spirit within me."* Psalm 51:10 (ESV)

Sundays are not only for rest and worship; they are also a time for spiritual recalibration. As a new week begins, this is the moment to invite the Lord to cleanse, renew, and prepare your heart for what lies ahead.

Whether last week brought celebration or challenge, today is a gift to reset.

Did you carry any burdens this week?

Did you pour yourself out in service, or maybe fall short in some areas?

Bring it all to the feet of Jesus. He specializes in renewal.

Let this be your prayer today:

> **Prayer:**
> Lord, renew my strength. Refresh my spirit. Ready my heart. Prepare me for the week ahead. I don't want to walk into this new week without You leading the way. Strip away the residue of the past week and fill me with Your wisdom, grace, and power. I need a fresh filling for a fresh start. In Jesus' name, Amen.

WEEK 28

MONDAY

Living Full — Even When Life Feels Empty

"A Cheerful Heart Has a Continual Feast." Proverbs 15:13–15 (NRSV)

I have a desktop flip devotion calendar on my desk, which is one of my readings after my personal devotion time. And today's verse is taken from Proverbs 15:13-15 (NRSV). The verse ends with "a cheerful heart has a continual feast."

The word continual caught my attention. Can we really be cheerful 24/7? Is that even possible in this world? I can understand having a feast here and there, but a continual feast and being cheerful?

How can I have that continual feast? I would love to.

Can you just imagine if we only had one emotion, a cheerful heart? Is that even possible?

What takes away our cheerful spirit?

Let's look at some of the causes for losing that joy:

When we rely on our own strength

When we bottle up all our disappointments, discouragements, and sorrow

When we rely on our bank balance

When we think we can handle it all

All the above brings only anxiety to our souls.

On the flip side, the Living Word talks about attaining this joy and sustaining that emotion. There is a fine line between happiness and joy.

Happiness mandates a happy event. It doesn't last. But joy, on the other hand, sticks around like a faithful friend, even during trials, because God has taken over and He keeps us in that place of joy.

There is a beautiful verse in Lamentations that we can all relate to:

"My soul has been excluded from peace; I have forgotten happiness." Lamentations 3:17 (NASB)

God didn't hand us joy on a platter and say we will not have other emotions. He is just asking you to trust Him with your situation. What does that mean? Transferring ownership—and the domino effect is your heart is free from all the other emotions, and what is left is joy. Is it easy to transfer? Not at all. It has to be a deliberate attempt.

"Rejoicing in hope, persevering in tribulation, devoted to prayer." Romans 12:12 (NASB)

Today, enjoy the continual feast that is being offered by God.

Prayer:
Lord, I confess that it's hard to be cheerful when my heart is weighed down with burdens. But You have shown me that true joy comes not from my circumstances but from trusting You. Help me to let go of everything that steals my peace and instead feast daily on Your promises. Teach me to transfer the weight of my worries into Your hands. Let my heart learn what it means to rejoice continually, even in trials. Thank You for offering me a joy that endures. Amen.

TUESDAY

Reflected Accurately

"Your light must shine before people in such a way that they may see your good works..." Matthew 5:16a (NASB)

Last night, this light captured my attention. Wow... reflecting accurately.

TUESDAY: *Reflected Accurately*

This is a light I use for my Zoom meetings. Even though the light is inside the room, what was mirroring on the window was strikingly clear. The reflection was accurate.

I started examining my heart — Am I emulating Christ accurately, or is it a touch-and-go? As I kept looking at the reflection, I felt like I was at a communion service, quietly examining myself.

How are we representing Christ today?
Can people see Christ in us?
Has the light lost its brightness?
Do we need to get recharged?
What causes you to lose your brightness?

A lot of questions, but perhaps these questions are necessary. I hope they will help you tweak your lifestyle so that your illumination is not distorted... but accurate.

Prayer:
Lord, search my heart today. Help me not to settle for a dim or distorted reflection of who You are. Recharge me with Your presence and realign me with Your purpose. If I've let the worries of life or the distractions of this world dim my light, reignite it. Let my actions, words, and thoughts reflect You clearly to those around me. Shine through me, not for my glory, but for Yours. In Jesus' name, Amen.

WEDNESDAY

A Solo Walk of Praise

"I will give thanks to You, because I am fearfully and wonderfully made; Wonderful are Your works, And my soul knows it very well."
Psalm 139:14 (NASB)

Today was a solo walk for me. I have never gone on a walk by myself—something new, different... but nice. I could set the pace of my walk. It reminded me of my walk with God. If I focus on God and not get distracted, I know my journey will be okay because He walks alongside me.

As I walked, I started thinking of my strong legs and realized how I had taken that strength for granted. One thing led to another, and as I walked briskly, I began thanking God for my strong legs, hands that could move, ears that could hear the chirping of the birds, eyes that could feast on the plush green grass, a heart that carries so many emotions, and the coordination of them all.

Wow. I just took them all for granted.

As I walked, I whispered a long overdue thank You to my God.

Prayer:
Lord, today I lift up a prayer of gratitude, for the simple things, the overlooked things, the taken-for-granted things. Thank You for the ability to walk, to see, to feel, to hear. Forgive me for the many times I've used these gifts without a thought of You.

And today, Lord, I also pray for those who have lost the use of any of these senses. May they feel Your nearness in ways that go beyond the physical. I pray they would sense Your guiding hand, Your mercy in abundance, and Your presence carrying them through this journey called life. Even with limitations, let joy overflow and let their hearts know they are fearfully and wonderfully made. In Jesus' name, Amen.

THURSDAY

Eyes That See, Ears That Hear

"But blessed are your eyes, because they see; and your ears, because they hear. For truly I say to you, that many prophets and righteous people longed to see what you see, and did not see it, and to hear what you hear, and did not hear it." Matthew 13:16-17 (NASB)

THURSDAY: *Eyes That See, Ears That Hear*

Another solo walk. I went out in the morning instead of my usual evening stroll. It was a different environment, almost like the Scripture verse: "blessed are your eyes because they see, and your ears because they hear."

I heard the birds chirping, squirrels hopping, the wind swishing through the trees, the beauty of the budding branches… and yes, check out the birds social distancing!

Wow. My eyes sure had a feast this morning.

Change up your strolling hours from time to time and you'll get a totally different perspective.

COVID-19 brought many of us out of our homes to stroll in a park, keeping our six feet of distance. But here I am, enjoying my stroll, and for the first time, really taking my time to enjoy all that He has created for us.

> **Prayer:**
> *Lord, thank You for the gift of sight and sound. Thank You for the beauty that surrounds us, often unnoticed in our daily rush. Help me to slow down and pay attention, to see the details of Your creation and hear the quiet whispers of Your presence. May my heart never grow dull to the wonder of Your handiwork. Open my eyes to see You more clearly and my ears to hear You more intimately. In Jesus' name, Amen.*

FRIDAY

Decluttering the Soul

> *"Your word is a lamp to my feet And a light to my path." Psalm 119:105 (NASB)*

Went for an early walk today since they were calling for a hot, humid day. It was a lot cooler once we stepped onto the entrance of the trail. Never have I enjoyed nature so much.

FRIDAY: *Decluttering the Soul*

Is it because I am slowly decluttering my mind?
Or is it because I don't have the stress of commuting anymore...?
What is it?
God has given me this pause to reflect on my walk—on my life.
I've been unloading the unnecessary load I was carrying, the kind of load that didn't even care whether I carried it or dropped it.
So I made the wise choice: I dropped what didn't matter... and chose to carry only what is near and dear to my heart.
Now you may ask me: What is near and dear to your heart?
My love for God.
My relationship with my loved ones.
My health—and their health.
Every time I walk the trails, I have this habit of standing at the crossroads and just being still. It's my way of asking for God's direction. It's a great visual for me.
I need His guidance for every step I take... and I love standing there and just looking.

> **Prayer:**
> *Lord, thank You for the gift of quiet moments where You help me sort through the clutter in my heart. Show me what to lay down and what to hold close. Help me not to carry what weighs me down or distracts me from Your path. Shine Your light on my steps. Speak clearly when I reach a crossroads. May Your Word continue to be my compass, and may my soul find peace in walking closely with You. Amen.*

SATURDAY

Same Sun, Different Growth

"For He causes His sun to rise on the evil and the good, and sends rain on the righteous and the unrighteous." Matthew 5:45 (NASB)

SATURDAY: *Same Sun, Different Growth*

It was just wonderful to go out and get some fresh air. As we entered the park, the rich green grass had a lush velvet look, and stepping on it gave a bouncy sensation. Nature is just so beautiful.

But as I looked around this vast piece of land, I noticed something unusual — the vegetation was so varied. I saw trees with new buds, burnt-up pinecone trees, fresh pinecone trees, evergreen trees... and as we walked a little further, there were dead branches and even dead trees.

All of these variations were found on the same piece of land. They all enjoyed the same sunshine. They all received the same rain. But the results were so different.

Our God is an impartial God.

This is the verse that popped into my head:

"... For He causes His sun to rise on the evil and the good, and sends rain on the righteous and the unrighteous." Matthew 5:45b (NASB)

It made me reflect: while God's provision is extended to all, what we do with what He gives us can lead to vastly different outcomes. Some grow, some thrive, some barely survive, and some wither. The sun shines. The rain falls. But growth depends on how deeply we're rooted, and whether we're receiving and responding to His care.

> **Prayer:**
> *Lord, thank You for being a faithful and impartial Provider. You shower Your blessings, sun and rain, on all of us. Help me not to take that for granted. Teach me to grow in every season, to root myself in Your Word, and to respond well to what You're giving me. Whether I'm in a budding season or one that feels dry, help me trust the One who sends both sun and rain. Amen.*

SUNDAY

The Power of Gathering

> *"And let us consider how to encourage one another in love and good deeds, not abandoning our own meeting together, as is the habit of some, but encouraging one another." Hebrews 10:24-25 (NASB)*

SUNDAY : *The Power of Gathering*

Sunday is a sacred invitation — to pause, to gather, to worship.

As you prepare your heart today, remember the importance of coming together with other believers. There's something beautiful about lifting your voice in worship alongside others, sitting under the Word, and letting God refresh your spirit through fellowship. Church is not just a building; it's a body. And you are a vital part of it.

So find your place, settle in, and be present in God's house.

> **Prayer:**
> *Lord, thank You for the gift of the church, a place to grow, to serve, and to be renewed. Help me enter Your presence with gratitude and expectation. Amen.*

WEEK 29

Monday

When You Feel Misunderstood

> *"He was in the world, and the world came into being through Him, and yet the world did not know Him. He came to His own, and His own people did not accept Him." John 1:10–11 (NASB)*

Ever feel misunderstood?
Like you don't belong?
Disrespected... dismissed?
Jesus did too.

Here's a pro tip: When you feel that way, and your emotions are spiraling in sadness, let those feelings connect you and draw you closer to the One who loved you first. You have something so very human in common with Jesus.

He was rejected by the very people He created. He understands. So when that ache rises, you can literally just pause and pray...

Lord, I surrender these emotions to You. Thank You for going through the pain of being human and experiencing these same things. You are my safe place, and in You—I am seen, known, and loved. And for that, I give You praise. Amen.

Prayer:
Lord, when I feel invisible or misunderstood, remind me that You see me, know me, and love me deeply. Anchor me in Your truth. Amen.

TUESDAY

Among the Weeds

> *"Allow both to grow together until the harvest; and at the time of the harvest I will say to the reapers, 'First gather up the weeds and bind them in bundles to burn them; but gather the wheat into My barn.'"*
> Matthew 13:30 (NASB)

Today, we lost a great servant of God.
His celebration of life service was so powerful.
In order to process what I heard, I needed to go for a walk.
God took me through a path of weeds.
I saw many different kinds, some pretty, some tall, some dainty. No matter how they looked, they were all still known as weeds.
Human beings can be like those weeds in different forms. One is indifferent, another proud and boastful. Some esteem themselves better than others.
Likewise, we are all considered weeds, until we receive the redemptive power of Christ.
Only His transforming grace can turn us from weeds into wheat.

Prayer:
God, even among the weeds of life, help me remember that Your redemptive power can turn any heart into wheat for Your harvest. Help me not to look down on others, but to see each person as a soul You long to redeem. Keep me humble, grateful, and aware that without You, I too am just a weed. Amen.

WEDNESDAY

No Shadow in the Light

> *"Every good thing given and every perfect gift is from above, coming down from the Father of lights, with whom there is no variation or shifting shadow." James 1:17 (NASB)*

Another solo walk today... enjoying the warm sunshine and the cool breeze. I could get used to this temperature.

I looked down and saw my shadow, and had some fun with it. When I was facing the sun, I didn't see any shadow. When I stood at an angle, I saw the shadow beside me. But when my back was toward the sun, I saw this big, black shadow in front of me.

That got me thinking...
If my eyes are fixed on the Son (get it?), there is no shadow—no fear. But when I try to balance the world and God, my walk becomes wobbly, and I start to see this monstrous shadow bringing doubt and worry.
When you walk alone, you have so many aah-ha moments.
I looked down and saw my shadow, and had some fun with it. When I was facing the sun, I didn't see any shadow. When I stood at an angle, I saw the shadow beside me. But when my back was toward the sun, I saw this big, black shadow in front of me.
I was reminded of something John MacArthur once said:
"The more you focus on yourself, the more distracted you will be from the proper path. The more you know Him and commune with Him, the more the Spirit will make you like Him."
When we walk in the light, the shadows fade.
But the moment we turn away, we begin to see fear, doubt, and confusion take form.

> **Prayer:**
> Lord, help me keep my eyes fixed on You, the true Light. When I'm tempted to look away or turn toward the world, remind me that the shadows I see are not from You. Keep the shadows of fear and doubt far from me. Help me to walk in confidence, steady and secure, because I'm walking toward You. Amen.

THURSDAY

A Pause

> "The Lord will protect you from all evil; He will keep your soul." Psalm 121:7 (NASB)

> "This is what the Lord says: 'Stand by the ways and see and ask for the ancient paths, where the good way is, and walk in it; then you will find a resting place for your souls.'" Jeremiah 6:16 (NASB)

> "He makes my feet like deer's feet, And sets me on my high places." 2 Samuel 22:34 (NASB)

All the effort my parents put into our spiritual walk came to the forefront today as I strolled through the park. Every scenario I encountered seemed to trigger a Scripture verse in my heart.

Thank you, Mom and Dad, for instilling in us the value of memorizing the Scriptures. What you sowed in faith is now bearing fruit in unexpected moments of reflection and comfort.

> **Prayer:**
> Father, thank You for the blessings of memory and Your living Word. Thank You for godly parents who planted Your truth deep within my heart. Help me to treasure Your Word each day and pass it on with the same care and love I received. Let Your truth rise up in me, especially in times of uncertainty, as a light and anchor for my soul. Amen.

FRIDAY: *Weed Day*

FRIDAY

Weed Day

> *"First gather up the weeds and bind them in bundles to burn them; but gather the wheat into My barn." Matthew 13:30b (NASB)*

Today was a weed day. While pulling weeds from our flower patch, I accidentally pulled out snapdragon seeds that Danny had sown. I didn't realize what they were at first—they were so small, easily mistaken for part of the overgrowth.

It made me pause and reflect.

Sometimes we blend in with the weeds around us, without even realizing it.

We allow certain attitudes, habits, or thoughts to take root, and before long, they start choking out the beauty God has planted within us. What was meant to flourish becomes buried under the clutter of what doesn't belong.

It's a good reminder to examine our hearts regularly.

To pause and ask: What have I allowed to grow that shouldn't be here?

Just as weeds can overtake a garden, so too can bitterness, pride, distractions, or fear take over the soul if left unchecked.

God's Word is clear, there will be a time of separating the wheat from the weeds. But He lovingly invites us to do the daily work of surrender and pruning now, while there's still time to grow and thrive.

Prayer:
Lord, search my heart. Uproot anything that doesn't belong, every hidden weed of resentment, fear, pride, or distraction. Help me to grow strong and rooted in Your truth. Nourish the beauty You've planted within me, and keep me from blending in with what You never intended to grow. May my life bear fruit that brings You glory. Amen.

SATURDAY

The Right Season

"There is an appointed time for everything. And there is a time for every matter under heaven" Ecclesiastes 3:1 (NASB)

Yesterday I was tempted to pick the mangoes off a tree. They looked full and ripe, but one bite revealed they weren't ready. The flesh was sour, and the texture still firm.

It got me thinking: sometimes in life, we try to rush things. We want the blessing now, the breakthrough now, the answer now. But just like a fruit, God's timing requires patience. What looks ready on the outside may still need more time on the inside.

Instead of plucking prematurely, we must trust the One who knows the seasons best. In the waiting, God is ripening our character, softening our hearts, and preparing us for what's to come.

Prayer:
Lord, help me to wait on Your timing. Teach me to trust that the fruit will be sweetest when it's in season. I surrender my timeline to You and choose to wait with faith. Amen.

SUNDAY

The Sacred Rhythm of Sunday

"I was glad when they said to me, 'Let's go to the house of the Lord.'" Psalm 122:1 (NASB)

SUNDAY: *The Sacred Rhythm of Sunday*

There's something sacred about Sunday mornings, the intentional pause, the gathering of God's people, the lifting of voices in praise, the Word going forth, and the reminder that we're not walking this journey alone.

Scripture encourages us not to forsake our own assembling together (Hebrews 10:25), and there's a reason for that. In a world that constantly pulls us in every direction, corporate worship centers us. It realigns our priorities, refreshes our spirit, and reminds us of the bigger picture — God is on the throne, and we are part of His body.

Church isn't just a building. It's a lifeline. It's where iron sharpens iron, where burdens are shared, where joy is multiplied, and where we get a glimpse of heaven on earth.

This morning, don't let sleep, schedules, or excuses rob you of what God wants to deposit in your spirit. Go to His house, not just out of habit, but with expectation.

The pew you sit in today might be the very place where God speaks directly to your heart.

> **Prayer:**
> *Lord, thank You for the gift of Sunday, for fellowship, for worship, and for the church. Help me not to treat it casually but to value it deeply. I come with an open heart today, ready to meet with You. Stir my spirit, speak to my soul, and align my steps with Yours. Let this day mark a fresh encounter with Your presence. Amen.*

WEEK 30

MONDAY

Jesus Will See You Through

> *"But I will sing of Your power; Yes, I will sing aloud of Your mercy in the morning; For You have been my defense And refuge in the day of my trouble." Psalm 59:16 (NKJV)*

Trust in the Lord and don't despair, He is a friend so true. No matter what your troubles are, Jesus will see you through.

This chorus has been playing in my head, and it feels so timely. There's so much going on around us — senseless violence, war, political unrest, personal struggles. Storms rage outwardly and inwardly. And in the midst of it all, this chorus rises in my spirit:

Sing, when the day is bright;
Sing, through the darkest night
Everyday, all the way,
Let us sing, sing, sing!

But how do we sing when everything is shaking?

This is where trust comes in. Praising God even in the midst of pain is not just possible; it's powerful. It shifts our focus and begins a transfer within: pain into praise. Trust turns into testimony. And no, it doesn't come naturally. But it's a spiritual muscle we can build.

Try it. Hum a song of praise in the middle of frustration. Sing aloud when your heart is heavy. I've found that even when my family doesn't say anything, they know, "Ah, she's singing again." But only I know that something sacred is happening inside me.

Friends, don't let your soul become a parched land. Our God offers Living Water.

TUESDAY: *A Friend Like No Other*

> **Prayer:**
> Lord, help us choose praise over despair. Train our hearts to trust You no matter the circumstance. Fill the dry places with Your Living Water, and teach us to keep singing until breakthrough comes. Amen.

TUESDAY

A Friend Like No Other

> *"I no longer call you servants, because a servant does not know his master's business. Instead, I have called you friends..." John 15:15 (NIV)*

Last Sunday, a preacher spoke of my dad, describing him as someone you could open your heart to — a true friend. It got me thinking... Can I call Jesus my Friend?

We call Him Lord, Savior, Healer, but what about Friend? That title implies intimacy. No pretense. Just you, as you are. The good, the bad, the confused, the messy. And you know what? He welcomes it.

A true friend listens. A true friend stays. A true friend will speak truth with grace. That's Jesus.

The Bible says Abraham was called a friend of God. Imagine being identified like that in heaven! Are we cultivating the kind of relationship where Jesus could call us friends?

May that be our aim, not just to serve Him, but to walk with Him, talk with Him, open up to Him like we would our dearest companion.

> **Prayer:**
> Lord, among all the names we call You — Savior, Healer, Provider — let me never forget that You also call me friend. Help me lean into that intimacy and walk closely with You each day. Amen.

WEDNESDAY

Living for Others

> *"And do not forget to do good and to share with others, for with such sacrifices God is pleased." Hebrews 13:16 (NIV)*

Take a look at creation:
   The flowers bloom — for whom?
   The trees offer shade — to whom?
   The rivers flow — who benefits?
   The sun shines — who receives its warmth?
   The answer to all these? Us. Creation gives freely.

So what about us? Are we pouring ourselves out for others the way creation does?

God made the world with generosity, and He made us in His image. If we're holding back, protecting our time, guarding our hearts, hoarding our energy, maybe it's time to release that grip and live for others.

Unused gifts go stale. Don't let your compassion rust. Don't let your encouragement go silent. Pour it out.

Even Jesus, the King of Kings, came not to be served, but to serve. What an example to follow.

Prayer:
Lord, let our lives be rivers, not reservoirs. Help us give freely, our time, our love, our gifts, for the sake of others and for the glory of Your name. Amen.

THURSDAY

Don't Forget the Sacrifice

"And what does the Lord require of you but to do justice, to love kindness, and to walk humbly with your God?" Micah 6:8 (NASB)

Every September 11th, I stand outside my office and watch the wreaths being laid in memory of those lost. It's solemn and moving. But a day later, we all return to our routines.

Isn't that how it was for the Israelites, too? Once a year, they brought an unblemished lamb to the temple — a ritual. But Jesus changed everything. He didn't come to offer an annual sacrifice. He became the sacrifice. Once and for all.

So why do we live like He's still hanging on that cross once a year?

What if we remembered every day — the lashes, the nails, the blood, the pain... and the love behind it all?

Remembering His sacrifice daily will change the way we live. It softens the heart, silences the grumbling, and calls us back to holiness.

Prayer:
Lord, don't let me take Your sacrifice lightly. Remind me of the price You paid, and let that remembrance shape my words, my thoughts, and my walk. Amen.

FRIDAY

His Word is My Anchor

"Therefore you shall lay up these words of Mine in your heart and in your soul..." Deuteronomy 11:18 (NKJV)

FRIDAY : *His Word is My Anchor*

We visited a friend with serious health issues — oxygen tank, wheelchair, and pain. But instead of focusing on his suffering, he was writing down God's promises.

That visual stuck with me. Instead of wallowing, he was anchoring himself in God's Word. Writing it down. Declaring it.

We all have verses hanging in our homes, not because they're pretty decor, but because they steady us.

The Living Word of God:
Wipes our tears
Brings hope
Offers comfort
Calms our nerves
Directs our steps
Let His Word electrify your spirit.

> **Prayer:**
> Lord, help us not just to read Your Word, but to treasure it. Etch it into our hearts, and let it be the anchor in every storm we face. Amen.

SATURDAY

Sitting or Serving?

"...but few things are needed—or indeed only one. Mary has chosen what is better, and it will not be taken away from her." Luke 10:42 (NIV)

Hospitality gets an A+. But fellowship? That's the gold.

Martha welcomed Jesus but missed time with Him. She was in the kitchen while Mary was at His feet. Do we do the same?

We clean and serve, getting everything picture-perfect, but we miss the very presence of the One we're preparing for.

Jesus isn't looking for spotless counters. He's looking for surrendered hearts.

SUNDAY: *Worship and Fellowship*

Let's stop "doing" and start "being." Be present. Be open. Sit at His feet. That's where transformation happens.

> **Prayer:**
> Lord, I don't want to be so busy serving that I miss You. Slow me down. Center me at Your feet. Let me choose what is better. Amen.

SUNDAY

Worship and Fellowship

"I was glad when they said to me, 'Let's go to the house of the Lord.'"
Psalm 122:1 (NASB)

There's something sacred about Sunday mornings — the intentional pause, the gathering of God's people, the lifting of voices in praise, the Word going forth, and the reminder that we're not walking this journey alone.

Scripture encourages us not to forsake assembling together (Hebrews 10:25), and there's a reason for that. In a world that constantly pulls us in every direction, corporate worship centers us. It realigns our priorities, refreshes our spirit, and reminds us of the bigger picture — God is on the throne, and we are part of His body.

Church isn't just a building; it's a lifeline. It's where iron sharpens iron, where burdens are shared, where joy is multiplied, and where we get a glimpse of heaven on earth.

This morning, don't let sleep, schedules, or excuses rob you of what God wants to deposit in your spirit. Go to His house, not just out of habit, but with expectation. The pew you sit in today might be the place God chooses to speak directly to your heart.

> **Prayer:**
> Lord, thank You for the gift of Sunday, for fellowship, for worship, and for the church. Help me not to treat it casually but to value it deeply. I come with an open heart today, ready to meet with You. Amen.

WEEK 31

MONDAY

Killjoy or Joy-Filled?

> *"Though the fig tree should not blossom, nor fruit be on the vines... yet I will rejoice in the Lord; I will take joy in the God of my salvation."* Habakkuk 3:17-18

Killjoy — it's a word we often use casually, but spiritually, it can run deep. Emotions like anxiety, discouragement, worry, bitterness, and unmet expectations become joy-stealers. We look for joy in situations, people, and comfort, but the kind of joy that lasts doesn't come from circumstances; it comes from Christ.

There was a time when I found myself tangled in frustration, and joy seemed far away. But as I began to lean into God's promises, something shifted. I would wake up with my heart smiling, not because everything was perfect, but because the JOY GIVER had sealed my spirit.

Some days, joy feels like a dance in the soul — intangible, but undeniably real. Not everyone will understand it, but when your source is Jesus, joy is immovable.

Prayer:
Thank You, Lord, for being the source of my joy. Even when circumstances threaten to steal it, help me to hold fast to You — my joy that transcends all understanding.

Tuesday

Radical Obedience

> *"His mother said to the servants, 'Whatever He tells you, do it.'"*
> *John 2:5 (NASB)*

At the wedding in Cana, Mary said to the servants, "Do whatever He tells you." Simple words. Profound obedience. The miracle followed their obedience, not before.

Obedience often defies logic. Sometimes it's small, a quiet nudge to pray. Other times, it's large, a bold step into the unknown. But every act of obedience deepens our faith and draws us closer to the heart of God.

The servants didn't know the outcome. They weren't given the plan. They simply obeyed.

Are we willing to obey even when it doesn't make sense?

There's a divine chain reaction in the Kingdom:
Trust begets obedience
Obedience begets reward
Reward begets joy
Joy begets contentment
Let's live out our begets.

Prayer:
Lord, help me to obey You without hesitation. When logic fails and outcomes are unclear, remind me that obedience always leads me closer to You. Teach me to trust Your voice above all else, and to walk in faith, even when the path is uncertain. I want to live a life where trust leads to obedience, and obedience leads to joy. Amen.

WEDNESDAY

When It Rains, It Pours

"Come to Me, all who labor and are heavy laden, and I will give you rest." Matthew 11:28 (NASB)

Have you ever had a day where every shelter leaks and every fix fails?

Like playing Whack-a-Mole with your problems — solve one, and three more pop up.

Life's storms come in waves, and sometimes… you're just tired.

But Jesus says, "Come to Me."

Not fix it yourself. Not hustle harder. Just come.

Whatever it is, physical sickness, emotional weight, spiritual confusion, take it to the Lord in prayer. Lay it down before the One who holds rest in His hands.

Prayer:
Lord, the waves feel relentless some days. Teach me to come to You first, not last. Remind me that I don't have to carry every burden alone. Quiet my anxious thoughts and give my soul the deep rest that only You can provide. I trust You with what's too heavy for me to hold. Amen.

THURSDAY

The Eye of the Storm

"For the Lord of armies says this: 'After glory He has sent Me against the nations that plunder you, for whoever touches you, touches the apple of His eye.'" Zechariah 2:8 (NASB)

THURSDAY: *The Eye of the Storm*

In a hurricane, the calmest place is the eye, while chaos swirls all around it.

Spiritually, Jesus is that calm in our storm.

You may feel like the winds are howling, and everything around you is falling apart, but in Him, there is refuge.

You are the apple of His eye.

No matter the pressure, the trials, or the weariness, the center of God's heart is peace for His children. The storm may rage, but the eye, His presence, remains still.

Stay there. Dwell there.

It's the safest place to be.

Prayer:
Lord, thank You for being my shelter in every storm. When life feels unstable, center me in Your presence. Remind me that I am the apple of Your eye and never outside of Your care. Help me to rest in the calm You offer, even when the winds of life roar around me. Let Your peace guard my heart today. Amen.

FRIDAY

When the Day Runs Wild

"Come to Me, all who are weary and burdened, and I will give you rest." Matthew 11:28 (NASB)

Yesterday was a domino day.

One mishap led to another, lentils spilled on the floor, onions had gone bad, fruit flies were swarming, and curtain nails were yanked from the wall. Just as I was ready to rest, someone casually asked, "Hope you rested well?"

I wasn't sure what exhausted me more, the chaos or the question.

Sound familiar?

When our mind races and our day unravels, it's time to slow down.
God invites us into His Word for the serenity we crave.
The world may be noisy, but His whisper brings peace.
Rest isn't found in finishing the to-do list.
It's found in surrendering it.

> **Prayer:**
> *Lord, when my day runs wild, anchor me in You. Calm my spirit and hush the noise around me. Remind me that rest is not earned; it's gifted. I receive it today, not because I have everything under control, but because I trust the One who does. Amen.*

SATURDAY

Watch and Pray

> *"It is God who arms me with strength and keeps my way secure."* 2 Samuel 22:33 (NIV)

We are weak, no denying that. But Jesus meets us in our weakness and says, "Watch and pray." Like an outlet powers a device, our spirit needs a connection to Christ. Prayer is that power line.

The enemy only needs a crack, a deflating tire, a weary heart, a distracted mind. But prayer tightens the seal. Prayer strengthens the soul. Start your day plugged in.

If you've been running low, today is the day to reconnect. Prayer is our lifeline, and His strength is our fuel.

> **Prayer:**
> *Lord, I confess my weakness. But in You, I find my all in all. Help me to stay connected, watchful, and prayerful in all things.*

SUNDAY

Worship and Fellowship

> *"I was glad when they said to me, 'Let's go to the house of the Lord.'"*
> *Psalm 122:1 (NASB)*

There's something sacred about Sunday mornings — the intentional pause, the gathering of God's people, the lifting of voices in praise, the Word going forth, and the reminder that we're not walking this journey alone.

Scripture encourages us not to forsake assembling together (Hebrews 10:25), and there's a reason for that. In a world that constantly pulls us in every direction, corporate worship centers us. It realigns our priorities, refreshes our spirit, and reminds us of the bigger picture — God is on the throne, and we are part of His body.

Church isn't just a building; it's a lifeline. It's where iron sharpens iron, where burdens are shared, where joy is multiplied, and where we get a glimpse of heaven on earth.

This morning, don't let sleep, schedules, or excuses rob you of what God wants to deposit in your spirit. Go to His house, not just out of habit, but with expectation. The pew you sit in today might be the place God chooses to speak directly to your heart.

Prayer:
Lord, thank You for the gift of Sunday, for fellowship, for worship, and for the church. Help me not to treat it casually but to value it deeply. I come with an open heart today, ready to meet with You.

WEEK 32

Monday

Perfect Peace

> *"You will keep in perfect peace those whose minds are steadfast, because they trust in you." Isaiah 26:3*

Woke up with this verse traveling through my mind, brainwashing me in the best way to take action. Two phrases popped out: perfect and steadfast.

Let's self-examine:
What is the status of my mind this morning?
Is it at peace?
If not, why not?

Every promise in Scripture comes with a responsibility. This peace is reserved for those whose minds are steadfast. Like a diabetic who checks their sugar level daily, we need to check the pulse of our spiritual walk to make necessary adjustments.

Christian maturity is about constant tweaks. Left unmonitored, we drift into complacency. So, is your mind fixed on Him today? Is peace reigning in your heart?

> **Prayer:**
> Lord, help my mind remain steadfast on You. When my thoughts drift, reel me back in. I trust You — anchor my soul in Your perfect peace.

TUESDAY

Surrounded by Favor

"Surely, LORD, you bless the righteous; you surround them with your favor as with a shield." Psalm 5:12 (NIV)

Do you consider yourself a favored child of God? His favor isn't to be taken lightly; it brings unexpected blessings at unexpected times through unexpected people.

Esther, a young Jewish girl, found favor with the king, not by chance, but by divine design. How much more favor awaits those who walk with God?

When we trust and obey, we walk right into God's storehouse of favor. It's inexhaustible. Let us not just ask for favor, but recognize and steward it well when it shows up.

Prayer:
Lord, thank You for surrounding me with Your favor like a shield. Teach me to walk in it with humility and gratitude.

WEDNESDAY

Be Specific

"This is the confidence we have in approaching God: that if we ask anything according to His will, He hears us." 1 John 5:14 (NIV)

WEDNESDAY: *Be Specific*

Our God isn't distant or detached; He desires to be part of the smallest details of our lives. So why do we pray vague prayers?
Be specific:
If you're brokenhearted, name it.
If you're discouraged, describe it.
If you're sick, detail it.
It's not about helping God understand; He already knows. It's about deepening the relationship. Just like we only share our innermost thoughts with trusted friends, so God invites us to come close and share the details.

> **Prayer:**
> *Lord, thank You for listening so intimately. Help me not to hold back but to bring everything — the specific, the raw, the real — to You.*

THURSDAY

God Is Still at Work

> *"Being confident of this, that he who began a good work in you will carry it on to completion until the day of Christ Jesus." Philippians 1:6 (NIV)*

We often beat ourselves up when life doesn't unfold as we planned. But perfection isn't the goal; progress is. God is still at work.
Like a goldsmith purifying metal, God is removing the impurities in us. Our failures, fears, and setbacks are all part of His shaping. He is preparing us to be faultless and flawless before His throne.
Don't give up. Trust the process.

> **Prayer:**
> *Lord, You're not finished with me yet. I place every broken part into Your hands — refine me, shape me, and prepare me for Your glory.*

Friday

Revealed Treasures

> *"Nothing will be able to separate us from the love of God that is in Christ Jesus our Lord."* Romans 8:38-39

To reveal means to unveil, to uncover hidden treasure. When we wait on God, He often reveals His will in the most unexpected ways — through a word, a dream, a person, or even a trip.

A visit to the seven churches of Revelation brought the Word to life for me. Each church echoed warnings and encouragements still relevant today — hard work without love, faithfulness amidst persecution, lukewarmness in faith.

The Christian journey is one of faith, yes, but God also gives us tangible glimpses of His truth. Keep your heart expectant; He's always revealing.

Prayer:
Lord, thank You for the glimpses You give me of Your will and Your love. Let me never lose my sense of wonder as I walk with You.

Saturday

Same Soil, Different Growth

> *"Like newborn babies, crave pure spiritual milk, so that by it you may grow up in your salvation."* 1 Peter 2:2

SATURDAY: *Same Soil, Different Growth*

This morning, I noticed my Christmas cactus, each tip at a different stage. Some are ready to bloom, others are just peeking. Same soil, same water, different growth.

It reminded me of the body of Christ. We're all growing, but not at the same pace. Some are thriving, others are just budding. And that's okay.

Let's be encouragers, not envious. Let's teach and guide those newer in faith and humbly learn from those further ahead. Growth isn't uniform, but it's beautiful.

> **Prayer:**
> *Lord, thank You for the unique journey You've set for each of us. Help me encourage others in their growth without comparison or pride.*

SUNDAY

Worship and Fellowship

"I was glad when they said to me, 'Let's go to the house of the Lord.'" Psalm 122:1 (NASB)

There's something sacred about Sunday mornings — the intentional pause, the gathering of God's people, the lifting of voices in praise, the Word going forth, and the reminder that we're not walking this journey alone.

Scripture encourages us not to forsake assembling together (Hebrews 10:25), and there's a reason for that. In a world that constantly pulls us in every direction, corporate worship centers us. It realigns our priorities, refreshes our spirit, and reminds us of the bigger picture — God is on the throne, and we are part of His body.

Church isn't just a building; it's a lifeline. It's where iron sharpens iron, where burdens are shared, where joy is multiplied, and where we get a glimpse of heaven on earth.

SUNDAY: *Worship and Fellowship*

This morning, don't let sleep, schedules, or excuses rob you of what God wants to deposit in your spirit. Go to His house, not just out of habit, but with expectation. The pew you sit in today might be the place God chooses to speak directly to your heart.

Prayer:
Lord, thank You for the gift of Sunday, for fellowship, for worship, and for the church. Help me not to treat it casually but to value it deeply. I come with an open heart today, ready to meet with You.

WEEK 33

Monday

From Acquaintance to Intimacy

> *"You, God, are my God, earnestly I seek you; I thirst for you, my whole being longs for you, in a dry and parched land where there is no water." Psalm 63:1*

They say absence makes the heart grow fonder, but in relationships, especially with God, distance often leads to disconnect. When we don't stay in close communion with Him, our relationship can become mechanical, a ritual instead of a relationship.

Think about how human relationships fade when we're not intentional. That same principle applies spiritually. Our walk with God cannot be sustained on "quick prayers" and hurried devotionals. We need the kind of closeness where our heart says, "I gotta have it!" Like the biggest size at Cold Stone Creamery.

Let's move from acquaintance-level faith to an abiding intimacy with our Savior.

Prayer:
Lord, rekindle my longing for You. Stir my heart beyond routines, and draw me into deep communion. I don't want a casual relationship; I want a 'gotta have it' faith.

TUESDAY

When Health Becomes the Prayer

> *"Beloved, I pray that all may go well with you and that you may be in good health, just as it is well with your soul." 3 John 1:2 (ESV)*

"Health is wealth."

It's a phrase we've all heard, and maybe even nodded at in agreement. But it often remains a distant truth until sickness knocks on the door of someone we love, or our own body begins to break down. Then suddenly, the phrase becomes personal… and prayerful.

When you are tending to someone who's ill, watching them fight fatigue, pain, or uncertainty, it shifts your perspective. It refines your petitions. You stop taking health for granted. Good health becomes a treasured request, lifted repeatedly before the Lord.

Scripture reminds us that God cares about our physical well-being just as much as He does our spiritual condition. He is the giver of good gifts, and health is one of them. Exodus 23:25 promises that when we serve Him, "He will bless our bread and water, and take sickness away from among us." What a powerful promise to pray over ourselves and those we love.

Let's be intentional today, not just in asking for healing, but in thanking Him for the health we do have. And may we commit to honoring our bodies as temples of His Spirit, walking in wellness and wisdom.

Prayer:
Lord, thank You for the gift of health. Bless me and those I love with strength, healing, and vitality. May we steward our bodies as temples of Your Spirit. And when we're weak, be our strength and our healer. In Jesus' name, Amen.

WEDNESDAY

Shadow of Surrender

> *"The heart of man plans his way, but the Lord establishes his steps."*
> *Proverbs 16:9 (ESV)*

Waking up and stretching, I noticed the shadow of my hand cast across the ceiling, and it stirred something deep in me.

A raised hand can mean many things: praise, surrender, petition, or dependence. That morning, it felt like a mix of all four. In that quiet moment, I saw more than a silhouette on the wall — I saw a reflection of my soul.

We make our plans, write out our lists, and try to map the path ahead. But sometimes, God gently reminds us that it's not our plans that matter most; it's our posture. A posture of surrender. A heart yielded to His will. A willingness to trust even when the way isn't clear.

Sometimes the deepest faith is found not in the steps we take, but in the hands we raise.

What does your shadow say today? Is it busy and restless, or surrendered and still? Whether you're celebrating or struggling, take a moment to lift your hands. In faith. In praise. In surrender.

Prayer:
Lord, I lift my hand in praise and surrender. Establish my steps today. Even when I don't know the way, I trust the One who does. Amen

Thursday

"I'll Be Praying for You" — A Sacred Promise

> *"Confess your sins to one another and pray for one another, that you may be healed." James 5:16 (ESV)*

"I'll be praying for you." We say it often, sometimes with deep sincerity, sometimes as a reflex. But how often do we pause and do it?

Life moves fast. Our minds are crowded. Good intentions slip through the cracks. That's why I've started writing prayer requests down — in a journal, in my Notes app, even on sticky notes. Because intercession isn't just a kind gesture; it's a sacred promise. A commitment made before both man and God.

James 5:16 reminds us that healing, both spiritual and physical, is connected to our prayers for one another. When believers gather to pray, there's power. Heaven leans in. Chains break. Hearts are softened. Miracles unfold.

Prayer meetings may not be trendy. They may not be full. But the impact is immeasurable. God moves when we pray.

Let's be more than well-wishers. Let's be faithful intercessors.

Prayer:
Lord, help me to honor the sacred responsibility of prayer. Make me faithful to intercede when I say I will. Let my words align with my actions. Remind me that when I lift others up, You lean down with grace and power. Amen.

Friday

Release the Emotions

> *"God is our refuge and strength, an ever-present help in trouble."*
> *Psalm 46:1 (NIV)*

There's a sacred strength in releasing.

When my husband was diagnosed with cancer, I remember one long drive when I finally let it all out — the tears, the fears, the grief, and all the "what ifs." I cried until there was nothing left to cry. That emotional release didn't weaken me. It prepared me. It made room for strength. I could finally stand in the "what next" because I had let go of the weight of "what now."

Everyone processes pain differently. Some cry. Some go quiet. Some serve. Some sleep. But what's universal is this: we all need God in the process. He is our IV of strength, dripping courage, peace, and grace into our weary souls, one slow, steady drop at a time.

Whether you're facing loss, sickness, disappointment, or heartbreak, don't bottle it up. Don't pretend it's not there. Release it, not just into the air, but into the hands of the One who truly understands. There's healing in that kind of surrender.

> **Prayer:**
> *Lord, I pour out my emotions at Your feet. Be my strength and fortress. Help me process pain with You beside me. Drip Your grace into every broken place. In Jesus' name, Amen.*

SATURDAY

Hands That Satisfy

"You open Your hand and satisfy the desire of every living thing."
Psalm 145:16 (NASB)

God's hand is open.

That image, an open hand, speaks volumes about His nature. It tells us He's not withholding, reluctant, or distant. He's generous, attentive, and near. His open hand is a symbol of provision, protection, and love.

Just as He satisfied the Samaritan woman's thirst with living water, He promises to satisfy the deepest longings of our hearts. This isn't about fleeting pleasures or surface-level fixes. This is about soul-level satisfaction; the kind that lingers, the kind that quiets restlessness, the kind that can't be replicated by anything this world offers.

Psalm 145:16 doesn't say He gives just enough to get by. It says He satisfies — fully, generously, lovingly. That's who He is.

So whatever you're yearning for today — peace, purpose, clarity, strength — take it to the One whose hand is already open and extended toward you.

> **Prayer:**
> Lord, You know my heart's desire. I come to You with open hands and expectant faith. Satisfy me with Your presence and provision. Let my soul find contentment in You alone. Amen.

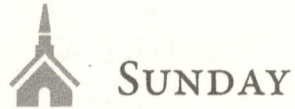

Renewal and Readiness

> *"But those who wait for the Lord will gain new strength; they will mount up with wings like eagles, they will run and not get tired, they will walk and not become weary." Isaiah 40:31 (NASB)*

Sunday is a sacred reset, a time to pause, worship, and get our bearings again. As we gather in His presence, our spirit finds renewal, and our strength is replenished.

Maybe the past week was draining, emotionally, spiritually, or physically. But today, you don't have to strive. Just come. Be still. Receive. Let the worship lift your eyes, and let the Word realign your heart.

You're not just resting; you're being readied.

Prayer:
Lord, thank You for this day of reset. Renew my strength and sharpen my focus. Prepare me for the week ahead, anchored in You.

WEEK 34

MONDAY

Thanksgiving

"In everything give thanks; for this is the will of God for you in Christ Jesus." 1 Thessalonians 5:18 (NASB)

It was just an ordinary morning, coffee brewing and the house quiet, when I felt a sudden urge to give thanks, not for anything grand or miraculous, but for the simple fact that my husband was still here. We've walked through health scares that shook us to our core. Times when fear tried to strangle hope. And yet here we are breathing, laughing, and leaning on God together.

Thanksgiving isn't always about tables piled high or answered prayers that look the way we imagined. Sometimes it's about finding joy in what remains, peace in the storm, and comfort in God's nearness. Gratitude has a way of shifting our perspective, not because everything is perfect, but because God is present.

When we practice thanksgiving, we invite heaven into our ordinary. We recognize God's fingerprints in the mundane. We remember that even when we can't control our circumstances, we can control our response, and gratitude is a powerful one.

What can you thank God for today? Even if your heart is heavy or your prayers feel unanswered, pause and thank Him. Not because everything feels good, but because He is good.

Prayer:
Lord, thank You for Your goodness that never wavers. Even in the hard moments, help me to see Your hand and whisper praise. Let gratitude be my rhythm and trust be my song. Amen.

Tuesday

Hope

> *"Now may the God of hope fill you with all joy and peace in believing, so that you will abound in hope by the power of the Holy Spirit." Romans 15:13 (NASB)*

There's something sacred about holding on when everything around you is falling apart. That kind of hope doesn't come from wishful thinking or shallow optimism; it's rooted in knowing the God who never fails.

I've been reflecting on the story of Hannah. She prayed year after year for a child, enduring misunderstanding, cultural pressure, and personal pain. And yet, she never stopped coming back to the Lord. Her hope wasn't just in having a baby; it was in the One who heard her cries. Then there's Daniel, exiled and surrounded by ungodliness, thrown into a lion's den, and yet his hope remained unshaken because it was anchored in God, not his surroundings.

Hope doesn't deny reality. It doesn't ignore the ache. But it chooses to believe that God is still writing the story, even when we're stuck in the middle chapters.

Maybe today you're holding onto a promise that seems long overdue. Maybe you're trying to muster faith for something that feels impossible. I want to remind you that you serve the God of hope. And when your hope is placed in Him, it's never in vain.

Prayer:
Lord, fill me with hope that is grounded in who You are. Remind me that You are working behind the scenes even when I can't see it. Let joy and peace guard my heart as I wait on You. Amen.

WEDNESDAY

Peace

> *"Peace I leave you, My peace I give you; not as the world gives, do I give to you. Do not let your hearts be troubled, nor fearful." John 14:27 (NASB)*

Peace is one of those things we often associate with quiet spaces — a walk in nature, a candle-lit room, a slow morning. But true peace, God's peace, isn't dependent on stillness around us. It lives deep within us, even when life is loud.

There have been times I've walked into situations full of tension or uncertainty and felt an unexplainable calm wash over me. It wasn't because everything had worked out. It wasn't because I knew the outcome. It was because I knew the One who holds the outcome.

Jesus promised His peace, not a peace we create, but one He gives. The kind that makes no sense to the world. The kind that steadies a trembling heart, silences anxious thoughts, and reminds us that we're not alone in the storm.

Maybe you're not in a tranquil season right now. Maybe your mind is racing, your calendar is full, your heart is heavy. But even here, in the swirl of real life, peace is available. Not the world's version, which is temporary and easily shaken, but the eternal peace of Christ.

Take a breath today. Invite His peace to meet you where you are. Let His presence still your soul.

Prayer:
Jesus, You are the Prince of Peace. Speak calm over the chaos inside me. When the world is noisy and overwhelming, remind me to anchor my soul in You. Amen.

Thursday

Grace

> *"And He has said to me, 'My grace is sufficient for you, for power is perfected in weakness.' Most gladly, therefore, I will rather boast about my weaknesses, so that the power of Christ may dwell in me."*
> 2 Corinthians 12:9 (NASB)

Grace is hard to wrap our minds around. It's undeserved, unearned, and freely given, and yet, we often struggle to receive it fully. We try to tidy up before coming to God, as if He didn't already see the mess. We try to earn His love, forgetting that He gave it before we ever got it right.

Paul knew what it meant to rely on grace. With a thorn in his flesh, a weakness he prayed three times to be removed, he was met not with deliverance but with reassurance: "My grace is sufficient."

That phrase is life-changing. It means God's strength meets us right where we feel weakest. His grace doesn't eliminate every trial, but it sustains us through them. It covers our flaws, lifts our heads, and empowers us to keep moving forward.

Think about your own life. Where do you feel least capable? Where are you weary or falling short? That's exactly where grace wants to step in. Not to shame you, but to remind you that God's power shines brightest in those cracks.

Prayer:
Lord, thank You for grace that meets me in my weakness. I don't have to have it all together; I just need to rest in You. Help me receive Your grace freely and extend it to others. Amen.

FRIDAY

Forgiveness

> *"Bearing with one another, and forgiving each other, whoever has a complaint against anyone; just as the Lord forgave you, so must you do also." Colossians 3:13 (NASB)*

Forgiveness is not a feeling; it's a decision. And sometimes, it's one we have to make over and over until healing settles into our bones.

I've had to learn this the hard way. I've carried the weight of words that wounded and actions that disappointed. I've wrestled with the ache of being let down, of trusting and being hurt. But unforgiveness doesn't protect us; it poisons us. It builds walls where God wants to bring healing. It keeps us tied to a moment when God wants to free us for the future.

When Jesus taught about forgiveness, He didn't put a limit on it. He modeled it, hanging on a cross, looking at His executioners, and saying, "Father, forgive them." That kind of mercy is hard to grasp, but that's the standard we've been called to follow.

Forgiveness doesn't mean what happened was okay. It means we're choosing not to be held captive by it anymore. It's not about excusing the pain; it's about releasing the power it has over us.

Is there someone you need to release today? Maybe it's someone else. Maybe it's yourself.

Prayer:
Lord, forgiveness is hard, but I know it's necessary. Help me to let go of what's behind so I can walk in freedom. Remind me of how much I've been forgiven so I can forgive others with grace. Amen.

SATURDAY

Motherhood

"Her children rise up and bless her; her husband also, and he praises her..." Proverbs 31:28 (NASB)

I thought I understood the strength of a woman until I truly began to see my mother through the lens of time and trials.

Motherhood is one of the most sacred, unseen callings. It's full of quiet sacrifices, sleepless nights, whispered prayers, and moments where strength must show up even when exhaustion threatens to take over. I've watched my mother serve with grace and grit, choosing joy in hard seasons, and love even when love wasn't returned in equal measure.

There were times I didn't fully understand her decisions, her tone, her "no" that felt like a loss in the moment. But as I grew older, I began to see her heart — fierce, faithful, and fixed on God. Her strength wasn't flashy; it was resilient. Her wisdom didn't come from books, but from walking closely with the Lord.

If you've been blessed by a praying mother, a guiding aunt, a spiritual mentor, or any woman who stood in the gap for you, take a moment today to bless her back. And if you are that woman, still pouring out, still pressing forward, still planting seeds in silence, know this: God sees every act. Every cup of water. Every diaper change. Every late-night prayer. You are doing holy work.

Prayer:
Lord, thank You for the gift of mothers and spiritual mothers. Strengthen those who are pouring out. Remind them that their labor in You is never in vain. May they feel seen, valued, and deeply loved today. Amen.

 ## SUNDAY

A Day to Refocus

> *"This is the day that the Lord has made; Let us rejoice and be glad in it." Psalm 118:24 (NASB)*

Sunday is more than just the end of the week; it's the beginning of your next chapter. It's a reset. A divine pit stop to fuel your spirit before life picks up again on Monday.

Gather with fellow believers. Soak in the Word. Sing out your praise. Be still in His presence.

Let today be your reminder that no matter what last week held, God is giving you a fresh page. So go to church, be encouraged, and carry His peace into the week ahead.

Prayer:
Father, thank You for Sundays. Thank You for quiet moments, joyful songs, and the blessing of community. Let today mark the start of a week filled with Your purpose. Amen.

WEEK 35

MONDAY

Close Your Eyes: Who Is God to You?

> *"Lord, help me return to childlike faith—a heart that sees You as kind, caring, and close. Strip away the noise of grown-up worries, and let me see You for who You are: my Savior, my Shepherd, my Friend. Amen." Luke 18:16 (ESV)*

I asked a group of Sunday school children, ages 4 to 6, to close their eyes and answer a simple question: Who is God?

Their answers were sincere and direct:

"He is kind."

"He cares for me."

"He protects me."

"He gives me food."

"He died on the cross for me."

No theological jargon. No hesitation. Just truth, flowing from the hearts of children who trust fully and love deeply. It was humbling.

So today, I turn that question to you and me:

Who is God to me?

Is He the One who lifted me when no one else saw my pain?

Is He the Father who listened when the world was too loud?

Is He my peace in chaos, my shelter in storm, my light in darkness?

Is He the reason I keep going even when I don't feel strong?

Let's pause.

Take a deep breath. Close your eyes.

And without overthinking, simply answer:

Who is God to me?

Let your heart speak. Let your soul answer.

TUESDAY: *Let Me Be Singing*

> **Prayer:**
> Lord, help me return to childlike faith—a heart that sees You as kind, caring, and close. Strip away the noise of grown-up worries, and let me see You for who You are: my Savior, my Shepherd, my Friend. Amen.

TUESDAY

Let Me Be Singing

"They shall sing of the ways of the Lord..." Psalm 138:5

"Bless the Lord, oh my soul
Oh my soul
Worship His holy name
Sing like never before
Oh my soul
I'll worship Your holy name..."
— From "10,000 Reasons" by Matt Redman

I've found myself singing this song over and over again lately, even though, at first, I only knew the first few lines by heart. Something about the melody and the message kept pulling me in, so I decided to look up the full lyrics.

What truly gripped me were these lines:
"Sing like never before,"
"Whatever lies before me,"
"Let me be singing..."

Isn't that the posture our hearts should always carry? A melody of praise, no matter what lies ahead. Yet, if we're honest, we know it's not always easy. There are days when praise feels like a foreign language, when heaviness clogs the pathways of joy, and even a whisper of worship feels out of reach.

But here's what I've learned: when we release our burdens to God, the blockage lifts. When we shift our focus from the weight of our worries to the worthiness of our Savior, the song rises again. Our soul begins to stir, and before we know it, the melody flows freely.

So today, no matter what you're walking through, let your soul declare:

"Whatever may pass and whatever lies before me, let me be singing when the evening comes."

Let this be your anthem:

"I will sing of Your strength..." Psalm 59:16

"I will sing aloud of Your steadfast love..." Psalm 59:16

"My tongue will sing of Your word..." Psalm 119:172

Is there a heaviness in your heart that's blocking your song? Release it to the Lord today. Let Him lift the weight and restore your melody.

What situation in your life feels heavy right now? Write it down and offer it up to God. Then write a few lines of praise to sing over your circumstances.

Prayer:
Lord, restore the song in my soul. When heaviness threatens to silence me, help me lift my voice in praise. Let me sing of Your love and strength, no matter what lies before me. Amen.

WEDNESDAY

Do My Best, Not Be the Best

"Whatever you do, work at it with all your heart, as working for the Lord, not for human masters." Colossians 3:23 (NIV)

"I want to be the best."

How often do we hear this from children, and how often do we silently echo it in our adult minds?

There's a subtle but powerful difference between wanting to be the best and striving to do our best. The first leans into pride and comparison;

Wednesday: *Do My Best, Not Be the Best*

the second leans into humility and wholehearted effort. One seeks applause from others; the other seeks approval from God.

The world teaches us to measure worth by rankings, awards, and visibility. But Jesus teaches us to measure faithfulness by the heart behind the act. Remember the widow with two mites? In the eyes of others, she gave little. But in Jesus' eyes, she gave her best, her all. And that's what mattered.

Today, let's realign our perspective. We're not called to outshine others; we're called to be faithful stewards of what God has entrusted to us. Whether it's two mites or two talents, give it your all.

Stop asking, "Am I the best?" And start asking, "Did I give God my best?"

Where in my life am I striving to be the best instead of doing my best? How can I shift that mindset this week?

> **Prayer:**
> *Lord, free me from the trap of comparison and the pride of being the best. Help me to focus on doing my best, with sincerity and humility. May my effort bring You joy, and may my heart stay anchored in pleasing You above all. Amen.*

THURSDAY

Steward of His Creation

"In the beginning God created the heavens and the earth." Genesis 1:1

From the very first verse in the Bible, we see the heart of a Creator—deliberate, orderly, intentional. Genesis 1 isn't just a timeline of creation; it's a portrait of divine preparation. God didn't create us first. Instead, He carefully formed everything we would need—light, sky, land, vegetation, sun, moon, stars, birds, sea creatures, animals, and then He created man and woman.

Why? Because He wanted us to walk into a world already equipped for us. That's the kindness of our God.

Thursday: *Steward of His Creation*

Let's slow down and look at just Day One:

He created light and separated it from darkness. Before the invention of electricity, darkness meant rest. Perhaps God, in His infinite wisdom, knew we would need a rhythm—light for work, darkness for stillness. Even the sequence of light and night was lovingly orchestrated for our well-being.

One of my favorite parts of creation is watching a flower bud slowly open into full bloom. It begins tightly closed, then, almost silently, it bursts into color. How could anyone say there is no God? Creation testifies to Him in every petal, every sunrise, every drop of rain.

And yet, we often overlook the marvel around us. We walk through life surrounded by artistry and provision, yet we rarely pause to acknowledge the Artist.

We are not just inhabitants of this earth; we are stewards of it.

Stewards pause to admire. Stewards protect. Stewards give thanks.

So, take a moment today and look around. Let your senses wake up to what God has made:

The breeze. The birdsong. The budding tree. The colors in the sky.

Let your heart whisper, "How awesome is our God."

> **Prayer:**
> Lord, forgive me for the times I've taken Your creation for granted. Open my eyes to the wonder around me—the things You lovingly prepared before I even existed. Help me be a good steward of all You've made. Teach me to pause, to marvel, and to give thanks daily. Amen.

Friday

The Lord Stood By Me

"But the Lord stood by me and gave me strength." 2 Timothy 4:17 (ESV)

Friday: *The Lord Stood By Me*

> *"The Lord is my light and my salvation; whom shall I fear?*
> *The Lord is the strength of my life; of whom shall I be afraid?"*
> *Psalm 27:1 (ESV)*

We had just finished our night prayer and settled into a time of quiet reflection when this powerful verse struck my heart: "The Lord stood by me."

Pause for a moment. Say it out loud: The Lord stood by me.
Doesn't it stir something deep within you?
Suddenly, fear loses its voice.
Anxiety begins to fade.
And your heart... finds rest.
These five simple words carry enough power to calm any storm.

It reminds me of watching a child walk hand-in-hand with their parent. There's no fear, no hesitation. They walk in full trust, knowing someone stronger is beside them. The parent doesn't need to explain every step; the child just knows they're safe.

So I ask you:
Who are you walking next to?
Fear creeps in when we forget who's with us.
Anxiety takes over when we lose sight of God's presence.
But Scripture is full of reminders that we are not alone.

Just like Paul, who endured isolation, persecution, and trials, we too can find strength, not from our circumstances, but from the One standing by us.

The next time fear knocks or loneliness sets in, pause and ask, "Who is standing next to me?"

If the answer isn't the Lord, it's time to shift your focus. But if it is the Lord, then breathe easy. You're not alone. You never were.

Prayer:
Lord, thank You for standing by me in every storm, every valley, and every quiet moment of fear. When I forget, remind me again that I'm never alone. Help me walk in peace and confidence, not because life is easy, but because You are beside me. Amen.

Saturday

What Are We Waiting For?

> *"If anyone, then, knows the good they ought to do and doesn't do it, it is sin for them." James 4:17 (NIV)*

How often do we delay doing something with the excuse that we'll "get to it later?" We postpone sending the message, taking the first step, making the call, applying for the job, or saying "yes" to what God has laid on our hearts. We shift into procrastination mode, often convincing ourselves that we're just waiting for the right time.

To me, procrastination is as good as not doing it at all.

One phrase that I hope my family and friends remember me for is this:

"Tomorrow is not promised to anyone, so do what you need to do now."

I once heard a quote that struck me like a lightning bolt to the spirit:

"Procrastination is the arrogant assumption that God owes you another opportunity to do tomorrow what He gave you the grace to do today."

How many of us are guilty of this? We delay that act of kindness, that phone call, that conversation, that ministry… not realizing we may be forfeiting the very grace that God has supplied for today.

Let's reflect on Jonah.

God told him to go to Nineveh. Jonah delayed—he ran. But God's call didn't change. Jonah's detour didn't cancel the assignment; it just prolonged the process. Eventually, Jonah obeyed, but not without consequence.

We may shake our heads at Jonah, but how many of us have done the same?

Delayed the hard conversation.
Postponed the dream.
Ignored the prompting.
We say:
"I'm too tired."
"I'm not ready."
"I'll wait for a better moment."
But what if now is the right moment?

Saturday: *What Are We Waiting For?*

God gives grace for today. He gives strength for the now. When He calls, He equips, even when it feels uncomfortable or inconvenient.
So let me ask:
What has God placed on your heart that you've been putting off?
What dream, calling, or step of faith are you delaying?
Is fear stopping you? Perfectionism? Doubt?
Don't let delayed obedience become disobedience.

Prayer:
Lord, forgive me for the times I've said "later" to what You wanted me to do today. Help me to recognize when I'm delaying out of fear, pride, or comfort. Stir up a sense of urgency in my spirit. Let me move with purpose and obedience. I trust Your timing, and today, I say yes. Amen.

Sunday

A Day to Refocus

"This is the day that the Lord has made; Let us rejoice and be glad in it." Psalm 118:24 (NASB)

Sunday is more than just the end of the week; it's the beginning of your next chapter. It's a reset. A divine pit stop to fuel your spirit before life picks up again on Monday.

Gather with fellow believers. Soak in the Word. Sing out your praise. Be still in His presence.

Let today be your reminder that no matter what last week held, God is giving you a fresh page. So go to church, be encouraged, and carry His peace into the week ahead.

Prayer:
Father, thank You for Sundays. Thank You for quiet moments, joyful songs, and the blessing of community. Let today mark the start of a week filled with Your purpose. Amen.

WEEK 36

Monday

Walk the Talk

> *"But be doers of the word, and not hearers only, deceiving yourselves." James 1:22 (ESV)*

I came across a heartwarming video recently. A father and son were strolling through a quiet park when the dad gently asked,
"Son, what would you like to be when you grow up?"
The boy thought for a moment and replied,
"Daddy, when I grow up, I want to read the Bible with coffee in my other hand."
He didn't say, "I want to be like you."
But oh, how deeply that simple sentence revealed his heart.
He had been watching his father, observing the quiet rhythms of his faith. The image of his dad reading the Bible every morning with a cup of coffee left a lasting impression. That daily discipline, that simple act of devotion, had shaped his aspirations.
Children notice. They don't always announce it, but they're watching.
Whether it's parents, grandparents, teachers, or mentors, little eyes are always observing.
And that leads me to a question that we must all reflect on:
Are we walking the talk?
Do our lives reflect the Christ we preach about?
Are we emulating Jesus in the small things—how we speak, how we react, how we treat those around us?
Is our faith visible in how we love and how we serve?
You don't need to be on a platform to make an impact. Sometimes, the most powerful sermons are preached in the kitchen, during a car ride, or at the breakfast table with coffee and a worn-out Bible.

Monday: *Walk the Talk*

Your habits matter. Your reactions matter. Your walk matters. Because someone is watching, and more than what you say, they will remember how you lived.

Let us live lives so consistent and sincere that when others observe us, even quietly, they are inspired to want more of God.

> **Prayer:**
> *Lord, forgive me for the times I've spoken about righteousness but failed to live it. Help me to walk in a way that reflects Your love, Your patience, and Your truth. Let my life preach louder than my words. May the next generation see You in me—and may I never forget that I am always planting seeds with my actions. In Jesus' name, Amen.*

TUESDAY

Feeling Alone in a Sea of People

"I will never leave you nor forsake you." Hebrews 13:5 (NIV)

Have you ever found yourself surrounded by people, family, coworkers, even friends, and yet felt utterly alone?

It's a strange kind of emptiness. On the outside, you're part of the crowd. But inside, you feel invisible. People greet you, even smile at you, but they don't really see you. You're present, but not felt. Needed, but not known.

Sometimes this feeling sneaks in because life moves so fast. Everyone is buried in their own responsibilities, their own worries, their own agendas. And unintentionally, you get lost in the shuffle. Other times, it stems from being overlooked or taken for granted. You show up for others, you support them, you do the things no one notices, and in return, you're met with silence or a shallow connection.

It can be discouraging. Even heartbreaking.

But then comes this truth, whispering into that hollow space:

"I will never leave you nor forsake you." Hebrews 13:5 (NIV)

Those were Jesus' words—personal, intimate, steady. His promise wasn't dependent on how many people gather around you or how loudly others affirm you. His presence is not seasonal or circumstantial. It's constant. He walks beside you in the crowd. He sees what others miss. He knows the unseen weight you carry. And He never treats your presence as optional or your heart as forgettable.

Even King David felt this way:

"Though my father and mother forsake me, the Lord will receive me." Psalm 27:10 (NIV)

God doesn't just notice you; He welcomes you. He gathers you close when the world keeps you at a distance. He fills the silence with His nearness and the loneliness with His love. So today, if you're feeling alone in a sea of people, pause and listen, not to the noise of the crowd, but to the gentle voice of the One who has never left your side.

When was the last time you felt unseen, even in the company of others?

What would it look like to invite God into that moment right now?

Write about a moment when you felt isolated despite being around people. Then write a response as if Jesus were speaking directly to you in that moment. Let His words remind you that you are deeply loved and never forsaken.

> **Prayer:**
> Lord, thank You for seeing me when no one else seems to. For staying close when others drift away. Fill the empty spaces of my heart with Your love. Help me rest in the truth that I am never truly alone, for You are with me. Amen.

WEDNESDAY

Hearers or Doers?

> "But be doers of the word, and not hearers only, deceiving yourselves." James 1:22 (ESV)

Wednesday: *Hearers or Doers?*

How often do we hear, yet slack off on the doing part? It's just human nature.

Think back to childhood. Obedience wasn't instant, was it? When our parents told us to put away our toys, did we jump to it? Probably not. As teenagers, when asked to clean our rooms, we often delayed or ignored it altogether. That hesitation is a picture of human tendency, to listen but not act.

Have you ever listened to a powerful sermon or read a Scripture that stirred your heart, only to walk away unchanged?

James doesn't sugarcoat his message. He says that if we only hear the Word but fail to live it, we are deceiving ourselves. It's like looking in a mirror, noticing the mess, and then doing nothing about it. God's Word is not just meant to inform us; it's meant to transform us.

Today, we're surrounded by opportunities to consume spiritual content. Sermons, podcasts, devotionals, and Bible studies are all at our fingertips. But spiritual maturity isn't revealed in how much we hear or highlight. It's seen in how much we obey.

God isn't asking for perfection. He desires surrender. A heart that says, "Lord, help me live this out," pleases Him more than one that says, "Amen," on Sunday and forgets Him on Monday.

Ask yourself:

Am I merely listening to the Word, or am I living it?

Where in my life is God prompting action, not just understanding?

What steps can you take today to be a doer of the Word?

> **Prayer:**
> *Lord, forgive me for the times I've heard Your Word but walked away unchanged. Help me not to be just a hearer, but a doer — someone who puts faith into action. Give me the courage to obey, even when it's hard. I don't want to deceive myself with empty knowledge. I want to live a life that reflects Your truth. In Jesus' name, Amen.*

THURSDAY

Shake the Dust and Keep Moving

> *"And whoever does not receive you nor listen to your words, as you leave that house or city, shake the dust off your feet." Matthew 10:14 (NASB)*

As Christians, we often carry a deep passion to see the world transformed by the love of Christ. We pray, preach, and share, hoping that everyone we encounter will be moved to repentance and faith. It's a noble desire, a reflection of God's own heart for the lost. But sometimes, that desire meets resistance. The response isn't always what we hoped for. Doors close. Hearts remain hard. Eyes stay blind.

Even Jesus, the Son of God, faced rejection. In His own hometown, among His own people, He was dismissed. And yet, He didn't force the message. He didn't linger where He wasn't welcome. He moved on to the next town, the next heart, the next opportunity.

Matthew 10:14 is a gentle reminder from Jesus to let go of the outcomes we can't control. If someone refuses to receive the message of hope, it's not our job to argue them into the Kingdom. We are called to sow seeds, not to force them to grow.

Maybe you've poured into someone for months or even years, and their heart seems unchanged. Maybe your words are met with indifference or mockery. Don't let discouragement take root. The seed of truth has been planted. Your labor is not in vain.

Shake off the dust, not in bitterness, but in freedom. The harvest is plentiful. There are souls waiting to hear. Keep walking. Keep speaking. Keep loving. Someone else is ready to listen.

Is there someone I've been trying to reach who continues to reject the message of Christ?

How can I lovingly release them to God's timing and focus on the next open door?

> **Prayer:**
> Lord, thank You for the privilege of sharing Your Word. Help me to serve faithfully and to release what I cannot control. When rejection comes, remind me that even You were turned away. Strengthen my heart to keep moving forward, one soul at a time. Give me eyes to see where You are working and a heart willing to follow wherever You lead. Amen.

FRIDAY

The Joy

"The joy of the Lord is your strength." Nehemiah 8:10 (NIV)

I was sitting in my living room the other day, staring at the words framed on my wall: "Today I choose joy." Every time my eyes landed on it, my heart would recalibrate—resetting itself to align with that truth. It became more than decor. It became a daily decision.

One day, I felt prompted to take that sign down and hang it in my office instead. Not long after, four coworkers stopped by. As we chatted, one of them suddenly locked eyes with the wall. He paused and then said, "You know what? That's what I'm going to do. No one is going to disturb that joy."

He continued, "My mom died of cancer, my brother, who never smoked, died of lung cancer, and my sister also died of cancer. I'm left with no one, but I'm going to choose joy. Thank you."

I didn't share this story to say I deserve a pat on the back. Not at all. That small act of moving a sign wasn't about me; it was a prompting from God. A gentle nudge that turned into a blessing for someone in deep pain.

Friend, today as you step out of your house or into your workplace, choose joy—a joy rooted in the Lord, a joy no one can steal. At a recent Bible study, someone asked, "Has anyone ever asked you at work, 'Why are you always smiling?'" What a beautiful opening to share the source of our joy—Jesus.

What is one practical way you can choose joy today, no matter your circumstances?

Has someone in your life needed to see joy in you lately?

Be the joy. Share the joy. Reflect the joy.

> **Prayer:**
> *Lord, help me to choose joy even when life feels heavy. Let my heart find its strength in You, and may others see Your joy shining through me. Use even the smallest acts to speak hope to someone else. Amen.*

SATURDAY

Planted to Withstand

> *"They will be like a tree planted by the water that sends out its roots by the stream. It does not fear when heat comes; its leaves are always green. It has no worries in a year of drought and never fails to bear fruit." Jeremiah 17:8 (NIV)*

Every year, before the first frost, we cut down the ornamental banana plant outside my house. We cover it with mulch to shield it from the harsh winter cold. And every spring, almost miraculously, it begins to sprout again — lush, green, and tall — bringing a tropical feel right to our doorstep. No matter how low it's cut, it always comes back. How? The roots. Deep beneath the surface, they remain unshaken, strong, and alive.

This simple plant teaches a powerful lesson about our spiritual life. When life cuts us down, through disappointments, grief, or hardship, do we stay rooted? Or are we only planted at the surface, vulnerable to the elements?

Saturday: *Planted to Withstand*

The strength of that banana plant lies in its roots. And so should ours, not in ourselves, but in the unshakable truth of God's Word. Unless we are deeply rooted in Him, the storms of life can knock us down and keep us down. But when we are grounded in the Word, we may bend, but we will not break.

Ask yourself today: What is the condition of your spiritual roots? Are you planted deeply or loosely hanging on? Are there areas in your life that need a little tending, small tweaks before they grow into deeper problems?

Invite the Lord to be your firm foundation. With Him, even in the toughest seasons, your leaves will stay green, and you will still bear fruit. What "winter" season are you facing right now?

How can you dig your roots deeper in the Word of God this week?

Is there a small issue in your life that God is prompting you to address before it grows?

Prayer:
Lord, thank You for being the solid ground beneath me. Strengthen my roots in You. Help me remain unshaken through life's trials. When I feel cut down, remind me that You are still at work — reviving, restoring, and preparing me to rise again. In Jesus' name, Amen.

Sunday

A Day to Refocus

"This is the day that the Lord has made; Let us rejoice and be glad in it." Psalm 118:24 (NASB)

Sunday is more than just the end of the week; it's the beginning of your next chapter. It's a reset. A divine pit stop to fuel your spirit before life picks up again on Monday.

SUNDAY: *A Day to Refocus*

Gather with fellow believers. Soak in the Word. Sing out your praise. Be still in His presence.

Let today be your reminder that no matter what last week held, God is giving you a fresh page. So go to church, be encouraged, and carry His peace into the week ahead.

Prayer:
Father, thank You for Sundays. Thank You for quiet moments, joyful songs, and the blessing of community. Let today mark the start of a week filled with Your purpose. Amen.

WEEK 37

Monday

Eternity in Our Hearts

> *"He has made everything beautiful in its time. He has also set eternity in the human heart; yet no one can fathom what God has done from beginning to end."* Ecclesiastes 3:11 (NIV)

There's something remarkable tucked into the middle of this verse: "He has also set eternity in the human heart." That line carries weight. It's easy to get caught up in the beauty of the world around us—the mountains, the oceans, the laughter of children, and even the comforts of daily life. Yet, in all His careful and magnificent creation, God left a space in our hearts that can't be filled by anything here. That space whispers of something greater—of eternity.

It's as if God built a homing device inside each of us, a constant internal reminder that this life is not all there is. While He has given us much to enjoy on this earth, He has deliberately left something just out of reach, something to look forward to. Why? Because He never intended for us to get too comfortable here. This is not our final destination.

There is nothing wrong with living well, with enjoying the blessings we've been given. But we must live with an awareness that we are only passing through. We're not called to plant our roots too deeply in the soil of this world. We are sojourners, travelers on our way home.

So, friends, don't settle. Don't kick back in life's recliner and say, "This is it. I've arrived." No, no, no. Keep moving forward. Keep your eyes on what lies ahead. Live with a mindset fixed on things above. We were created for eternity, and our hearts will never truly be at rest until we are home with Him.

> **Prayer:**
> Lord, forgive us for the times when we've gotten so entangled in the temporary that we've neglected the eternal. Turn our hearts back to You. Help us live with a kingdom mindset, grateful for our blessings, but never consumed by them. Thank You for providing so richly for us and for allowing us to be stewards of what You've given. Make us Kingdom people, Lord. Detach us from the grip of this world and anchor us in the hope of eternity. Purge our hearts of anything that keeps us from You. In Your name, Amen.

TUESDAY

Breathe on Me, O Breath of God

> *"Then the Lord God formed the man of dust from the ground and breathed into his nostrils the breath of life, and the man became a living creature." Genesis 2:7 (ESV)*

One night at Bible Study, we practiced the songs for Sunday worship. One of the hymns we'll be singing is "Breathe on Me." Such a beautiful, soul-stirring hymn. I'll include the YouTube link at the end so you can listen.

O breathe on me, O Breath of God,
Fill me with life anew,
That I may love the things You love,
And do what You would do.
O breathe on me, O Breath of God,
Until my heart is pure;
Until my will is one with Yours,
To do and to endure.
O breathe on me, O Breath of God,
So shall I never die,
But live with You the perfect Life

Broken Hearts Held by God: Week 37

Tuesday: *Breathe on Me, O Breath of God*

For all eternity.

From the very beginning, breath was more than oxygen. God didn't just form man; He filled him. That divine breath turned dust into being. And yet, how often do we, the once-breathed-upon, now walk around spiritually dry?

There are moments, perhaps even seasons, when we feel lifeless, simply going through the motions. We pray, but our words feel flat. We read Scripture, but our hearts remain unmoved. In those dry and weary places, our soul cries out: "Breathe on me, O Breath of God."

It is a plea not just for comfort, but for resurrection. A cry of the soul to be revived, resuscitated by the only One who gives true life.

Ezekiel was taken to a valley of dry bones—brittle, lifeless, scattered. God asked him, "Can these bones live?" Then came the instruction: "Prophesy to the breath." And as Ezekiel obeyed, breath entered those bones, and they stood—alive, strong, restored (Ezekiel 37:5–10).

That same breath, the Spirit of the living God, is still at work today. He revives the weary, restores the broken, and empowers the faint-hearted.

When you're spiritually fatigued, whisper this simple but powerful prayer: "Breathe on me, O Breath of God."

Then wait.

Wait for His Spirit to stir the dry places in your soul. Wait for the warmth of His presence to reach the cold corners of your heart. Wait for fresh wind, fresh vision, and renewed purpose to rise within you.

Have you ever seen someone being resuscitated? It's an emotional moment. A lifeless body is pressed, jolted, pleaded with to breathe again. That is the image I see when I say, "Lord, breathe on me." I need more than a nudge; I need resurrection.

We don't just need a breath from God. We need to be filled with the breath of God.

Prayer:
Come, Holy Spirit. Revive my dry spirit. Reignite my passion. Remind me that life apart from You is no life at all. Breathe on me, O Breath of God, until I am fully alive again—in You. Amen.

WEDNESDAY

Emoji World: When LOL Meets G-O-D

"The writing on the wall was written by a hand sent from God."
Daniel 5:24 *(paraphrased for modern emoji users)*

We live in a world where a conversation can go something like this:
HYD? How are you doing?
IDF. I am doing fine.
HBU? How about you?
DF. Doing fine
And that's the depth of today's emotional connection. We've got acronyms for everything—LOL, IKR, BRB, TTYL, SMH, and my favorite: IDK (I Don't Know), which is often followed by IMO (In My Opinion), which is a nice way of saying "I don't know, but I'm still going to give you advice."

Sometimes I think we'd need Daniel himself to come and interpret half our texts, just like he did with the mysterious writing on the wall. If he lived today, he'd walk into our group chats and say, "Hmm... this means your days of clarity have been numbered, your text has been weighed and found wanting, and your emoji use has divided your friendships!"

But let's get serious for a second (just a second—I promise). Are we having deep conversations anymore? Or have we boiled everything down to "LOL" and the occasional fire emoji? Are we truly connecting with others, or just hitting "♥" on their posts and moving on?

God didn't send His Son so we could live in acronym autopilot. He wants real conversations with us—no filters, no abbreviations, no perfect punctuation needed. Just you, Him, and an honest heart. Imagine texting God:
Me: "IDK what to do."
God: "TRUST ME."
Me: "SMH. Life's hard."
God: "IKR. I walked it too. Just follow Me."

WEDNESDAY: *Emoji World: When LOL Meets G-O-D*

Me: "LOL, okay."
God: "❤"
Let's not emoji our way out of intimacy with God. Instead of quick phrases, let's make time for real prayers. Instead of 😢, tell Him what's breaking your heart. Instead of 😠, confess what's frustrating you. And when you're 😊, give Him praise!

Because here's the truth: no acronym can ever summarize the depth of love He has for you. But if you had to try...
GOD:
Grace
Over
Drama.
Now that's a status worth sharing.

> **Prayer:**
> *Lord, help me log out of surface-level living and log into real conversations—with You and with the people You've placed in my life. Thank You for being the God who speaks clearly, listens patiently, and never uses read receipts. Amen.*

THURSDAY

Keep Us Grounded, Lord

> *"The Lord your God has been with you; you have not lacked a thing." Deuteronomy 2:7 (paraphrased)*

Memories came flooding in today as I recalled arriving in this land as a young mother 39 years ago. I remembered the struggles of settling in, the uncertainties we faced, and the quiet prayers whispered in the dark. But more than anything, I remembered how God sent just the right kind of angel at just the right hour, time and again. My tears flowed freely, uncontrollably—tears of overwhelming gratitude.

THURSDAY: *Keep Us Grounded, Lord*

We raised our family here. And now, as we walk into the sunset years of our lives, my heart keeps echoing the same simple prayer: "Lord, keep my family grounded. Help us never to forget our humble beginnings."

It was a deep conviction, a nudge from the Spirit that reminded me how easily we go about our busy days without pausing to remember where we started. How often we forget the manna moments, the quiet provisions, the unseen grace.

A thousand tongues would not be enough to express my gratitude for His leading. The verse that rose up in my heart was this: "Your clothes did not wear out and your feet did not swell during these forty years" (Deuteronomy 8:4). In other words, our shirts didn't have holes, and neither did our shoes.

Take a moment today. Pause. Reminisce. Look back on the journey from then to now and whisper thanks to the One who carried you every step of the way.

Prayer:
Lord, anchor our hearts in gratitude. May we never lose sight of where You've brought us from. Keep us grounded, humble, and always remembering that it was Your hand that led us, fed us, and carried us. Amen.

FRIDAY

Be the Night Light

"You are the light of the world. A city that is set on a hill cannot be hidden." Matthew 5:14 (NKJV)

I was looking at this little night light the other day, the kind that turns on automatically when the room gets dark. But as soon as I switched on the overhead light, the night light faded. It went into conservation mode, no longer glowing. The brightness of the room made it feel like it had no more purpose.

FRIDAY: *Be the Night Light*

Our lives can sometimes feel like that night light. In the hustle and bustle of daily life, it's easy for our light to grow dim. We blend into the noise, the motion, the crowd. Is it hard to stand out and shine? Absolutely—because when you carry the light of Christ, you often feel like the minority. But the closer we draw to Him, the more we become intentional about being the light. His light through us can shine brighter than anything around if we're unashamed to carry His name.

So, how is your light shining today?

As we grow older, we often install night lights throughout our homes, not for decoration, but for direction. They keep us from stumbling. No one tells those lights when to turn on; they just do. Even if they're the only light in the room, they faithfully do their job.

Be like that night light. Shine where it's dark. Shine even if you're the only one. Shine quietly, gently, consistently. You never know whose path you're helping illuminate.

Isn't it amazing how God uses the simplest things to speak to us? He knows how easily we get distracted or discouraged. So He leaves us little reminders, like a glowing night light, to keep us grounded and faithful. We are remnants of His grace in a dark world. Let's shine unashamedly.

Prayer:
Lord, help me to shine for You, even in small, quiet ways. Remind me that I don't have to be the brightest, just faithful. Let Your light shine through me today. Amen.

SATURDAY

Hear My Song, Lord

"He put a new song in my mouth, a hymn of praise to our God. Many will see and fear the Lord and put their trust in him." Psalm 40:3 (NIV)

SATURDAY: *Hear My Song, Lord*

I woke up with a song on my lips, not a prayer, not a plea, but a melody. The Gaither Band's beautiful chorus rang through my heart before my feet even hit the floor:
Hear my song, Lord,
You fill me with music.
Hear my words, Lord,
You fill me with praise.
Take this moment, I just can't waste it,
This one is Yours, Lord; I give You this day.

What a shift from our usual mornings filled with petitions, "Lord, hear my prayer..." Today, it was "Hear my song, Lord." What a powerful way to start the day, wrapped in gratitude and praise rather than worry or request.

He is so worthy of our praise, day and night. And for those of us who have been redeemed, He has put a song in our mouths. It's not just any tune; it's a song of hope, a song of joy, a song of promise. And this song can carry us through even the hardest moments if we let it.

Whatever you are facing today, don't lose the song. Don't let the chaos of the day drown out the melody He's given you. Let your praise rise before the problems. Let your worship go ahead of your worry.

So today, as I fold laundry, respond to emails, run errands, or sit in silence, this one is Yours, Lord. I give You this day, and I'll let the song You've placed in my heart rise freely from my lips.

Don't let the enemy steal your melody. Lift your voice, even if it's cracked or weary, and let Him hear your song.

> **Prayer:**
> *Lord, You fill me with music and cover me with praise. No matter what comes my way today, help me keep my song. Let my life be an offering of worship to You, not just in words, but in attitude, in heart, and in sound. Thank You for placing a song in my spirit that reminds me of who You are. I give You this day. Amen*

Sunday: *The Sacred Rhythm of Sunday*

Sunday

The Sacred Rhythm of Sunday

Sundays are more than a date on the calendar. They are sacred invitations. God ordained a rhythm—six days of work and one day of rest. Not just rest from labor, but rest "in Him."

Have you fallen into the habit of skipping church because of exhaustion or busyness? Reorder your steps. There is joy in the sanctuary. Healing in the worship. Encouragement in the Word. Connection in community.

We weren't made to walk this life alone. Sunday worship reminds us that we're part of something bigger—a body, a family, the Church. Even when life feels heavy, the joy of Sunday can lift our hearts.

"I was glad when they said to me, 'Let us go into the house of the Lord.'" Psalm 122:1 (NIV)

Prayer:
Lord, remind me that Sunday is not just a tradition, but an invitation. Help me show up, worship deeply, and leave renewed. Thank You for the sacred rhythm of rest and fellowship. Amen.

WEEK 38

Monday

When Doubt Creeps In

> *"Now the serpent was more crafty than any of the wild animals the Lord God had made. He said to the woman, 'Did God really say, "You must not eat from any tree in the garden"?'" Genesis 3:1 (NIV)*

> *"But when you ask, you must believe and not doubt, because the one who doubts is like a wave of the sea, blown and tossed by the wind." James 1:6-7 (NIV)*

"Did God really say?"

That one question from the serpent in the garden was enough to plant the first seed of doubt. It's subtle, isn't it? Doubt doesn't scream; it whispers. But that whisper can cause even the strongest to waver.

I've experienced it firsthand. I remember starting a new job, eager and confident. I would complete a task and submit it, thinking I'd done everything right. But then my supervisor would glance at it and ask, "Are you sure?" And just like that, all my confidence would crumble. That simple question planted doubt.

We see it again and again in Scripture.

Moses, handpicked by God to lead His people, still asked, "Who am I that I should go?" Despite hearing God's voice directly, Moses wrestled with inadequacy.

The father of the sick boy in Mark 9:24 cried out, "I do believe; help me overcome my unbelief!" Jesus honored his honesty and healed the boy.

Monday: *When Doubt Creeps In*

Peter—bold, courageous Peter—stepped out of the boat to walk on water. But the moment he took his eyes off Jesus and looked at the storm, he began to sink. And still, Jesus reached out and caught him.

Even spiritual giants had their moments of doubt. The beautiful truth? God didn't disqualify them. He met them in their doubt, restored their faith, and strengthened them for the journey ahead.

So, what kind of doubt are you facing today?

Are you doubting God's provision?

His healing power?

His ability to restore?

His presence in your storm?

Let the Word remind you: God is faithful. His promises are true. And His love does not waver, even when your faith does.

But remember what James writes: Doubt makes us unstable, like a wave tossed by the wind. Faith and doubt cannot co-exist. One will silence the other.

Choose today which one you'll give voice to.

Prayer:
Lord, how often doubt sneaks into my thoughts, sometimes quietly, sometimes forcefully. But You are steady, sovereign, and good. Help me silence every voice that questions Your truth. Strengthen my belief. Replace every doubt with confidence in You, my faithful and loving Father. In Jesus' name, Amen.

Tuesday

A Bible That's Falling Apart

"I have stored up your word in my heart, that I might not sin against you." Psalm 119:11

"The unfolding of your words gives light; it imparts understanding to the simple." Psalm 119:130

TUESDAY: *A Bible That's Falling Apart*

> *"The grass withers, the flower fades, but the word of our God will stand forever." Isaiah 40:8*

> *"Your words were found, and I ate them, and your word was to me the joy and rejoicing of my heart." Jeremiah 15:16*

A.W. Tozer once said, "A Bible that's falling apart usually belongs to someone who isn't." That quote has stayed with me for years.

When I hold my husband's Bible or my father's, I see pages torn and worn thin. The margins are filled to the brim with notes. Ink has bled through from years of study, and some letters are smudged, perhaps from tears that fell while reading God's promises in moments of sorrow. These Bibles are precious trophies of faith. They've been used, and more importantly, lived through.

I'm reminded of a story I heard in Sunday school:

A father sends his son off to college with a new Bible and one piece of advice—"Read it every day."

The son nods, says goodbye, and goes off to begin his new chapter in life.

Month after month, he calls home, asking for money. Each time, the father asks, "Son, have you read your Bible today?"

"Yes, Dad," the son replies, though he hadn't.

One day, the son receives the devastating news that his father has passed. Overwhelmed with grief, he finally opens the Bible for the first time, and tucked inside, between the pages, he finds envelopes with money, one for each month he had called. If only he had read the Word... he would have also received the provision.

What a powerful image. When we neglect the Word, we miss out—not just on wisdom or encouragement, but on the tangible blessings God may have hidden for us within its pages.

Did you eat His Word today?

Did you devour it like Jeremiah, who said, "I ate them, and Your Word was the joy and rejoicing of my heart"?

Or did you rush through a quick "one-minute devotion" hoping it would be enough?

Friends, reading the Word is our only spiritual ammunition to face the challenges of the day. Not a podcast, not a quote, not even a sermon, nothing replaces the living Word in your hands.

WEDNESDAY: *In His Time*

> **Prayer:**
> Lord, forgive me for the times I've taken Your Word lightly. Stir within me a hunger—not just for a verse, but for deep communion with You through Scripture. Let my Bible bear the marks of use, not neglect. May I be found, like Jeremiah, feeding on Your words and finding joy in every one of them. Amen.

--- WEDNESDAY ---

In His Time

> *"He has made everything beautiful in its time."* Ecclesiastes 3:11a (NIV)

Last night I was watching a testimony, and something the speaker said struck a deep chord. He asked, "Why is it that when we pray, we give God a deadline?"

Lord, I need to hear from You in three days.

We may not say it exactly that way, but in our hearts, we often set our own timeline for how and when we expect God to act.

But who are we to give God a deadline?

As soon as he said that, a familiar chorus rose in my spirit—the old Maranatha song:

In His time, in His time, He makes all things beautiful in His time.

Oh, how often we need to be reminded of that simple truth.

Maybe today you're waiting for an answer, and the silence feels louder than ever. Maybe your heart is growing impatient, your faith a little wobbly. That's when the word complete must rise up:

Complete trust.
Complete faith.
Complete hope.

Not half-hearted, not rushed, not conditional. But total surrender—complete submission to His will, His plan, and yes, His timing.

And what does He promise?
That He makes all things beautiful in His time.

> **Prayer:**
> Lord, forgive me for rushing Your process. Help me to rest in complete trust, faith, and hope. I choose to release my timeline and surrender to Yours—because Your timing is always perfect. Amen

---

THURSDAY

More Valuable Than Sparrows

> *"Look at the birds of the sky, that they do not sow, nor reap, nor gather crops into barns, and yet your heavenly Father feeds them. Are you not much more important than they?" Matthew 6:26 (NASB)*

I have a bird feeder, and I love sitting by the window to watch the sparrows. Tiny and feeble, they brave the outdoors—rain, wind, snow, and sun. They don't plant seeds, harvest crops, or store food in barns. And yet, somehow, they're fed.

Who feeds them? Our Heavenly Father does.

If God is that mindful of the birds, creatures without voice, shelter, or plans, how much more is He mindful of us? We, His children. We, who were created in His image. In Matthew 6, Jesus asks this question plainly: "Are you not of more value than they?"

So today, if your heart is anxious, weary, or overwhelmed, snuff it all out with this truth: You are of more value.

More than the sparrows. More than the lilies. You are known, seen, and cherished.

> **Prayer:**
> Lord, remind me of my worth in Your eyes. When I feel small or forgotten, let the birds remind me that You are near, and that I am deeply loved. Amen.

Friday

Keep It Real

> *"Finally, brothers and sisters, whatever is true, whatever is honorable, whatever is right, whatever is pure, whatever is lovely, whatever is commendable... think about these things." Philippians 4:8 (NASB)*

Here's one of my pet peeves: Society has conditioned us to be overly diplomatic and politically correct. We're taught to say just enough to keep the peace, to sugarcoat the truth, to avoid rocking the boat. But in all that careful editing, we lose something important—we lose our authenticity.

Why can't we just be real?

My kids love to tease me: "No mincing words with Mom!" And you know what? I take no offense. I'd rather speak the truth in love than hide behind a smoky mirror of polite pretense. There's something powerful about walking in truth, not brashly, not carelessly, but with clarity, courage, and compassion.

The Bible doesn't tell us to think on what's popular. It says to think on what is true, honorable, right, and pure. How can we do that if we're constantly walking on eggshells, afraid to speak with conviction? Jesus Himself didn't tiptoe around the truth; He spoke with love but never diluted His message.

Realness doesn't mean being harsh. It means being anchored. It means letting your words be a reflection of your heart—seasoned with grace but rooted in truth. The world doesn't need more filters. It needs believers who are real, honest, and Spirit-led.

So let's keep it real—with kindness, with humility, and with truth.

Prayer:
Father, help me walk in truth today. Strip away any fear of offense, and teach me how to speak with grace and clarity. May my words reflect what is true, honorable, and pure. Keep me grounded in You, and help me never lose my voice in a world that craves silence. Amen.

Saturday

Assignment from Above

> *"And God spoke to Israel in visions of the night and said, 'Jacob, Jacob.' And he said, 'Here I am.'"* Genesis 46:2 (NASB)

> *"Then I heard the voice of the Lord, saying, 'Whom shall I send, and who will go for Us?' Then I said, 'Here am I. Send me!'"* Isaiah 6:8 (NASB)

When God places a thought on your heart, it's not random; it's a divine assignment. Whether it's a burden to pray for someone, a prompting to serve, or an idea that keeps resurfacing in your spirit, it's often heaven's way of saying, "I have something for you to do."

But here's the reality: we often hesitate. We question whether we heard Him right. We wonder if we're qualified. We stall, waiting for confirmation after confirmation, hoping the assignment will pass to someone else.

But if God gave it to you, He already factored in your weaknesses, your hesitations, and your history. He knows who He's calling, and still calls you anyway.

Picture God as the Divine VP of Purpose, carefully delegating specific tasks to specific people, not by accident but by intentional design. He assigns you not because you're the most talented, but because He knows you're available. He's just waiting for your response: "Here I am."

That's what Jacob said. That's what Isaiah said. That's what we are invited to say, too.

So today, if your heart stirs with something that seems bigger than you, don't run. Don't overanalyze it. Simply answer the call. God is not looking for perfect vessels, just willing ones.

Prayer:
Lord, I'm ready to receive my assignment. Give me ears to hear when You speak, and the courage to say "Here I am" without hesitation. Equip me with

Sunday: *Worship and Fellowship*

what I need to carry out what You place in my heart today. I may not feel ready, but I trust that You are. Amen.

Worship and Fellowship

> *"I was glad when they said to me, 'Let's go to the house of the Lord.'"*
> Psalm 122:1 (NASB)

There's something sacred about Sunday mornings, the intentional pause, the gathering of God's people, the lifting of voices in praise, the Word going forth, and the reminder that we're not walking this journey alone.

Scripture encourages us not to forsake assembling together (Hebrews 10:25), and there's a reason for that. In a world that constantly pulls us in every direction, corporate worship centers us. It realigns our priorities, refreshes our spirit, and reminds us of the bigger picture — God is on the throne, and we are part of His body.

Church isn't just a building; it's a lifeline. It's where iron sharpens iron, where burdens are shared, where joy is multiplied, and where we get a glimpse of heaven on earth.

This morning, don't let sleep, schedules, or excuses rob you of what God wants to deposit in your spirit. Go to His house, not just out of habit, but with expectation. The pew you sit in today might be the place God chooses to speak directly to your heart.

Prayer:
Lord, thank You for the gift of Sunday, for fellowship, for worship, and for the church. Help me not to treat it casually but to value it deeply. I come with an open heart today, ready to meet with You.

WEEK 39

Monday

You Are Not Alone

> *"Be strong and courageous. Do not be afraid or terrified because of them, for the Lord your God goes with you; he will never leave you nor forsake you." Deuteronomy 31:6 (NIV)*

Several things were weighing heavily on me, and I didn't sleep well, waking up frequently throughout the night. But when I woke up that morning, the first song I heard was "Oh My Soul, You're Not Alone."

Oh, my soul
Oh, how you worry
Oh, how you're weary, from fearing you lost control
This was the one thing you didn't see coming
And no one would blame you, though
If you cried in private
If you tried to hide it away so no one knows
No one will see, if you stop believing

Oh, my soul
You are not alone
There's a place where fear has to face the God you know
One more day, He will make a way
Let Him show you how, you can lay this down
'Cause you're not alone

God knows how to bring peace into our hearts. That morning, He used a song. Though we've tasted God's love, sometimes our

Monday: *You Are Not Alone*

circumstances drag us into a place of feeling alone. But our God, true to His promise, never leaves us. He steps into our situations with a word, a verse, or even a song.

> **Prayer:**
> Lord, thank You for reminding me that I am never alone. Help me recognize Your presence even when my heart feels heavy. Amen.

TUESDAY

Red Lights and Stop Signs

"He has made everything beautiful in its time." Ecclesiastes 3:11 (NKJV)

Everyone has dreams. Hopes. Longings. We envision the future with bright colors and bold outcomes. But the problem is, they don't always materialize right away. And that waiting period? It can be hard. Painful, even. We live in a world that thrives on instant results, fast fixes, and same-day delivery. But God doesn't operate on human timelines. He works in eternity. He sees the big picture.

And along the way to fulfillment, we often hit red lights.

Delays. Detours. Disappointments. Sometimes it feels like every direction we turn has a stop sign waiting for us. A job doesn't come through. A door that once looked wide open suddenly slams shut. A prayer seems unanswered or at least unheard.

But here's the truth: red lights are not rejections; they're reminders.

Reminders to pause. To breathe. To trust. To remember that we don't drive this journey, He does.

God isn't just interested in delivering the dream. He's refining you for it. There are lessons in the waiting. There's growth in the delay. Sometimes He holds back the answer because the soil of your heart needs time to be prepared for the beauty He's about to plant.

Ecclesiastes 3:11 doesn't say He makes some things beautiful. It says everything. That includes the mess, the delays, the failures, the "not yets," and the moments that didn't make sense. Everything becomes beautiful when it's surrendered to His perfect timing.

So if you're surrounded by red lights right now, don't panic. Don't take a shortcut. Don't try to run ahead. Wait. Because what He's preparing is worth it. And when the light finally turns green, you'll step into something more beautiful than you imagined—right on time.

> **Prayer:**
> *Lord, give me the patience to wait on Your perfect timing. When I see red lights and feel stuck, remind me that You are still working behind the scenes. Keep me from rushing ahead and help me trust that You are making all things beautiful—in Your time. Amen.*

WEDNESDAY

Don't Withhold Good

> *"And do not neglect doing good and sharing, for with such sacrifices God is pleased." Hebrews 13:16 (NASB)*

At home, I often say, "God hasn't given you this intelligence so you can keep it tucked away." Whether at work or in the kitchen ☺, I've noticed a curious pattern: people tend to withhold knowledge, not because they're unkind, but often because they're insecure.

At work, the hesitation might sound like this: "If I share this, what if they get the credit instead of me?"

In the kitchen: "I'm not giving away that secret ingredient—what if she makes it better than I do?"

Let's be honest, we've all had those moments! But if we truly remember the Source of our gifts, we'll realize there's no need to hoard

Wednesday: *Don't Withhold Good*

them. God didn't bless us to make us look good. He blessed us to be a blessing to others.

The wisdom, the talent, the creativity, the problem-solving skills, even your secret spice blend, all of it is a divine deposit from God. When you withhold those gifts, you're not protecting yourself; you're actually limiting what God could be doing through you.

Hebrews 13:16 reminds us that God is pleased when we share, when we do good, and when we give of ourselves. It might feel small, offering a tip to a coworker, teaching someone a recipe, mentoring someone younger, but in the Kingdom, these are holy sacrifices.

So be intentional. Share what you know. Encourage someone who's just starting out. Lift up others instead of competing with them. When we give freely, we reflect the generosity of the Giver Himself.

> **Prayer:**
> *Father, help me to freely share the gifts You've given me, without fear, without competition, and without hesitation. Remind me that every good thing in me comes from You, and You've given it so I can bless others. Make me generous with my wisdom, my kindness, and my knowledge. Amen.*

Thursday

When God Closes the Door

"Rest in the Lord and wait patiently for Him..." Psalm 37:7 (NASB)

"'For My thoughts are not your thoughts, nor are your ways My ways,' declares the Lord. 'For as the heavens are higher than the earth, so are My ways higher than your ways...'" Isaiah 55:8-9 (NASB)

Children and adults alike, we want things now. We're wired for speed. Fast answers. Immediate gratification. Same-day delivery. We make

THURSDAY: *When God Closes the Door*

plans and expect them to unfold just as we imagined. But what happens when God says "no," or "not yet"?

Sometimes, He gently, or not-so-gently, closes a door we were certain would swing wide open. Maybe it's a job opportunity that falls through. A relationship that unexpectedly ends. A ministry that doesn't gain traction. In those moments, we're tempted to question God's plan or even try to force our way in.

But trying to pry open a door God has closed doesn't show strength; it shows a lack of submission.

Waiting is hard. Yielding is harder. But trusting in God's timing and sovereignty is what faith is all about. He's not being cruel or careless. He's being God, the One who sees the end from the beginning. His "no" is often a setup for a better "yes." His redirection is never random. It's divine.

Psalm 37:7 calls us to rest and wait patiently. That doesn't mean passive sitting. It means releasing our clenched fists and open palms, saying, "Lord, I trust You more than I trust my plans." And Isaiah 55 reminds us why we can do that—His ways aren't just different; they are higher. Better. Wiser. Eternal.

So if you're standing in front of a closed door today, take a deep breath. Stop knocking. Don't try to pick the lock. Walk away with peace in your heart, knowing that God never closes a door without a reason, and He never leads without a purpose.

Prayer:
Lord, help me to stop banging on closed doors and trust Your divine detours. When things don't go my way, teach me to rest in Your sovereignty. I surrender my plans to Your perfect will and choose to follow where You lead. Amen.

FRIDAY

Give the Day Back

"Commit your works to the Lord, and your plans will be established."
Proverbs 16:3 (NASB)

Many of us start the morning with a familiar phrase: "Thank You, Lord, for a new day." And that's a beautiful beginning. Gratitude sets the tone. But here's a deeper question: how often do we actually give that day back to Him?

It's easy to thank God for the gift of a new morning, but then rush into it with our own agenda. Meetings to attend, errands to run, conversations to have, boxes to check. Before we know it, we've taken full control, planning, directing, and moving, without consulting the One who gave us the day to begin with.

But what if, instead, we paused to say:

"Lord, here is my day. You steer it. If I take control, I'll make wrong turns. But if You navigate, I'll walk in Your shadow—under Your protection, peace, and provision."

That's the heart behind Proverbs 16:3. God doesn't just want to be informed about our plans; He wants to be entrusted with them. When we commit our works to Him, He doesn't just bless them; He establishes them. He puts purpose behind the tasks, clarity in the chaos, and peace in the process.

Giving the day back doesn't mean we abandon responsibility; it means we align our to-do list with His will. We let Him speak into our decisions. We invite Him into the interruptions. We surrender the outcomes and trust that His presence goes before us.

And when we do that, something shifts. We move from striving to resting. From pressure to peace. From control to confidence, not in ourselves, but in Him.

We are truly blessed to be called His children. And as any loving Father would, He delights in walking through the day with us, guiding, correcting, blessing, and strengthening along the way.

> **Prayer:**
> Lord, I give this day to You. Every task, every meeting, every decision. Steer me in the right direction. Let my every step align with Your will and purpose. Keep me under Your covering as I walk in faith and obedience. Amen.

SATURDAY

Extraordinary in the Ordinary

> *"Be kind to one another, compassionate, forgiving each other, just as God in Christ also has forgiven you." Ephesians 4:32 (NASB)*

Elder David A. Bednar once said, "Ordinary people who faithfully, diligently, and consistently do simple things that are right before God will bring forth extraordinary results."

That quote lingers with me because it speaks to the heart of how God works.

So often, we chase big moments, grand gestures, public accomplishments, or titles that validate our efforts. But heaven's applause is often for the quiet, unseen faithfulness of everyday life.

Changing diapers at midnight. Sending a note of encouragement. Making a meal for someone in need. Choosing to forgive when no one else knows you were hurt. Showing kindness in a tense moment. These things may never go viral, but they matter deeply in the Kingdom.

The world may not notice the way you consistently show up. It may not applaud the patience you extend to someone who doesn't deserve it. You may not get a plaque or spotlight for choosing integrity when compromise would be easier. But your Heavenly Father sees it all.

And He is not unjust to forget your labor of love.

Glory fades. Awards gather dust. Accolades are forgotten. But the fruit of ordinary faithfulness, kindness, compassion, and forgiveness lasts for eternity. That's the stuff of heaven.

SATURDAY: *Extraordinary in the Ordinary*

So don't stop. Don't grow weary in doing the good, small things. The eyes of your Father are never blind to your obedience. He watches. He remembers. And in His time, He will reward openly what was done in secret.

Prayer:
Father, remind me that what I do in secret, You reward openly. Help me remain faithful in the small things, even when no one sees or applauds. Let my daily choices reflect the heart of Christ, and may I never underestimate the power of simple obedience. Amen.

SUNDAY

A Day to Refocus

"This is the day that the Lord has made; Let us rejoice and be glad in it." Psalm 118:24 (NASB)

Sunday is more than just the end of the week; it's the beginning of your next chapter. It's a reset. A divine pit stop to fuel your spirit before life picks up again on Monday.

Gather with fellow believers. Soak in the Word. Sing out your praise. Be still in His presence.

Let today be your reminder that no matter what last week held, God is giving you a fresh page. So go to church, be encouraged, and carry His peace into the week ahead.

Prayer:
Father, thank You for Sundays. Thank You for quiet moments, joyful songs, and the blessing of community. Let today mark the start of a week filled with Your purpose. Amen.

WEEK 40

Monday

Soul Temperature Check

> *"'I know your deeds, that you are neither cold nor hot; I wish that you were cold or hot. So because you are lukewarm, and neither hot nor cold, I will spit you out of My mouth.'"* Revelation 3:15-16 (NASB)

Is your soul hot or cold?

In our home, this is a running joke—my husband wears flannel while I'm dressed like it's beach weather. Opposites, all in good fun. But spiritually, this isn't a laughing matter. God isn't looking for mild, middle-ground faith. He desires a fiery, fervent love. Passionate. Alive.

Lukewarm Christians are half-committed, living in the safety of pretense. Not fully turned away, but not fully surrendered either. Comfortable enough to blend in, but not bold enough to stand out.

Jesus doesn't mince words; He'd rather us be cold or hot. At least cold can be honest. Lukewarmness masks apathy behind a spiritual disguise.

So today, check your soul's temperature. Has routine replaced relationship? Has comfort cooled your calling? Don't settle for spiritual mediocrity.

> **Prayer:**
> *Lord, ignite a fire in my soul. Forgive me for the times I've grown cold or indifferent. Reignite my heart. Let me burn passionately for You, consumed by love, not complacency. Amen.*

TUESDAY

Keep a Part of You Empty

> *"Bear one another's burdens, and thereby fulfill the law of Christ."*
> *Galatians 6:2 (NASB)*

There is so much brokenness in this world. Heartache often hides behind polite smiles and everyday conversations. Everyone we meet is likely carrying a quiet pain—grief, disappointment, stress, or fear. But in a culture that thrives on speed and surface-level interactions, how can we truly live with compassion and awareness?

The answer is simple, yet deeply spiritual:
Keep a part of you empty.
Empty enough to receive.
Empty enough to notice.
Empty enough to pause, to listen, and to love.

In my office at work, I have two chairs. One is for the usual back-and-forth—light-hearted chit-chat, quick questions, daily routines. But the other chair? It's sacred. It's the one I reserve, mentally and spiritually, for those who need a moment. For those who carry invisible weights and just need a place to land. Over the years, that chair has become a place of quiet ministry. Healing has happened there. Tears have fallen there. Sometimes no words are spoken, just presence, just listening.

But if I hadn't intentionally kept space in my day… in my heart… in my soul…

If I had filled every moment, every ounce of energy, every emotional shelf with busyness and self-preservation, there would've been no room left. No chair. No margin. No ministry.

Jesus didn't just come to save us; He came to show us how to walk with others in their pain. He wept with the grieving, paused for the forgotten, and touched the untouchable. He made room.

And He calls us to do the same.

We don't need to have the perfect words or solutions. Sometimes the greatest gift we can offer is availability, a willingness to be present and carry another's burden for just a little while.

> **Prayer:**
> Lord, help me not to fill my life so full that there's no room left for compassion. Keep a part of me empty, soft and available, for the broken, the burdened, and the weary. Let my presence reflect Yours, and let me be willing to carry what someone else can no longer hold alone. Amen.

WEDNESDAY

Held in My Brokenness

"You keep track of all my sorrows. You have collected all my tears in your bottle. You have recorded each one in your book." Psalm 56:8 (NLT)

To be in a place of brokenness is often to be in the very center of God's tender love. It's in those raw, shattered spaces, when we feel most undone, that His presence becomes undeniable. Michael Card once said, "To allow myself to be loved by God in my deepest brokenness is to experience a love that defies human comprehension." I've found that to be true.

There was a day I simply couldn't hold it together. The tears came without warning, and the weight I'd been carrying felt too heavy to shoulder another moment. I didn't want advice. I didn't want explanations. I just wanted someone to notice, someone to care.

That's when it happened. In the silence of that moment, I sensed eyes watching me, not with judgment, but with an overwhelming love. Then came something even more real: an invisible embrace. A grip so gentle, yet so firm, wrapped around me, like the arms of a parent scooping up their weeping child. I didn't see it with my eyes, but I knew I was being held.

And I heard His whisper: "I will never leave you nor forsake you."

That invisible grip stayed until the sobs quieted. He didn't rush me. He didn't scold me for being weak. He just held me. In that moment, I wasn't expected to be strong; I was simply invited to rest.

WEDNESDAY: *Held in My Brokenness*

Too often, we try to gather ourselves, to appear okay, to mask our pain under a smile or a busy schedule. But what if your most broken moment is also your most beautiful invitation to fall into the arms of a Father who catches every single tear?

He doesn't just see your pain; He honors it. He records it. He holds it. And most of all, He holds you.

So the next time your heart breaks, don't pretend. Don't push Him away. Lean in. Collapse if you need to. He's not going anywhere.

> **Prayer:**
> *Father, thank You for collecting every tear and holding me even when I feel like falling apart. I don't have to be strong when I'm with You. In my brokenness, I find the beauty of being fully known and fully loved. Hold me close until the storm passes, and remind me that even in the silence, You are still holding on. Amen.*

THURSDAY

Don't Let the Storm Stop You

> *"A generous person will be prosperous, and one who gives others plenty of water will himself be given plenty." Proverbs 11:25 (NASB)*

Storms have a way of narrowing our vision. When life is swirling and the winds of hardship blow hard against us, we tend to look inward, guarding our energy, protecting our emotions, conserving what little strength we have left. And yet, that's often the very moment God nudges us outward.

There were days when I had nothing left to give. Emotionally, I was running on fumes. Spiritually, I felt dry. But then someone would walk into my office, heavy with grief, uncertainty, or fear. They didn't need a sermon; they just needed a listening ear, a word of encouragement, a prayer whispered on their behalf. And somehow—somehow—God would meet me right there. He poured into me as I poured into them.

THURSDAY: *Don't Let the Storm Stop You*

That's the beauty of His Kingdom: even in our weakness, we're still useful.

God never asks us to wait for perfect conditions to serve Him. If we wait for the storm to pass before we open our mouths or extend our hand, we may never act at all. Our calling doesn't pause when life gets rough. In fact, it's in those vulnerable seasons that our ministry often carries the most weight because it comes from a place of dependence, not performance.

You don't need to be overflowing with energy to water someone else's soul. Just show up. Just be available. You are a steward of His life-giving Word, and even a drop of that living water can refresh a weary heart.

Let God use your storm, not just to shape you, but to strengthen someone else.

> **Prayer:**
> Lord, even when I feel empty, remind me that You are my source. Use me in every season, even the hard ones. Help me give from what You provide, and let my life be a vessel of encouragement for someone else today. Amen.

FRIDAY

Trust Over Whys

> *"For we do not have a high priest who cannot sympathize with our weaknesses... let's approach the throne of grace with confidence."*
> *Hebrews 4:15-16 (NASB)*

Sometimes, our joy slips away, not because God has changed, but because we've become entangled in the "Why, God?" cycle. It's a place many of us know too well. When circumstances don't make sense, when grief hits unexpectedly, or when prayers seem unanswered, the questions begin to swirl.

Why didn't You stop this, Lord?

FRIDAY: *Trust Over Whys*

Why now? Why me? Why them?

Mary and Martha voiced those very questions when their brother Lazarus died. "Lord, if You had been here…" was their cry (John 11:21, 32). It's a cry many of us have echoed. But what they couldn't see was the bigger plan—the resurrection, the miracle, the glory that was coming. We often forget: even in our pain, God is still writing a glorious story.

There's nothing wrong with asking God why. He invites honest prayers. But if we stay stuck in the why, we can miss the Who—the One who stands with us in our sorrow and walks us through the fire.

God doesn't promise we'll always understand. But He does promise His presence, His comfort, and His grace. Hebrews reminds us that we serve a High Priest who is not distant or cold. Jesus understands our weaknesses. He feels our pain. And because of that, we are invited to approach the throne of grace, not with fear or confusion, but with confidence.

Even when we don't understand, we can trust. Trust that He's working all things together. Trust that He hasn't forgotten. Trust that His will is perfect, even when it doesn't match our expectations.

Let's choose faith over frustration. Let's replace our whys with worship.

> **Prayer:**
> *Father, help me to let go of what I don't understand and cling to what I know: You are good. You are sovereign. You are near. Even when I have questions, remind me that I can come boldly to Your throne, confident in Your love and grace. Teach me to trust You more. Amen.*

SATURDAY

Even If… He Is With Me

"Do not fear, for I have redeemed you; I have called you by name; you are Mine! When you pass through the waters, I will be with you,

> *and through the rivers, they will not overflow you. When you walk through the fire, you will not be scorched, nor will the flame burn you." Isaiah 43:1–3a (NASB)*

There's a holy kind of peace that comes when you can say:
"Even if... He is still with me."
Even if the diagnosis doesn't change.
Even if the job falls through.
Even if the prayers seem delayed.
Even if the worst happens... God is still faithful.

This passage from Isaiah has become a lifeline in many dark moments. It doesn't promise a life free of trials; it promises something far better: His presence through them.

"When you pass through the waters..."
"When you walk through the fire..."
These aren't ifs; they're whens. And yet, so is His promise:
"I will be with you."

That truth is breathtaking. He doesn't leave when things get hard. He doesn't step back when the storm rages. He enters the water with us. He walks into the fire beside us. And that changes everything.

This verse reminds us who we are:
Redeemed.
Called by name.
His.
Never alone.

You may not feel strong enough. You may not have the answers. But take heart—you don't need to. The One who holds the waters and commands the fire says, "You are Mine." And that promise is the anchor your soul needs today.

Prayer:
Lord, thank You for being with me, even in the fire, even in the flood. I don't have to be afraid because I am Yours. Help me hold tightly to Your promises and trust in Your presence, no matter what comes. Even if... I will not fear. Because You are with me. Amen.

SUNDAY: *Worship and Fellowship*

 SUNDAY

Worship and Fellowship

"I was glad when they said to me, 'Let's go to the house of the Lord.'"
Psalm 122:1 (NASB)

There's something sacred about Sunday mornings, the intentional pause, the gathering of God's people, the lifting of voices in praise, the Word going forth, and the reminder that we're not walking this journey alone.

Scripture encourages us not to forsake assembling together (Hebrews 10:25), and there's a reason for that. In a world that constantly pulls us in every direction, corporate worship centers us. It realigns our priorities, refreshes our spirit, and reminds us of the bigger picture — God is on the throne, and we are part of His body.

Church isn't just a building; it's a lifeline. It's where iron sharpens iron, where burdens are shared, where joy is multiplied, and where we get a glimpse of heaven on earth.

This morning, don't let sleep, schedules, or excuses rob you of what God wants to deposit in your spirit. Go to His house, not just out of habit, but with expectation. The pew you sit in today might be the place God chooses to speak directly to your heart.

Prayer:
Lord, thank You for the gift of Sunday, for fellowship, for worship, and for the church. Help me not to treat it casually but to value it deeply. I come with an open heart today, ready to meet with You.

WEEK 41

Monday

Daily Manna

"Give us this day our daily bread." Matthew 6:11 (NASB)

Wouldn't it be easier if God gave us a monthly supply of grace, wisdom, and strength — a spiritual stockpile to carry us through the ups and downs? But that's not how He works. He invites us into daily dependence.

Just like the Israelites received manna in the wilderness, fresh each morning, only enough for that day, God provides for us moment by moment. They couldn't gather extra for tomorrow. Why? Because He wanted them to return, to trust, to seek Him again when the sun rose.

God doesn't deal in leftovers or bulk deals. He gives us today's grace for today's needs. Tomorrow's grace will meet us when tomorrow comes.

So if you're feeling empty, unsure, or overwhelmed, don't look too far ahead. Just come to Him now. Ask for your portion. He is faithful.

Prayer:
Lord, thank You for today's manna — fresh, timely, and perfectly measured. Help me not to rush ahead or hoard what's meant for today. Teach me to rest in Your provision and meet with You each new morning. Amen.

TUESDAY

Rooted in Truth

"Sanctify them in the truth; Your word is truth." John 17:17 (NASB)

Good morning! In a world spinning with opinions, algorithms, and ever-changing headlines, truth can feel like a moving target. Values shift. Standards blur. Even facts seem up for debate. But one thing remains unshaken and unchanging, the Word of God.

God's Word isn't just a helpful suggestion or a good moral compass; it is truth. Eternal, pure, and unwavering. It cuts through confusion like a light in the fog. When you don't know what to believe, where to stand, or how to respond, Scripture is your safe place. Your anchor.

Jesus prayed, "Sanctify them in the truth..." That means He wants us to be set apart, shaped, refined, and strengthened by truth. Not culture. Not emotion. Not peer approval. But truth that sanctifies the soul.

The more deeply rooted we are in Scripture, the more unshakable we become. Like a tree planted by rivers of living water, we'll bear fruit in every season, not because life is easy, but because our roots go deep.

Prayer:
Lord, anchor me in Your truth. Let Your Word guide my steps, guard my heart, and shape my thinking. When the world feels loud and uncertain, remind me that Your truth is eternal. I want to be rooted in You, not swayed by trends, but sanctified by truth. Amen.

WEDNESDAY

Refined to Reflect

"The refining pot is for silver and the furnace for gold, But the Lord tests hearts." Proverbs 17:3 (NASB)

I once had the pleasure of watching a goldsmith at work, carefully removing impurities from a piece of metal. He held it in the fire, not for punishment, but with purpose, watching closely until he could see his reflection in the purified surface.

That's exactly how Christ works with us.

He uses the fire of life to remove the things that dull our shine — bitterness, gossip, anxiety, depression, pride — the things that distort His image in us. He keeps us in the refining fire not to harm us, but to shape us into something beautiful, something that reflects Him.

Sometimes those tests feel like spiritual boot camp. Our son went through one to become a cop — intense, exhausting, demanding. But it built him. It strengthened him. And it shaped him into someone ready for the job. God does the same with us.

When our hearts are tested, it's not to break us. It's to refine us.

So don't fight the fire. Don't run from the discomfort. Stay in the process. Let Him work.

Because when the refining is complete, we shine. We reflect our Maker.

We were created in His image, but somewhere along the journey, we got covered in the world's grime. Now, the Master Refiner calls us back. To be made new. To be restored.

Prayer:
Master Refiner, purify my heart. Remove what is not of You and help me reflect Your image. Amen.

THURSDAY

Eternity Is Too Long to Stay Silent

"For what does it benefit a person to gain the whole world, and forfeit his soul?" Mark 8:36 (NASB)

Fear of rejection.
Fear of ruining the relationship.
Fear of not having the right words.
But if we truly believe that eternity is at stake, then silence becomes the greater risk.
We spend so much of life chasing after things that won't last—comfort, achievement, approval, reputation. We protect people's feelings, preserve temporary peace, and hesitate to rock the boat.
Yet the soul, the only part of us that will live forever, often gets pushed aside. Not just our own soul, but the souls of those around us.
Mark 8:36 reminds us how tragic it would be to gain the whole world, only to lose what matters most. That truth isn't just about us; it's about our neighbors, our coworkers, our friends, and even those we love most.
You don't need to preach a sermon.
You don't need a theology degree or the perfect answers.
You simply need a heart that's willing.
Love boldly. Live authentically. Speak when God prompts. Share what He's done for you.
Because eternity is too long to stay silent.
And love refuses to keep quiet when hope is within reach.

Prayer:
Lord, break my heart for the people around me who don't know You. Give me both compassion and courage—compassion to care deeply, and courage to speak truth in love. Use my life to reflect eternity, and let my words carry the hope of salvation. In Jesus' name, Amen.

FRIDAY

Covenant of Love

> *"Then it shall come about, because you listen to these judgments and keep and do them, that the Lord your God will keep His covenant with you and His faithfulness which He swore to your forefathers."*
> Deuteronomy 7:12 (NASB)

I was mentally organizing my week (classic firstborn syndrome!) when I felt a prompting in my spirit, Deuteronomy 7:12. Curious, I opened my e-Bible, and there it was:

"If you pay attention to these laws and are careful to follow them, then the LORD your God will keep His covenant of love with you..."

That phrase, "if you pay attention," stopped me in my tracks. I had been arranging my plans, but God was inviting me to consider His.

How often do we make our relationship with God one-sided? We run to Him when we're in need, but do we consistently rededicate ourselves to Him? He longs not just for our checklist of prayers but for our heart. His covenant of love isn't a transaction; it's a relationship, one that requires our attention, obedience, and surrender.

This verse reminded me of the concept of yielding. It took time, but when I began the practice of rededicating myself each day, something shifted. My thoughts became more centered on Him. It became less about fitting God into my schedule and more about building my life around Him. Daily yielding says: Lord, I want more of You in my life.

In the business world, a handshake seals a deal. In the Kingdom of God, the covenant is sealed by love, and it starts with our "yes."

Are you experiencing His covenant of love today? If not, maybe it's time to realign your heart. Let's pause, check the posture of our spirit, and make the necessary tweaks to return to that beautiful place of intimacy with our promise-keeping God.

> **Prayer:**
> Lord, I rededicate my heart to You today. Thank You for Your faithfulness and covenant love. Keep me close, and help me live in alignment with Your Word. I want more of You. Amen.

SATURDAY

Gift Giving Like God

> *"For God so loved the world, that He gave His only begotten Son…"*
> *John 3:16 (NASB)*

Who taught us to give gifts?

It wasn't the department stores or social trends. It was God Himself. He set the standard by giving us the most extravagant gift of all: His only Son. Not a spare, not something unwanted — His very best.

John 3:16 isn't just a familiar verse; it's the foundation of our faith. My husband just finished a four-week sermon series on this Scripture, and I'll never look at it the same way again. It's more than a verse; it's a divine blueprint for how to love, how to sacrifice, and how to give.

So now the question is: What gift are we offering back to Him?

Is it something convenient or leftover? Are we giving out of routine, dropping an offering in the plate or wrapping something for someone who already has everything? Are we caught in the cycle of giving where closets are bursting and hearts are still empty?

Maybe it's time to step back and rethink our giving.

How about blessing someone who won't expect it, but truly needs it? The mail carrier who delivers through rain, snow, and heat.
The trash collector who hauls away your mess all year long.
The neighbor who's grieving and alone this season.
Or maybe the lonely soul who just needs the gift of your time.

Some gifts don't come in wrapping paper. They come through listening ears, shared tears, warm meals, and open arms. God's gift didn't come with a bow; it came with a cross.

You may not be able to give extravagantly, but you can give meaningfully. That's what makes it powerful. Love multiplies in the simplest acts.

Let's follow His example this season. Let's give in a way that reflects the Giver.

> **Prayer:**
> Lord, thank You for the gift of Your Son, the greatest gift I could ever receive. Teach me to give like You. Help me to notice those around me, and give not out of obligation, but out of love. Use my hands, my time, and my heart to bless someone today. Amen.

 SUNDAY

The Sacred Rhythm of Sunday

"I was glad when they said to me, 'Let's go to the house of the Lord.'"
Psalm 122:1 (NASB)

There's something sacred about Sunday mornings, the intentional pause, the gathering of God's people, the lifting of voices in praise, the Word going forth, and the reminder that we're not walking this journey alone.

Scripture encourages us not to forsake our own assembling together (Hebrews 10:25), and there's a reason for that. In a world that constantly pulls us in every direction, corporate worship centers us. It realigns our priorities, refreshes our spirit, and reminds us of the bigger picture — God is on the throne, and we are part of His body.

Church isn't just a building. It's a lifeline.

It's where iron sharpens iron, where burdens are shared, where joy is multiplied, and where we get a glimpse of heaven on earth.

Broken Hearts Held by God: Week 41

Sunday: *The Sacred Rhythm of Sunday*

This morning, don't let sleep, schedules, or excuses rob you of what God wants to deposit in your spirit. Go to His house, not just out of habit, but with expectation.

The pew you sit in today might be the very place where God speaks directly to your heart.

Prayer:
Lord, thank You for the gift of Sunday — for fellowship, for worship, and for the church. Help me not to treat it casually but to value it deeply. I come with an open heart today, ready to meet with You. Stir my spirit, speak to my soul, and align my steps with Yours. Let this day mark a fresh encounter with Your presence. Amen.

WEEK 42

MONDAY

Obedience Without the Bargain

"But whoever listens to me will live securely and will be at ease from the dread of evil." Proverbs 1:33 (NASB)

I found myself drawn to the excitement of the magi—wise men eagerly traveling to see the newborn King. They weren't dragging their feet. They were thrilled at the idea of seeing Jesus, guided by a star and driven by hope.

And then I read Proverbs 1:33, and suddenly I was a little kid again, standing before my mom, asking for a Gaylord ice cream (if you remember those, they looked like bright tennis balls on a stick). My mom would say, "If you finish all your food, then we can go get some." And you better believe I cleaned that plate fast! The reward was motivation enough.

From childhood to adulthood, we live in a world of conditions—if you do this, then you'll get that. We're conditioned to reel and deal, to negotiate, to earn our reward. But God doesn't work like that. He isn't holding blessings behind His back waiting for us to meet a quota.

Our Father simply says: Listen to Me. Obey Me. Trust Me. And when we do, we live securely, not just physically, but emotionally and spiritually. There's no dread of evil, no bargaining for peace. It's a promise: listen and live secure.

Are we as eager as the magi in our pursuit of Jesus? Are we following His voice with that same joy and anticipation? Or have we reduced our walk to a reward-based religion?

Let's lay down the deals. Let's listen because we love Him. Let's obey because He's worthy.

> *Prayer:*
> *Lord, help me to trust You without needing the incentive. May I obey not for what I'll get, but because of who You are. Let me listen eagerly and walk securely in the path You've set before me. Amen.*

TUESDAY

Should I or Should I Not?

> *"But seek first His kingdom and His righteousness, and all these things will be provided to you." Matthew 6:33 (NASB)*

Ezra Taft Benson once said, "When we put God first, everything else falls into proper place or drops out of our lives." What a powerful truth.

It's comforting to know that God takes the guesswork out of life. Honestly, I sometimes struggle just deciding what to wear to an event, let alone making major life choices! Forget life decisions; many of us can't even decide what to cook for dinner without polling the whole family. We are a people prone to indecision.

But here's the beauty of God's promise: Put Me first, and I'll take care of what stays and what goes.

He does the sorting. He knows what's essential and what's extra. What a relief! We don't have to overthink, second-guess, or carry the weight of wondering if we made the right choice. The Creator, the Master Designer of our lives, has already volunteered to handle that for us.

All He asks is simple: Seek Me first. That's it.

It's not a complicated formula; it's a daily rhythm. Wake up and say, "Lord, I surrender this day to You." Do it again tomorrow. And the next day. Over time, it becomes a lifestyle. When we live totally yielded, He takes the wheel and makes sure we don't end up in a ditch.

What a bargain! We give up control, and in return, we get peace, purpose, and divine direction.

So I challenge you: for the next two weeks, try this act of surrender every morning. Say it out loud. Pray it from your heart. Then watch how God faithfully aligns your path.

> **Prayer:**
> *Father, I'm tired of trying to figure everything out on my own. I surrender today and every day to You. Be the decision-maker in my life. Guide my thoughts, shape my choices, and lead me to what truly matters. Amen.*

WEDNESDAY

The Temptation of Warm Bread

"But he does not know that the dead are there, that her guests are in the depths of Sheol." Proverbs 9:18 (NASB)

(Proverbs 9:17 context: "Stolen water is sweet, and bread eaten in secret is pleasant.")

Lord, are You kidding me? You know us so well that You had this verse written down centuries ago, like a mirror exposing our hearts. Your Word truly is alive. It's not just a book; it's a manual for life, filled with insight that cuts right to the core.

I couldn't help but chuckle as I read this verse. My eyes fixated on the part about bread. Now you've got my attention! I love restaurants that serve fresh, from-the-oven-to-the-table bread—warm, soft, with a swipe of butter. On a cold, snowy morning like this one, I crave it even more.

But isn't that exactly how temptation works? We say we're on a diet, physically or spiritually, and yet in secret, we sneak that forbidden thing. We know it's not good for us, but the moment is too enticing. We indulge, and the satisfaction is fleeting. The result? Harm. To our bodies. To our souls. To our witness.

It's the same pattern that led Eve to take a bite. Just one moment of weakness… and the enemy pounced.

WEDNESDAY: *The Temptation of Warm Bread*

But God, in His goodness, already knew this about us. That's why He gave us a powerful promise through Paul in 2 Corinthians: "My grace is sufficient for you, for My power is made perfect in weakness."

In our weak moments, God offers strength. In our struggles, He provides a way of escape. His Word is timeless, just as relevant today as it was 2,000 years ago. That's why it's called the Book of Life.

Temptations will always exist. But we don't have to be victims of our cravings or our emotions. When your knees start to buckle, call on Him.

In that exact moment of temptation, just whisper: "Lord, Your grace is sufficient for me." He will strengthen you. He will uphold you.

So I ask, can you trust Him in your weakest moment?

Will you?

Prayer:
Lord, You know my weaknesses even better than I do. In those vulnerable moments, remind me that Your grace is enough. Help me to say no to what harms and yes to what brings life. Thank You for being my strength when I am weak. Amen.

THURSDAY

Victim or a Conqueror?

"If God is for us, who can be against us?" Romans 8:31 (NASB)

What's your state of mind this morning? Are you feeling discouraged? Disappointed? Maybe even hosting a pity party? It's okay to acknowledge those feelings, but don't stay there. Let God's Word reshape your mindset today. You were never meant to live as a victim. In Christ, you are a conqueror.

Whatever life has handed you, fear, pain, or confusion, God has already spoken into it:

Are you afraid?

THURSDAY: *Victim or a Conqueror?*

Matthew 8:26, "Why are you afraid, O you of little faith?" Then He rose and rebuked the winds and the sea, and there was a great calm.

Are you feeling helpless?

Isaiah 12:2, "God is my savior; I will trust him and not be afraid. The Lord gives me power and strength; he is my savior."

Are you lonely?

Loneliness can slowly drag you into depression. Don't go there, please.

Psalm 34:18, "The Lord is close to the brokenhearted and saves those who are crushed in spirit."

Are you weak?

Isaiah 41:10, "Do not fear, for I am with you; do not be dismayed, for I am your God. I will strengthen you and help you; I will uphold you with my righteous right hand."

Struggling with self-esteem?

That's a big one. It can sneak in through job disappointments, physical struggles, or just feeling unseen.

Hebrews 10:35-36, "So do not throw away your confidence; it will be richly rewarded. You need to persevere so that when you have done the will of God, you will receive what he has promised."

Are you doubting?

James 1:6-7, "But ask in faith, never doubting, for the one who doubts is like a wave of the sea, driven and tossed by the wind."

Facing temptation?

1 Corinthians 10:13, "No temptation has overtaken you except what is common to mankind. And God is faithful… He will also provide a way out so that you can endure it."

Feeling hopeless?

1 Peter 5:7, "Cast all your anxiety on Him because He cares for you."

Hurting from a broken relationship?

Psalm 147:3, "He heals the brokenhearted and binds up their wounds."

Are you grieving?

Psalm 73:26, "My flesh and my heart may fail, but God is the strength of my heart and my portion forever."

1 Thessalonians 4:13, "We do not grieve like those who have no hope…"

This year has been tough for our family—misunderstood, misrepresented, rejected, and walking through many storms. And yet, it's only

Thursday: *Victim or a Conqueror?*

the grace of God that has sustained us. I can stand today and confidently declare: "If God is for us, who can be against us?"

The enemy may have his field day, but the final verdict comes from the Lord.

Keep doing good. Keep trusting Him. I'm so grateful for the stories of Job, Joseph, and others in Scripture; they remind us that we are not alone and we are not powerless. The Christian walk isn't a cakewalk. But we don't walk it alone. You have a Savior who walks beside you through both the highs and the lows.

He is all you need.

So today, take off the victim mask and wear your conqueror crown. God's Word is your arsenal. His promises are your defense. And His Spirit within you makes all the difference.

1 John 4:4, "You are from God, little children, and have overcome them; because greater is He who is in you than he who is in the world."

Prayer:
Father, when I feel like a victim, remind me of who I am in You. Help me walk in confidence, not fear. In weakness, be my strength. In doubt, be my anchor. Today, I choose to be a conqueror. Amen.

FRIDAY

Blame Game

"If we confess our sins, He is faithful and righteous, so that He will forgive us our sins and cleanse us from all unrighteousness." 1 John 1:9 (NASB)

When Pharaoh saw Sarai, he couldn't help but notice her beauty. And Abraham's response? Not protection. Not courage. Not faith. Instead, he quickly said, "She is my sister."

Why? Because he was trying to save his own life.

Friday: *Blame Game*

In fact, this wasn't a spontaneous lie. It was a premeditated plan. Abraham had already told Sarai, "Please say you are my sister so that it may go well with me... and my life will be spared." (Genesis 12:13, paraphrased).

Sounds selfish, doesn't it? He was willing to put his wife in a dangerous, compromising position just to protect himself. What if Pharaoh had taken her in? What if God hadn't intervened?

But this isn't new. The pattern started in Eden.

When God confronted Adam in the garden, Adam immediately deflected: "The woman You gave me..."

Then Eve passed the blame to the serpent.

And Cain? After murdering his brother, he threw up his hands and said, "Am I my brother's keeper?"

It's a cycle as old as sin itself, blame-shifting to avoid owning up to our mistakes.

Let's bring this into modern times. Ask a child if they took a cookie, and nine times out of ten, the answer will be, "No!" Quickly followed by, "She took it first!"

We even had a rule in our home: if you own up to your mistake, the punishment will be lighter, or grace may even step in completely! 😊

Call it shifting the blame, throwing someone under the bus, or pointing fingers, this behavior is deeply ingrained in human nature. It gives a temporary relief from guilt, but it does nothing for healing or growth.

Contrast this with Jesus.

Blameless. Faultless. Pure. And yet, falsely accused. The religious leaders labeled Him a blasphemer, even though He was Truth itself. He didn't deflect. He didn't retaliate. He took on our guilt so we could be free.

Why, then, are we so quick to shift the blame when we have a Savior who invites us to confess?

The gospel isn't about perfection; it's about confession.

It's about coming clean, not pointing fingers.

It's about stopping the blame and starting the healing.

Let's be people who take responsibility, who admit when we're wrong, and who trust in the mercy of a Father who is more than ready to forgive.

Stop shifting. Start owning. That's where freedom begins.

> **Prayer:**
> Lord, forgive me for the times I've blamed others to protect myself. Give me the courage to own my mistakes, to walk humbly, and to receive the mercy You so freely offer. Thank You for being faithful, even when I fall. Amen.

SATURDAY

Deflated, But Not Defeated

> *"Do not be anxious about anything, but in everything by prayer and pleading with thanksgiving let your requests be made known to God. And the peace of God, which surpasses all comprehension, will guard your hearts and minds in Christ Jesus." Philippians 4:6-7 (NASB)*

Have you ever had one of those days where you feel like a deflated balloon? Drained. Zapped. Like someone pulled the plug on your energy and strength?

Maybe life has thrown one thing after another at you, challenges you didn't see coming, disappointments that cut deep, responsibilities that just keep piling up. You're tired. You've prayed. You've tried to push through. But now, you just feel empty.

In those moments, don't try to inflate yourself back up. Instead, let God breathe into you.

Only He can calm the chaos in your mind and bring peace to your anxious heart. The world offers temporary fixes—distractions, noise, even numbing—but God offers peace that surpasses understanding.

It doesn't always make sense. It doesn't always change the situation. But somehow, His peace guards us, keeps us steady, anchored, even when we're completely drained.

So what do you do when you feel deflated?

You pray. You plead. You give thanks in the middle of it all. You bring every need, big or small, to the Father. And in return, you receive something the world cannot give: divine peace.

Don't underestimate the power of that promise. Don't think your tired, anxious heart has to keep running on fumes.
Let His strength carry you. Let His peace protect you.
You may feel deflated, but in Christ, you are never defeated.

> **Prayer:**
> *Lord, I bring You my tired heart today. You know what I'm carrying. You know how drained I feel. Fill me again with Your strength. Guard my heart and mind with Your perfect peace. Amen.*

SUNDAY

Worship and Fellowship

"I was glad when they said to me, 'Let's go to the house of the Lord.'"
Psalm 122:1 (NASB)

There's something sacred about Sunday mornings, the intentional pause, the gathering of God's people, the lifting of voices in praise, the Word going forth, and the reminder that we're not walking this journey alone.

Scripture encourages us not to forsake assembling together (Hebrews 10:25), and there's a reason for that. In a world that constantly pulls us in every direction, corporate worship centers us. It realigns our priorities, refreshes our spirit, and reminds us of the bigger picture — God is on the throne, and we are part of His body.

Church isn't just a building; it's a lifeline. It's where iron sharpens iron, where burdens are shared, where joy is multiplied, and where we get a glimpse of heaven on earth.

This morning, don't let sleep, schedules, or excuses rob you of what God wants to deposit in your spirit. Go to His house, not just out of habit, but with expectation. The pew you sit in today might be the place God chooses to speak directly to your heart.

Sunday: *Worship and Fellowship*

> **Prayer:**
> Lord, thank You for the gift of Sunday, for fellowship, for worship, and for the church. Help me not to treat it casually but to value it deeply. I come with an open heart today, ready to meet with You.

WEEK 43

Monday

What Are We Waiting For?

> *"If anyone, then, knows the good they ought to do and doesn't do it, it is sin for them." James 4:17 (NIV)*

How often do we postpone doing something, telling ourselves we'll get to it later? Whether it's sending that text, applying for that job, or stepping out in faith, we shift into procrastination the moment we resist action. To me, procrastination is as good as not doing it at all. I believe my family and friends will remember me for these words: "Tomorrow is not promised to anyone, so do what you need to do now and not wait for tomorrow." I once heard a quote that struck a chord in my spirit: "Procrastination is the arrogant assumption that God owes you another opportunity to do tomorrow what He gave you the grace to do today."

How many times have we delayed something God placed on our hearts, whether it's reaching out to someone, starting a new ministry, writing that book, or simply obeying a nudge from the Holy Spirit? We tell ourselves, "I'll get to it later," but too often, later becomes never. We soothe our conscience with excuses: "I'm too tired." "I'll wait for the right time." "I'm not ready yet." But what if now is the right time? Delayed obedience quietly turns into disobedience.

Think of Jonah. He delayed. He ran. But God's calling didn't change. It's easy to shake our heads at Jonah until we realize we've fled our own Ninevehs, ignoring God's voice, hoping He'll bring it up again later under better circumstances. But God gives grace for the present. He gives strength for the now. And when He calls, He equips, even when it's uncomfortable or inconvenient. What has God placed on your heart

Tuesday: *A Head-to-Toe Inventory of God's Design*

that you've been putting off? Are fear or perfectionism stopping you from saying "yes"? What would it look like to trust His timing and move today?

> **Prayer:**
> *Lord, forgive me for putting off the very things You've called me to do. Help me to recognize when I'm delaying out of fear or doubt. Teach me to trust Your timing and walk in daily obedience. Today, I choose to say yes to what You've placed on my heart, for I believe tomorrow is not promised to anyone. And now is the time. Help me to get moving. Amen.*

TUESDAY

A Head-to-Toe Inventory of God's Design

> *"You were bought at a price. Therefore honor God with your bodies."*
> *1 Corinthians 6:20 (NIV)*

God has intricately crafted our bodies, not merely for function, but for purpose. Each part carries divine potential, and today, I pause to ask: Am I using all He gave me to glorify Him?
   Brain – to discern right from wrong, truth from deception.
   Eyes – to see the needs around me, not just the distractions
   Ears – to listen deeply, compassionately, without judgment.
   Mouth – to speak words of life, hope, and encouragement.
   Neck – to remain flexible, turning where God leads.
   Heart – to beat with genuine love for others.
   Chest – to carry courage and embrace the broken.
   Hands – to serve, give, and create generously.
   Legs – to walk intentionally in service, not comfort. After taking this inventory, I can say with honesty and humility:
   God is at work in me. He's not finished.

"Therefore, I urge you, brothers and sisters, in view of God's mercy, to offer your bodies as a living sacrifice, holy and pleasing to God—this is your true and proper worship." Romans 12:1 (NIV)

> **Prayer:**
> Lord, You formed me uniquely, every fingerprint, every heartbeat, a sign of Your artistry. Forgive me when I withhold what You created for Your glory. Teach me to offer my whole self as a living sacrifice.

WEDNESDAY

Steward of His Creation

"In the beginning God created the heavens and the earth." Genesis 1:1

When we look at the order of creation, we do not see chaos, but intentionality. Each day, God shaped the world with purpose:
Day One – Light and darkness (night and day)
Day Two – Sky and sea
Day Three – Land and vegetation
Day Four – Sun, moon, and stars
Day Five – Fish and birds
Day Six – Animals and mankind
Day Seven – He rested

What a beautiful, meticulous sequence. God could have created us first, but He didn't. Instead, He prepared everything for us before we even took our first breath. How incredible is that?

Take just Day One: He created light and separated it from darkness. Perhaps He knew we would need rest after a long day's work, so He gave us night, a time to pause and be still. Before electricity existed, darkness was a signal to stop, to breathe, to sleep. How thoughtful!

WEDNESDAY: *Steward of His Creation*

One of my favorite parts of creation is watching a bud bloom into a beautiful flower. One day, it's tightly closed; the next, it bursts open with color and life. How awesome is our God! The intricacy and quiet wonder of it all leave me in awe. For someone to say that there is no God—how baffling! Creation testifies of Him.

And yet, how easily we take it all for granted. We walk through life surrounded by beauty, complexity, and provision, and seldom stop to marvel at it. Creation wasn't random; it was lovingly orchestrated. We are not mere occupants of the earth; we are stewards of His masterpiece.

Let us live with eyes open and hearts aware of the divine fingerprints all around us.

How awesome is our God! As you wake up and see your surroundings, say a quick thank you to God for His awesome creation.

Prayer:
Thank you, God, for Your creation. Make me a better steward. Amen

THURSDAY

Put It in Grandma's Basket

"And let us consider how to stir up one another to love and good works, not neglecting to meet together, as is the habit of some, but encouraging one another—and all the more as you see the Day drawing near." Hebrews 10:24–25 (ESV)

"How good and pleasant it is when God's people live together in unity!" Psalm 133:1 (NIV)

"Two people are better off than one, for they can help each other succeed." Ecclesiastes 4:9 (NLT)

THURSDAY: *Put It in Grandma's Basket*

We often hear that Gen Z is the "digital native" generation. They are the first to grow up with the internet as part of daily life, gaining computer literacy at an incredibly young age. With that comes power—technological ability, instant information, limitless communication.

But with that power has also come something else: loneliness.

This generation doesn't need to physically meet up with friends; they can FaceTime. They don't have to think deeply, AI can write their essays. Their bodies have become their own islands, their world is accessible with a swipe. And honestly, it's not just Gen Z; we all are slipping into this rhythm.

There's a story of a grandmother who kept a basket near her front door. Anytime her children or grandchildren arrived, they were asked to drop their phones in the basket. It was a simple gesture, but a powerful, intentional act of being fully present.

It makes me wonder:

Is your connection only through Wi-Fi?

Are we living on autopilot, our eyes glued to screens while life passes by?

Have we traded real, messy, beautiful relationships for curated, filtered screen time?

Have you ever watched people cross the street, never looking up from their phones? It's not just young people. Adults, too, are succumbing to these habits.

We've become global communicators, yet can't have a meaningful conversation at the dinner table.

We've surrendered our thinking to AI, our downtime to apps, and our silence to screens.

So here's a word of caution:

Be intentional.

Don't let your device become part of your identity.

Look up. Look around.

Someone near you might need a smile, a kind word, a warm hug. But you'll only notice it if your phone goes in Grandma's basket. ☺

The Bible is clear—community matters.

Relationships matter.

Presence matters.

Let us stir one another to love. Let us not neglect meeting together. Let us choose connection, not just digital, but deeply human and spiritual.

Broken Hearts Held by God: Week 43

Friday: *The Straw That Broke the Camel's Back*

> **Prayer:**
> Lord, help us to be present again. Teach us to lift our eyes from our screens and see the people You have placed right in front of us. Where distraction has dulled our awareness, restore intentionality. Where convenience has replaced connection, renew our desire for real, meaningful relationships. Help us value community, cherish conversation, and choose presence over productivity. May we use technology wisely without letting it replace the gift of human connection You designed for us. Give us hearts that notice, hands that reach out, and lives that reflect Your love—face to face, not just screen to screen. Amen.

Friday

The Straw That Broke the Camel's Back

> *"Do not be anxious about anything, but in every situation, by prayer and petition, with thanksgiving, present your requests to God.*
>
> *And the peace of God, which transcends all understanding, will guard your hearts and your minds in Christ Jesus." Philippians 4:6–7 (NIV)*

The saying, "The straw that broke the camel's back," is a powerful metaphor.

Picture a camel carrying a load of straw. A single straw isn't heavy. But as more and more straws are added, the weight becomes unbearable. Eventually, one last straw tips the balance, and the camel collapses.

Isn't that how life works sometimes?

It's rarely the one small thing that breaks us. It's the accumulation of everything else—the worries we suppress, the disappointments we ignore, the hurts we never process. And suddenly, it's that one last email, one small comment, or missed moment that causes us to break down.

So let me gently ask:

FRIDAY: *The Straw That Broke the Camel's Back*

How are you doing today?
Is something weighing heavily on you?
Are you in the habit of bottling things up?

We've all been there. And the Bible is full of people who faced emotional weight, and found resilience and hope in God:

Hannah wept bitterly over her barrenness but poured her heart out to God in prayer.

Paul endured beatings, imprisonment, and rejection, yet clung to grace.

David, whom I often relate to, wrestled with fear, anger, and failure, and yet kept turning back to God.

None of them were perfect. But they brought their weight to the One who could carry it.

Friend, what are you waiting for?

I may sound like a broken record by always pointing you back to God, but that's only because I've lived through my own "last straw" moments. And every time, He has carried me.

Philippians 4 reminds us:

Don't bottle it up. Don't pretend it's fine.

Instead, present it to God.

And in exchange, He gives you peace that makes no earthly sense.

A peace that can guard your heart, even when your circumstances don't change.

> **Prayer:**
> *Lord Jesus, I'm not sure why You placed this thought in my heart in the middle of the day. You usually speak to me in the mornings. But here I am, obeying Your gentle nudge. I pray this message finds someone who is on the verge of collapse. For every person carrying too much, speak peace. Strengthen what's weak. Wipe away the tears they've been hiding. Lord, we transfer our burdens to You because You're strong enough to carry them all. In Your precious name we pray, Amen.*

SATURDAY

The Curved End of the Staff

> *"Yea, though I walk through the valley of the shadow of death, I will fear no evil; for You are with me; Your rod and Your staff, they comfort me." Psalm 23:4 (NKJV)*

Life often feels like a balancing act; when one foot falters, the other catches you to restore balance. But what happens when both feet slip, and you're falling into the valley?

This verse from Psalm 23 paints that very picture: walking through the valley of the shadow of death. It sounds ominous, doesn't it? Yet it doesn't end there. There's a promise tucked in: "Your rod and Your staff, they comfort me."

Let's talk about that staff.

The shepherd's staff wasn't just decorative; it was practical. The curved end of the staff was a tool of rescue. When a sheep wandered too far or slipped into a crevice, the shepherd would use that curved hook to gently draw the sheep back to safety.

The staff is also taller than the rod, designed to reach into places the shepherd can't easily go himself. Visualize this: a sheep falling deep into a valley. The shepherd doesn't climb down; he reaches with the staff. The curve hooks gently around the sheep's neck or leg, and he pulls it back to safety.

God's staff is like that. His power to rescue us runs deep. Even in the darkest valleys, whether of grief, failure, discouragement, or fear, He can reach you.

No valley is too deep for the shepherd's staff.

Friend, maybe today feels like a valley. Maybe the shadows seem long, and your footing feels weak. Take heart:

The curved end of His staff is already extended.

You will not hit rock bottom.

You are not too far gone.

The Shepherd is near, and His staff is steady.

Start your day with the quiet assurance that the shepherd's staff is within reach. Let it anchor your soul when anxiety stirs. Let it comfort your heart when disappointment visits. And let it remind you that you are never walking alone.

> **Prayer:**
> Lord, thank You that no valley is too deep for You to reach. Even when I can't see the way out, Your staff is already extended. Rescue me, steady me, and lead me beside still waters once again. Amen.

Sunday

The Sacred Rhythm of Sunday

"I was glad when they said to me, 'Let's go to the house of the Lord.'"
Psalm 122:1 (NASB)

There's something sacred about Sunday mornings, the intentional pause, the gathering of God's people, the lifting of voices in praise, the Word going forth, and the reminder that we're not walking this journey alone.

Scripture encourages us not to forsake our own assembling together (Hebrews 10:25), and there's a reason for that. In a world that constantly pulls us in every direction, corporate worship centers us. It realigns our priorities, refreshes our spirit, and reminds us of the bigger picture — God is on the throne, and we are part of His body.

Church isn't just a building. It's a lifeline.

It's where iron sharpens iron, where burdens are shared, where joy is multiplied, and where we get a glimpse of heaven on earth.

This morning, don't let sleep, schedules, or excuses rob you of what God wants to deposit in your spirit. Go to

His house, not just out of habit, but with expectation.

The pew you sit in today might be the very place where God speaks directly to your heart.

BROKEN HEARTS HELD BY GOD: Week 43

SUNDAY: *The Sacred Rhythm of Sunday*

Prayer:
Lord, thank You for the gift of Sunday, for fellowship, for worship, and for the church. Help me not to treat it casually but to value it deeply. I come with an open heart today, ready to meet with You. Stir my spirit, speak to my soul, and align my steps with Yours. Let this day mark a fresh encounter with Your presence. Amen.

WEEK 44

MONDAY

The Gift Found in Stillness

"Stop striving and know that I am God." Psalm 46:10a (NASB)

Brokenness isn't something we seek, but it often becomes the place where God speaks the loudest. When life cracks open our strength, and striving comes to a halt, we're finally quiet enough to hear Him. No more performing. No more pretending. Just stillness... and surrender.

It's in those moments, where we have nothing left to offer but our honesty, that His presence becomes undeniable.

God doesn't scold us in our weakness. He doesn't meet us with frustration or disappointment. Instead, He enters softly, with healing in His hands and compassion in His voice. He reminds us: You don't have to hold it all together. I'm here. I've got you.

The stillness isn't empty. It's full of grace.

When we stop striving, we start receiving. And in the quietness of surrender, we discover a truth that changes everything: His love has never depended on our strength, only on His mercy.

Prayer:
Lord, in my brokenness, meet me with Your grip of love. Quiet my heart, still my soul, and help me rest in the truth that You are God. Let me feel Your nearness and trust Your promises again. Amen.

TUESDAY

When Cracks Invite His Strength

> *"But the Lord stood with me and strengthened me."* 2 Timothy 4:17 (NASB)

Are there cracks in your heart, those quiet places where pain seeps in like water through a fracture? Sometimes it doesn't take much. A word spoken in anger. A closed door. A disappointment that lingers. All it takes is a sliver—and left unchecked, those cracks can grow. Slowly. Silently. Making room for fear, discouragement, or bitterness to settle in.

But here's the hope: You are not abandoned to your brokenness.

Paul, writing from prison, said, "The Lord stood with me and strengthened me." Not when things were easy, but in isolation. In need. In weakness.

That's our God. He doesn't walk away when we fracture. He steps in. He fills the gaps with grace. He doesn't just bind the wound; He becomes the strength we lack.

You don't have to patch yourself back together alone. The world may see cracks, but God sees an opportunity to pour in His power.

Prayer:
Lord, seal the cracks in my heart with Your peace. Let not the world seep in, but Your love overflow in me. When I am weak, be my strength. When I am broken, be my healer. Amen.

WEDNESDAY

You Are Wonderfully Made

> *"I will give thanks to You, because I am awesomely and wonderfully made; Wonderful are Your works, And my soul knows it very well."*
> Psalm 139:14 (NASB)

Some mornings begin with stillness, no rushing, no chaos, just a warm cup of coffee and a moment to breathe. But even on the calmest days, there's often a quiet current of self-doubt: Am I doing enough? Am I making a difference? Am I enough?

Psalm 139 quiets that swirl of insecurity with a bold, sacred truth: You are fearfully and wonderfully made.

You were crafted with care, knit together by the very hands that hung the stars. Every detail, every thread of your being, was intentionally designed by God. Even when the world's standards shout that you need to do more or be more, your identity remains unshaken. You are His. That's enough.

So lift your head, not in pride, but in confidence. You are the child of the King. Walk in the truth of who you already are.

Prayer:
Father, thank You for creating me with purpose. When self-doubt creeps in, remind me whose daughter I am. Help me walk in the strength and beauty You've placed within me. Amen.

THURSDAY

A Covenant That Cannot Be Shaken

> *"'For the mountains may be removed and the hills may shake, But My favor will not be removed from you, Nor will My covenant of peace be shaken,' Says the Lord who has compassion on you." Isaiah 54:10 (NASB)*

Lately, our church has been immersed in teachings about covenant and commitment, what it truly means to be unwavering in our word, especially before God. And it challenged me deeply.

Because life? It's anything but steady.

Mountains move. Hills shake. People shift. Promises are broken. Plans unravel.

But not with God. His covenant is anchored in His nature, not in our performance, not in our emotions, not in our ability to hold it all together. His peace remains, even when everything else feels uncertain. His favor stays, even when we feel undeserving.

That's the beauty of covenant. It's not a contract that can be canceled; it's a commitment rooted in compassion and faithfulness.

And as He is faithful, He calls us to reflect that faithfulness. To let our "yes" before Him carry weight. To treat our promises not as casual agreements, but as sacred declarations before a holy God.

So today, whether you're clinging to one of God's promises or reflecting on your own vows before Him, remember, He is the covenant-keeper. And He's calling us to mirror that steadfastness in return.

Prayer:
God, help me to be faithful to the covenants I make before You. Let my word be holy, my promises sincere, and my heart anchored in Your unshakable peace. Amen

FRIDAY

Keepers of the Covenant

> *"But the mercy of the Lord is from everlasting to everlasting for those who fear Him, And His justice to the children's children, To those who keep His covenant And remember His precepts, so as to do them."*
> Psalm 103:17–18 (NASB)

Maybe I didn't fully grasp the seriousness of keeping a covenant.

Maybe, like many of us, I thought I could coast on good intentions.

But God, in His mercy, gave me a chance to learn, not to punish, but to remind.

Covenants matter to Him. They always have.

God doesn't forget His promises. And He calls us to mirror that faithfulness, not just in word, but in action. He honors those who keep His covenant and remember His precepts so as to do them. Not just to memorize them, quote them, or nod along on Sundays, but to live them out.

His mercy, thankfully, is from everlasting to everlasting. He doesn't write us off when we fall short. But He does call us to rise higher, to take our commitments seriously, especially those made in His name.

So today, if you've made a vow to the Lord, spoken or silent, ask yourself: Am I living it? And if not, ask Him for the grace to start again.

> **Prayer:**
> Lord, forgive my forgetfulness. Remind me of every promise I've made before You. Help me honor every vow, living each day in full-hearted commitment. Amen.

SATURDAY

Commit and be Established

"Commit your works to the Lord, And your plans will be established." Proverbs 16:3 (NASB)

As I came down this morning, the aroma of coffee filled the air, and so did a quiet reminder from God's Word. Just one simple verse caught my eye: "Commit your works to the Lord..." And suddenly, I was fully awake, spiritually and physically.

How often do we charge into the day with our own plans, mapping out every detail, trying to steer the ship of our lives with precision? But today's verse invites us to a better way: to place our efforts in God's hands first, not last.

When we commit our works to Him, it's not about abandoning our responsibilities; it's about surrendering control. It's about acknowledging that no matter how detailed our calendar is, only God can establish what truly matters.

So before the to-do list takes over, take a moment to commit it all to the One who sees the full picture. Let Him steer. Let Him establish.

Prayer:
God, today I place my plans in Your hands. Steer the boat of my life, and I will rest in Your direction. Amen.

SUNDAY

The Power of Gathering

> *"And let us consider how to encourage one another in love and good deeds, not abandoning our own meeting together, as is the habit of some, but encouraging one another." Hebrews 10:24–25 (NASB)*

Sunday is a sacred invitation — to pause, to gather, to worship.

As you prepare your heart today, remember the importance of coming together with other believers. There's something beautiful about lifting your voice in worship alongside others, sitting under the Word, and letting God refresh your spirit through fellowship. Church is not just a building; it's a body. And you are a vital part of it.

So find your place, settle in, and be present in God's house.

Prayer:
Lord, thank You for the gift of the church, a place to grow, to serve, and to be renewed. Help me enter Your presence with gratitude and expectation. Amen.

WEEK 45

Monday

The Weight of the Calling

"Nevertheless, each person should live as a believer in whatever situation the Lord has assigned to them, just as God has called them." 1 Corinthians 7:17 (NIV)

"Each of you should use whatever gift you have received to serve others, as faithful stewards of God's grace in its various forms... so that in all things God may be praised through Jesus Christ." 1 Peter 4:10–11 (NIV)

So many breaking news stories flash across our screens every day. But one moment that struck me deeply was the installation of a new Pope. As the camera zoomed in on his face, you could see the emotion, the gravity, the burden of the role being placed on his shoulders.

His teary eyes...

His trembling lips...

His visible awareness of the immense responsibility...

I've watched that reel multiple times, not out of religious sentiment, but because I get goosebumps every time I see the emotion in his face. It's the weight of a sacred calling. It's the realization that life is about to change, not for self-glory, but for service.

And it made me ask:

When God calls us, do our hearts tremble the same way?

Do the nerves on our face sense the holy weight of the assignment?

Do we shed tears of humility when we realize God chose us, cracked vessels, for His Kingdom work?

MONDAY: *The Weight of the Calling*

Friends, when God calls you to serve in His vineyard, your burden should carry that kind of intensity. Not in pressure or fear, but in passion. With passion comes burden. With burden comes obedience. And obedience leads to purpose.

Unlike the Pope, who may feel isolated under the weight of his position, God never calls you without walking with you.

Unlike the Pope, who goes through intercessors like Mother Mary, we have direct access to the throne of God through Christ.

I use the image of the Pope not to elevate a person, but to help you visualize the sacred weight of being called by God. Your calling may not come with cameras and a balcony, but the moment you said yes to God's assignment, heaven noticed. And so should you.

You may not be wearing a robe or standing before millions.

But if God has assigned you a task, however big or small, carry it with reverence.

Prayer:
Lord, may we never take our calling lightly. Thank You for choosing ordinary people to carry out Your extraordinary mission. Fill us with reverence, passion, and obedience as we walk in the purpose You've assigned to us. Give us the strength to serve, and may all glory go to You. In Jesus' name, Amen.

TUESDAY

Anxiety and the Killjoy

"When anxiety was great within me, your consolation brought me joy." Psalm 94:19 (NIV)

Anxiety.

According to the Mayo Clinic, it's defined as "intense, excessive, and persistent worry and fear about everyday situations. Fast heart rate, rapid breathing, sweating, and fatigue may occur." That's a mouthful.

TUESDAY: *Anxiety and the Killjoy*

I'd summarize it in one word: Killjoy.
Now, the younger generation would probably disagree. They live by a different motto: "Just chill." Have you noticed how little seems to cause them stress? Ask them anything, and the response is usually, "Mom, just chill," or in my case, "Just go with the flow," as my daughter lovingly reminded me the other day.
To me, that sounds like drifting aimlessly. But let's be real, we all go through different phases of anxiety throughout life:
As children, waiting on exam results
As young adults, hoping for job offers
As singles, longing for the right life partner
As parents, navigating the unknowns of raising children
As older adults, concerned about health, legacy, or financial security
There are so many triggers, and if we're not careful, we find ourselves tangled in an unending web of anxiety.
Let me share a small moment from just this morning:
I was trying to reserve a flight seat, hoping to avoid being sandwiched between two people, and the website kept throwing errors. My anxiety levels started to creep up. Over a seat, of all things! Isn't it amazing how even the smallest hiccups can trigger that anxious spiral?
Now scroll back up and read the verse again:
"When anxiety was great within me, your consolation brought me joy."
This verse isn't just poetry; it's a powerful truth. Though the Bible was written thousands of years ago, the Word is still alive and active. It meets us in our modern worries, big or small.
So what's triggering your anxiety this morning?
Health?
Finances?
Your children?
Job pressure? Etc.
Whatever it is, inhale the Life-Giving Word. Let the Word settle into the crevices of your worry. Transfer that anxiety to the One who actually invites you to do so.
"Cast all your anxiety on Him because He cares for you." 1 Peter 5:7
Nothing in this world should be a Killjoy, because we serve the God of joy unspeakable, joy that surpasses understanding, joy that cannot be explained, only experienced.

So hush your soul.
Breathe.
Let that joy rise quietly within.
Oh, and by the way... I did end up getting a seat.
That anxiety? Totally uncalled for. 😊

> **Prayer:**
> *Lord, thank You for being our steady place when anxiety tries to shake us. Remind us that Your Word is life, comfort, and joy, especially in the moments when fear creeps in. Teach us to breathe deeply of Your promises and release what we were never meant to carry alone. In Jesus' name, Amen.*

WEDNESDAY

When My Foot Slipped

"When I said, 'My foot is slipping,' your unfailing love, Lord, supported me." Psalm 94:18 (NIV)

I came across this verse about a week ago, and it's been echoing in my heart ever since. I kept wondering, how could I bring this to life with a visual we all can relate to? And then, like a light bulb, it hit me.

Have you ever stood at the edge of the seashore, hesitant to go deeper into the water? You twist your feet firmly into the sand, hoping the waves won't carry you away. I know I have, especially since I'm not one to venture too far in.

Now take that image and apply it to this verse: "My foot is slipping..." That's life sometimes, isn't it? It feels like the rug's been pulled out from under us, a moment of instability, panic, or complete helplessness.

That's how it feels when our footing isn't planted firmly on Christ, the Rock.

But the verse doesn't end with the slipping. It says, "Your unfailing love, Lord, supported me."

Wednesday: *When My Foot Slipped*

Even when life feels shaky, His love never shifts. It's the steadying hand, the secure foundation.

Here's another picture that brings this truth to life: Years ago, on a trip to Israel, one of our group members, frail and elderly, wanted to be baptized in the River Jordan. The riverbed was slippery, and she struggled to find her footing. So the pastor gently told her, "Put your feet on my feet." He anchored her as she was lowered into the water.

What a powerful image. That was love, on a human scale.

Now imagine the unfailing love of Christ. How much more secure are we when our feet rest on His?

So I ask you today:

Are you feeling unstable?

Do certain areas of your life feel out of control?

Are you struggling to fully surrender?

Here's the hard truth: partial surrender is no surrender at all.

But the beautiful truth? His unfailing love is always extended toward you. It's your support when your foot slips. It's your anchor when life's waves try to knock you down.

Prayer:
Lord, when my footing feels unsure, remind me that Your unfailing love is what holds me up. Help me not to grasp at false stability but to plant my feet firmly on You. I don't want to surrender halfway; I want to stand, fully anchored in Your love. In Jesus' name, Amen.

THURSDAY

Don't Let the Little Foxes In

"Catch us the foxes, the little foxes that spoil the vines, for our vines have tender grapes." Song of Solomon 2:15 (NKJV)

THURSDAY: *Don't Let the Little Foxes In*

For the longest time, I've wanted to write about broken relationships, especially in marriages.

To all the couples out there:

Try to resolve your issues within the four walls of your own bedroom.

Please don't be influenced by peers, co-workers, friends, or even well-meaning family members. Every marriage is different. There is no cookie-cutter formula.

If you feel the need to share with someone close to you, pray first. And be sure the person you're confiding in has one goal: to help unite you with your spouse, not to pour gasoline on the fire. Remember, they're only hearing your side.

Instead, take your issues:

To God.

To your pastor.

Or to a trained marital counselor.

Why?

Because not everyone is a marital counselor.

Not everyone is mature enough to give wise advice.

Not everyone is looking out for your best interest.

Not everyone has a pure motive.

So many marriages have been destroyed, not because of the original problem, but because of the wrong advice that followed.

Be wise. Be prayerful. Guard your marriage.

Don't let a third person into your covenant. God is the only third person who belongs in that union.

To those who mean well and want to help:

If you're not a pastor or a trained counselor, stop giving marital advice.

It's natural to be biased when your friend is hurting, but that's where trained counselors and godly leaders excel. They offer wisdom without partiality.

Marriages are like fingerprints, each one unique.

What worked for your marriage may not work for your friend's. What healed your wounds may not heal theirs.

So to those seeking help:

Seek counsel from godly sources.

Go to your pastor.

Find a mature elder.

THURSDAY: *Don't Let the Little Foxes In*

Look for someone trained to walk with you through this sacred covenant.

As Song of Solomon 2:15 warns, "The little foxes spoil the vines." Don't ignore the small things that sneak in and destroy something beautiful.

Marriage is sacred. You made a covenant before God and His people. Protect it.

Preserve your marriage; don't let the little foxes in your vineyard.

> **Prayer:**
> *Lord, we lift up every couple walking through conflict. Teach us to be wise about who we allow to speak into our relationships. Help us protect the covenant of marriage with humility, prayer, and discernment. Strengthen marriages, restore broken places, and guard every union from the little foxes that seek to divide. In Jesus' name, Amen.*

FRIDAY

When the Door Is Shut

Jesus said to him, "I am the way, the truth, and the life. No one comes to the Father except through Me." John 14:6 (NKJV)

In the wee hours of this morning, I decided to sit on the deck for a time of quiet meditation. The birds were singing, and a gentle breeze brushed my face; it was the perfect setting to spend time with the Lord.

But sure enough, I stepped outside without checking the latch, and it locked me out.

Thus began my journey of impatience. I banged on the door for over 15 minutes. No one came. I called and texted, no response. Eventually, I made my way down the steps and circled around to enter through the front door.

As I sat back down, the story of Noah and the Ark came to mind. Noah had been proclaiming God's Word while building an ark on dry

FRIDAY: *When the Door Is Shut*

land. People mocked him and ignored the message. Then the rains came. The floodwaters rose. And by the time they realized he was right, it was too late. The door of the ark had been sealed shut by God. No human hand could open it.

Unlike my situation, where I found another way in, there is only one Door into God's Kingdom. Jesus said, "I am the Way, the Truth, and the Life."

Friends, we are living in a season of grace. But Matthew 7 reminds us of a coming day of accountability:

"Not everyone who says to Me, 'Lord, Lord,' shall enter the kingdom of heaven... Then I will declare to them, 'I never knew you; depart from Me.'" Matthew 7:21-23 (NIV)

Just like I kept knocking and no one answered, many will one day knock on Heaven's door, but it will be too late. Can you imagine hearing those heartbreaking words from the Lord: "I never knew you, depart from Me"?

Yet today, the invitation is still open. Revelation 3:20 says:

"Behold, I stand at the door and knock. If anyone hears My voice and opens the door, I will come in..."

What grace! The door is still open—for now. But just like in Noah's day, there will come a time when it will be sealed, and no man can open it.

We're all sailing on what I like to call the Boat of Grace. Stay afloat by staying surrendered. Stay inside the ark of His presence by receiving Him.

And for those of us already saved, we have a responsibility. Our loved ones, friends, and even strangers need to hear about this Door before it's too late. Plant seeds. Speak life. Live with urgency. Maybe you've drifted away, come back now. The time of grace is still here, but it's slipping away.

> **Prayer:**
> *Father God, thank You for showing us the power of a closed and an open door this morning. Forgive us for taking Your grace for granted. We pray for family and friends who are far from You—may they open the door of their hearts and receive You. Lord, we are living in a time of grace. Let our burden increase for those who don't yet know You. Make us intentional. Use us as Your disciples. And may none of our loved ones ever hear those words, "I never knew you." In Jesus' name, Amen.*

SATURDAY

No Experience Required

> *"The Lord does not look at the things people look at. People look at the outward appearance, but the Lord looks at the heart."* 1 Samuel 16:7 (NIV)

"I'm not qualified."
"I don't have the experience."
"I've never done this before."
With thoughts like these, we demotivate ourselves before we even begin.

Think of a job interview. You walk in as a recent graduate, full of enthusiasm. But the interviewer says, "Great qualifications, but you lack hands-on experience." That's how the world operates.

Now, just to bring a little smile to your morning, I have a plaque hanging above my stove that reads:

"Kitchen help needed, no experience required." ☺

And that, my friends, is exactly how God's Kingdom works.

God's qualification system is beautifully simple: He's looking for a willing heart. That's it. He's not concerned about résumés, portfolios, or perfect speech. He simply says, "Come, and I will train you." What an anxiety-free qualification!

Sadly, in many churches today, there are abundant gifts that go unused, gifts lying dormant because people believe they aren't ready, skilled, or good enough. But God says, "If you're pliable, I'll shape you."

Our willingness to serve is a reflection of our yielded spirit. God desires hearts that are soft, teachable, and available.

Just like the plaque in my kitchen reminds me, no experience required, so it is with God. He molds us, shapes us, and fills the gaps. Unlike the world, where inexperience can cost you an opportunity, in God's Kingdom, willingness is the only requirement.

So, how willing are you to be used by God? Don't disqualify yourself from Kingdom work. He already knows your potential and will equip you to serve His purpose.

> **Prayer:**
> Lord, forgive us for disqualifying ourselves with excuses. Often we say, "That's not my gift," or "I'm not ready." But You're only asking for a willing and pliable heart. Help us to yield. Thank You that no service in Your Kingdom goes unnoticed. Shape us, mold us, and use us today, no experience required. In Jesus' name, Amen.

Sunday

Worship and Fellowship

"I was glad when they said to me, 'Let's go to the house of the Lord.'"
Psalm 122:1 (NASB)

There's something sacred about Sunday mornings, the intentional pause, the gathering of God's people, the lifting of voices in praise, the Word going forth, and the reminder that we're not walking this journey alone.

Scripture encourages us not to forsake assembling together (Hebrews 10:25), and there's a reason for that. In a world that constantly pulls us in every direction, corporate worship centers us. It realigns our priorities, refreshes our spirit, and reminds us of the bigger picture — God is on the throne, and we are part of His body.

Church isn't just a building; it's a lifeline. It's where iron sharpens iron, where burdens are shared, where joy is multiplied, and where we get a glimpse of heaven on earth.

This morning, don't let sleep, schedules, or excuses rob you of what God wants to deposit in your spirit. Go to His house, not just out of habit, but with expectation. The pew you sit in today might be the place God chooses to speak directly to your heart.

SUNDAY: *Worship and Fellowship*

> **Prayer:**
> Lord, thank You for the gift of Sunday, for fellowship, for worship, and for the church. Help me not to treat it casually but to value it deeply. I come with an open heart today, ready to meet with You.

WEEK 46

MONDAY

The Weight of the Calling

> *"Nevertheless, each person should live as a believer in whatever situation the Lord has assigned to them, just as God has called them." 1 Corinthians 7:17 (NIV)*

> *"Each of you should use whatever gift you have received to serve others, as faithful stewards of God's grace in its various forms... so that in all things God may be praised through Jesus Christ." 1 Peter 4:10–11 (NIV)*

So many breaking news stories flash across our screens every day. But one moment that struck me deeply was the installation of a new Pope. As the camera zoomed in on his face, you could see the emotion, the gravity, the burden of the role being placed on his shoulders.

His teary eyes...

His trembling lips...

His visible awareness of the immense responsibility...

I've watched that reel multiple times, not out of religious sentiment, but because I get goosebumps every time I see the emotion in his face. It's the weight of a sacred calling. It's the realization that life is about to change, not for self-glory, but for service.

And it made me ask:

When God calls us, do our hearts tremble the same way?

Do the nerves on our face sense the holy weight of the assignment?

Do we shed tears of humility when we realize God chose us, cracked vessels, for His Kingdom work?

BROKEN HEARTS HELD BY GOD: Week 46

MONDAY: *The Weight of the Calling*

Friends, when God calls you to serve in His vineyard, your burden should carry that kind of intensity. Not in pressure or fear, but in passion. With passion comes burden. With burden comes obedience. And obedience leads to purpose.

Unlike the Pope, who may feel isolated under the weight of his position, God never calls you without walking with you.

Unlike the Pope, who goes through intercessors like Mother Mary, we have direct access to the throne of God through Christ.

I use the image of the Pope not to elevate a person, but to help you visualize the sacred weight of being called by God. Your calling may not come with cameras and a balcony, but the moment you said yes to God's assignment, heaven noticed. And so should you.

You may not be wearing a robe or standing before millions.

But if God has assigned you a task, however big or small, carry it with reverence.

Prayer:
Lord, may we never take our calling lightly. Thank You for choosing ordinary people to carry out Your extraordinary mission. Fill us with reverence, passion, and obedience as we walk in the purpose You've assigned to us. Give us the strength to serve, and may all glory go to You. In Jesus' name, Amen.

TUESDAY

From a Lion's Mane to a Horse's Tail"

"The glory of young men is their strength, gray hair the splendor of the old." — Proverbs 20:29 (NIV)

Yesterday I was chatting with a dear friend of mine and the conversation was about hair and she commented how her hair went 'from a lion's mane to a horse's tail'. Now that got my brain on over drive.

TUESDAY: *From a Lion's Mane to a Horse's Tail"*

A lion's mane is often a symbol of strength, dignity, and leadership. In the animal kingdom, the mane of a male lion announces his maturity and commands respect. It's majestic, full, and speaks of power. Likewise, a horse's tail has a different kind of beauty — long, flowing, graceful — but it also serves a functional purpose: to swat away flies and protect from irritation. On a side note, I have always admired the straight, silky tail of a horse ☺.

Life sometimes takes us from seasons where we feel like the lion — bold, strong, unshaken — to seasons where we may feel more like the horse — still purposeful, but perhaps quieter, less visibly powerful, more protective than dominating. Both are beautiful in their own way, and both reflect God's design.

The key point to observe is both had a role in the animal kingdom..

The lion's mane reminds us of seasons of courage, public victories, and God-given authority. The horse's tail reminds us of the quieter seasons — of service, endurance, and quiet resilience. One is not greater than the other; they simply mark different chapters of our journey.

Don't despise the season you're in. If you're in your lion's mane stage, lead well and point others to Christ. If you're in your horse's tail stage, be faithful in the behind-the-scenes work God has given you. Both bring glory to Him when lived in obedience.

Prayer:
Lord, teach me to value the season I'm in. Whether I'm roaring like a lion or serving quietly like a faithful horse, may my life bring You glory in every chapter.

WEDNESDAY

When My Foot Slipped

"When I said, 'My foot is slipping,' your unfailing love, Lord, supported me." Psalm 94:18 (NIV)

BROKEN HEARTS HELD BY GOD: Week 46

WEDNESDAY: *When My Foot Slipped*

I came across this verse about a week ago, and it's been echoing in my heart ever since. I kept wondering, how could I bring this to life with a visual we all can relate to? And then, like a light bulb, it hit me.

Have you ever stood at the edge of the seashore, hesitant to go deeper into the water? You twist your feet firmly into the sand, hoping the waves won't carry you away. I know I have, especially since I'm not one to venture too far in.

Now take that image and apply it to this verse: "My foot is slipping..." That's life sometimes, isn't it? It feels like the rug's been pulled out from under us, a moment of instability, panic, or complete helplessness.

That's how it feels when our footing isn't planted firmly on Christ, the Rock.

But the verse doesn't end with the slipping. It says, "Your unfailing love, Lord, supported me."

Even when life feels shaky, His love never shifts. It's the steadying hand, the secure foundation.

Here's another picture that brings this truth to life: Years ago, on a trip to Israel, one of our group members, frail and elderly, wanted to be baptized in the River Jordan. The riverbed was slippery, and she struggled to find her footing. So the pastor gently told her, "Put your feet on my feet." He anchored her as she was lowered into the water.

What a powerful image. That was love, on a human scale.

Now imagine the unfailing love of Christ. How much more secure are we when our feet rest on His?

So I ask you today:

Are you feeling unstable?

Do certain areas of your life feel out of control?

Are you struggling to fully surrender?

Here's the hard truth: partial surrender is no surrender at all.

But the beautiful truth? His unfailing love is always extended toward you. It's your support when your foot slips. It's your anchor when life's waves try to knock you down.

> **Prayer:**
> *Lord, when my footing feels unsure, remind me that Your unfailing love is what holds me up. Help me not to grasp at false stability but to plant my feet firmly on You. I don't want to surrender halfway, I want to stand, fully anchored in Your love. In Jesus' name, Amen.*

Thursday

For Such a Time as This

> *"Then Mordecai told them to reply to Esther, 'Do not think to yourself that in the king's palace you will escape any more than all the other Jews. For if you keep silent at this time, relief and deliverance will rise for the Jews from another place, but you and your father's house will perish.'"* Esther 4:13–14

The story of Esther has always fascinated me. The boldness of one woman, positioned in a palace, used to save her people—it's nothing short of remarkable. Yet before Esther's great act of courage, we see her hesitation. She carefully explained the palace rules, the danger, and the risk of approaching the king uninvited.

But Mordecai's response cut through her fear: "Do not think that just because you are in the palace, you will escape." His words remind us that God's placement in our lives is never accidental. Esther was not in that palace by chance—she was there for such a time as this.

How often do we forget that truth in our own lives? By God's grace, we have been elevated, blessed, and given opportunities. Yet sometimes, instead of using those opportunities to reach back and help others, we choose comfort. We help only when it is convenient, when it doesn't "get grease on our shirt." But the needs around us don't wait for convenience. Helping often requires sacrifice—our time, our comfort, sometimes even our reputation.

Esther risked everything because she remembered who she was and where she came from. That's something I've always reminded my boys: "Keep your head on your shoulders, and never forget your humble beginnings." It is natural for us to forget when God elevates us. But elevation is never meant to isolate—it's meant to position us for service.

Today, be like Esther. Remember where God brought you from, and use where He has placed you now to lift someone else. You may be exactly where you are "for such a time as this."

Friday: *When the Door Is Shut*

> **Prayer:**
> *Lord, give me the courage to step out of comfort and into obedience. Help me not to forget where You brought me from, and to use where I am today to bless and help others, even if it costs me something. Amen.*

Friday

When the Door Is Shut

"Jesus said to him, 'I am the way, the truth, and the life. No one comes to the Father except through Me.'" John 14:6 (NKJV)

In the wee hours of this morning, I decided to sit on the deck for a time of quiet meditation. The birds were singing, and a gentle breeze brushed my face; it was the perfect setting to spend time with the Lord.

But sure enough, I stepped outside without checking the latch, and it locked me out.

Thus began my journey of impatience. I banged on the door for over 15 minutes. No one came. I called and texted, no response. Eventually, I made my way down the steps and circled around to enter through the front door.

As I sat back down, the story of Noah and the Ark came to mind. Noah had been proclaiming God's Word while building an ark on dry land. People mocked him and ignored the message. Then the rains came. The floodwaters rose. And by the time they realized he was right, it was too late. The door of the ark had been sealed shut by God. No human hand could open it.

Unlike my situation, where I found another way in, there is only one Door into God's Kingdom. Jesus said, "I am the Way, the Truth, and the Life."

Friends, we are living in a season of grace. But Matthew 7 reminds us of a coming day of accountability:

FRIDAY: *When the Door Is Shut*

"Not everyone who says to Me, 'Lord, Lord,' shall enter the kingdom of heaven... Then I will declare to them, 'I never knew you; depart from Me.'" (Matthew 7:21-23)

Just like I kept knocking and no one answered, many will one day knock on Heaven's door, but it will be too late. Can you imagine hearing those heartbreaking words from the Lord: "I never knew you, depart from Me"?

Yet today, the invitation is still open. Revelation 3:20 says:

"Behold, I stand at the door and knock. If anyone hears My voice and opens the door, I will come in..."

What grace! The door is still open for now. But just like in Noah's day, there will come a time when it will be sealed, and no man can open it.

We're all sailing on what I like to call the Boat of Grace. Stay afloat by staying surrendered. Stay inside the ark of His presence by receiving Him.

And for those of us already saved, we have a responsibility. Our loved ones, friends, and even strangers need to hear about this Door before it's too late. Plant seeds. Speak life. Live with urgency. Maybe you've drifted away, come back now. The time of grace is still here, but it's slipping away.

> **Prayer:**
> *Father God, thank You for showing us the power of a closed and an open door this morning. Forgive us for taking Your grace for granted. We pray for family and friends who are far from You; may they open the door of their hearts and receive You. Lord, we are living in a time of grace. Let our burden increase for those who don't yet know You. Make us intentional. Use us as Your disciples. And may none of our loved ones ever hear those words, "I never knew you." In Jesus' name, Amen.*

SATURDAY

No Experience Required

> *"The Lord does not look at the things people look at. People look at the outward appearance, but the Lord looks at the heart." 1 Samuel 16:7 (NIV)*

"I'm not qualified."
"I don't have the experience."
"I've never done this before."
With thoughts like these, we demotivate ourselves before we even begin.

Think of a job interview. You walk in as a recent graduate, full of enthusiasm. But the interviewer says, "Great qualifications, but you lack hands-on experience." That's how the world operates.

Now, just to bring a little smile to your morning, I have a plaque hanging above my stove that reads:

"Kitchen help needed, no experience required." 😊

And that, my friends, is exactly how God's Kingdom works.

God's qualification system is beautifully simple: He's looking for a willing heart. That's it. He's not concerned about résumés, portfolios, or perfect speech. He simply says, "Come, and I will train you." What an anxiety-free qualification!

Sadly, in many churches today, there are abundant gifts that go unused, gifts lying dormant because people believe they aren't ready, skilled, or good enough. But God says, "If you're pliable, I'll shape you."

Our willingness to serve is a reflection of our yielded spirit. God desires hearts that are soft, teachable, and available.

Just like the plaque in my kitchen reminds me, no experience required, so it is with God. He molds us, shapes us, and fills the gaps. Unlike the world, where inexperience can cost you an opportunity, in God's Kingdom, willingness is the only requirement.

So, how willing are you to be used by God? Don't disqualify yourself from Kingdom work. He already knows your potential and will equip you to serve His purpose.

> **Prayer:**
> Lord, forgive us for disqualifying ourselves with excuses. Often we say, "That's not my gift," or "I'm not ready." But You're only asking for a willing and pliable heart. Help us to yield. Thank You that no service in Your Kingdom goes unnoticed. Shape us, mold us, and use us today—no experience required. In Jesus' name, Amen.

Sunday

Worship and Fellowship

"I was glad when they said to me, 'Let's go to the house of the Lord.'"
Psalm 122:1 (NASB)

There's something sacred about Sunday mornings, the intentional pause, the gathering of God's people, the lifting of voices in praise, the Word going forth, and the reminder that we're not walking this journey alone.

Scripture encourages us not to forsake assembling together (Hebrews 10:25), and there's a reason for that. In a world that constantly pulls us in every direction, corporate worship centers us. It realigns our priorities, refreshes our spirit, and reminds us of the bigger picture — God is on the throne, and we are part of His body.

Church isn't just a building; it's a lifeline. It's where iron sharpens iron, where burdens are shared, where joy is multiplied, and where we get a glimpse of heaven on earth.

This morning, don't let sleep, schedules, or excuses rob you of what God wants to deposit in your spirit. Go to His house, not just out of habit, but with expectation. The pew you sit in today might be the place God chooses to speak directly to your heart.

SUNDAY: *Worship and Fellowship*

> **Prayer:**
> Lord, thank You for the gift of Sunday, for fellowship, for worship, and for the church. Help me not to treat it casually but to value it deeply. I come with an open heart today, ready to meet with You.

WEEK 47

Monday

Leave the Thinking to the Conductor

> *"You will keep him in perfect peace, whose mind is stayed on You, because he trusts in You." Isaiah 26:3 (NASB)*

I once read that overthinking kills our happiness. And let's be honest, overthinking is practically a sport for many women! ☺ It breeds anxiety, fear of the unknown, and a thousand imaginary worries.

But God gives us a better way.

In Isaiah 26:3, we're reminded that peace comes when our minds are stayed on Him. Psalm 73:23 comforts us with this truth: "I am continually with You; You hold my right hand." And of course, Matthew 6:34 echoes loudly: "Do not be anxious about tomorrow, for tomorrow will be anxious for itself. Sufficient for the day is its own trouble."

Are you restless about something today? Are you giving your worry wings? Clip them. Let Him fly the plane while you sit back in the co-pilot seat and say, 'Lord, You take the controls. I trust You.'

Prayer:
Lord, quiet my thoughts when they race ahead of You. Help me to fix my eyes on You, not the 'what ifs.' Thank You for the promise of perfect peace. I trust You to lead me. Amen.

TUESDAY

Anchored Love

> *"We have this hope as an anchor for the soul, firm and secure."*
> *Hebrews 6:19a (NIV)*

There's something deeply comforting about the image of an anchor — steady, grounded, unwavering. In a world where feelings fluctuate, and relationships can be unpredictable, anchored love is a rare treasure. It is the kind of love that doesn't shift with moods or seasons. It stays.

Just like a ship confidently rests in place when its anchor is dropped, we too can find rest in a love that holds fast. Whether it's the divine love of God or a God-reflecting love shared on earth, anchored love doesn't run when the waves rise. It endures. It remains.

Blessed are those who find such love here on earth — steady, kind, and unwavering. But even if earthly love fails, God's anchored love never will. His love is the anchor for our souls, firm and secure, never letting go, even in the fiercest storm.

Let your heart be tethered to that kind of love today, divine, steady, and unshakable.

Prayer:
Father, thank You for Your love that anchors me when life feels uncertain. When relationships disappoint, and emotions run high, help me rest in Your constant, unchanging love. Teach me to reflect that kind of love to others, stable, secure, and rooted in grace. In Jesus' name, Amen.

WEDNESDAY

Held in the Hollow

"See, I have inscribed you on the palms of My hands..." Isaiah 49:16 (NASB)

When life feels like it's spinning, emotionally, mentally, or spiritually, there is comfort in knowing you are held. Not loosely. Not temporarily. But firmly and tenderly in the very hands of God.

We live in a world where even the strongest support systems can falter. People disappoint. Circumstances change. But the hands of God are unwavering. His grip doesn't slip. His embrace doesn't weaken. His love doesn't loosen its hold when we cry, question, or even doubt.

The hollow of His hand is a place of belonging. It's where the weary are steadied, the anxious are calmed, and the broken are cradled. It's where your name is engraved, not written in pencil, not tattooed with ink, but inscribed. That's permanent love. That's divine stability.

You may feel like you're losing your grip, but take heart, He's not losing His hold on you.

Prayer:
Lord, thank You for holding me in the hollow of Your hands. When everything around me feels uncertain, let me feel the security of Your love. Remind me that I am not forgotten and never abandoned. I am held, anchored, and engraved in the hands of the Almighty. Amen.

THURSDAY

A Love That Doesn't Walk Away

"For the mountains may be removed and the hills may shake,
But My favor will not be removed from you,
Nor will My covenant of peace be shaken,"
Says the Lord who has compassion on you. Isaiah 54:10 (NASB)

There's a kind of love that stays, even when the mountains crumble, and the storms shake everything you thought was steady. That's God's love.
It doesn't walk away when you're too tired to pray.
It doesn't give up when you fall short again.
It doesn't withdraw when the world turns its back on you.
God's love is not just kind; it's committed. It's not based on how lovable we are, but on how unchanging He is. We may go through moments where we question everything: "Am I enough? Will I ever be fully loved? Who can I trust?"
But this verse silences all the noise. Even if the mountains fall, even if everything else collapses, God's covenant of peace will not be shaken. His love isn't fragile or fickle. It's anchored in a promise, sealed by His compassion.
You don't have to earn it. Just receive it. And rest in it.

Prayer:
Father, thank You for a love that doesn't leave when I'm at my lowest. When the world around me shifts, anchor me in the truth of Your covenant. Let me live today knowing that I am loved deeply, steadily, and eternally. In Jesus' name, Amen.

Friday

Held When I Can't Hold On

*"I am continually with You;
You have taken hold of my right hand." Psalm 73:23 (NASB)*

Sometimes, we're not strong enough to hold on.
Grief loosens our grip.
Exhaustion makes us slip.
Doubt tells us to let go.
But this verse shifts the pressure. He has taken hold of your hand.
We aren't holding on to God as much as He's holding on to us. That changes everything.
Take a moment and look at the cover of this book. See the hollow of God's palm, the open hand that holds many broken hearts. That hand isn't frail or distant. It's divine. It's strong enough to hold your sorrow, your confusion, and your slipping faith.
He holds you, not just when you're standing tall, but especially when your knees buckle, and your strength runs dry.
Even if your grip fails, His never will.
You are safe in His grasp. He doesn't let go when things get hard. In fact, that's when He grips tighter.

Prayer:
Lord, thank You for holding me when I don't have the strength to hold on. When my emotions overwhelm me, when fear clouds my vision, help me rest in the safety of Your hand. I'm not alone. I'm not lost. I'm held in the hollow of Your palm. In Jesus' name, Amen.

Saturday

Unshaken

> *"I have set the Lord continually before me;*
> *Because He is at my right hand, I will not be shaken." Psalm 16:8*
> *(NASB)*

Life is unpredictable; a phone call can change everything. A loss, a diagnosis, a betrayal. Suddenly, what once felt stable begins to tremble beneath us.

But David, the psalmist, teaches us a powerful truth: stability doesn't come from circumstances but from presence. "I have set the Lord continually before me..." — in other words, I keep Him in view.

And because the Lord is at his right hand, his place of action, decision, and strength, he declares: "I will not be shaken."

That's not denial. That's faith.

David still faced battles, betrayal, and wilderness seasons. But he learned that with God beside him, even shaking ground couldn't make him fall.

Are you facing something today that feels like it's pulling the rug out from under you? Are emotions, memories, or fears threatening your peace?

Keep the Lord before you. Let His presence be your anchor, His Word your guide, and His love your firm foundation.

The ground may shake, but you don't have to.

Prayer:
Lord, life shakes me more than I care to admit. But I'm learning to keep You ever before me. Let Your nearness steady my heart and guide my steps. I don't want to lean on emotions or shifting circumstances. You are my unshakable ground. Amen.

SUNDAY

The Power of Gathering

> *"And let us consider how to encourage one another in love and good deeds, not abandoning our own meeting together, as is the habit of some, but encouraging one another." Hebrews 10:24-25 (NASB)*

Sunday is a sacred invitation — to pause, to gather, to worship.

As you prepare your heart today, remember the importance of coming together with other believers. There's something beautiful about lifting your voice in worship alongside others, sitting under the Word, and letting God refresh your spirit through fellowship. Church is not just a building, it's a body. And you are a vital part of it.

So find your place, settle in, and be present in God's house.

Prayer:
Lord, thank You for the gift of the church, a place to grow, to serve, and to be renewed. Help me enter Your presence with gratitude and expectation. Amen.

WEEK 48

Monday

The War Within

"For the flesh desires what is contrary to the Spirit, and the Spirit what is contrary to the flesh. They are in conflict with each other..."
Galatians 5:17a (NIV)

The Christian walk is not a carefree cruise; it's a battleground.
Many of us want the comfort of a cruise ship—calm waters, good food, spiritual sunbathing. But truthfully, we've been enlisted onto a battleship. One that requires alertness, readiness, and the full armor of God. The Spirit of God and the desires of our flesh are constantly at war within us. It's not a skirmish. It's full-on combat.
There's an old saying: "Give an inch and they'll take a yard." That's exactly how the enemy operates. Give the flesh a little room, just a small compromise, a tiny slip, a brief moment of justification, and it will soon consume every corner of your heart. Before you know it, your sensitivity to the Spirit begins to dull. Discernment fades. Conviction softens. And spiritual laziness creeps in.
But you don't have to live defeated.
Ephesians 6 tells us to be fully armed—helmet, shield, sword, and all. We don't fight alone, and we don't fight in our strength. The same Spirit that raised Jesus from the dead dwells in you. That's resurrection power. That's battle-winning strength. But it requires vigilance. You must suit up daily.
Don't let your guard down. Don't let your heart be a playground for compromise. Stay awake. Stay armored.

> **Prayer:**
> Lord, how easily we slack off in our Christian walk. Forgive us for when we've laid down our armor and let the enemy creep in through open doors. Help us to be alert, fully suited in Your armor, and aware of the battle that rages within. Let Your Spirit win every war inside our hearts. Amen.

TUESDAY

Dressed to Stand

> *"Put on the full armor of God, so that you can take your stand against the devil's schemes." Ephesians 6:11 (NIV)*

There's a reason Paul doesn't say, "Hold the armor nearby." He says to put it on. Because in spiritual battles, proximity won't protect you; preparation will.

The armor of God isn't just symbolic. It's practical. The belt of truth keeps lies from slipping in. The breastplate of righteousness guards your heart. The shield of faith extinguishes flaming arrows. Every piece matters, because the battle is real.

We don't face flesh and blood enemies, but the unseen forces that chip away at our peace, whisper lies into our minds, and tempt us with easy roads that lead to destruction. If we don't intentionally armor up each day, we're walking into battle exposed.

So don't forget your armor today, not just part of it. All of it.

> **Prayer:**
> Lord, clothe me today in Your full armor. Fasten truth around my life, guard my heart with righteousness, and let my shield of faith be strong. I will stand firm in You. Amen.

WEDNESDAY

Watch the Gates

"Guard your heart above all else, for it determines the course of your life." Proverbs 4:23 (NLT)

Gates are meant to control what comes in and what goes out. Your eyes, ears, and mind are gates to your heart. What are you letting in?

The flesh is sly. Sometimes the attack doesn't come in the form of obvious sin but in subtle compromise. A small indulgence here, a justifying thought there. Before long, what once stirred conviction now feels normal.

Spiritual warfare often begins with entertainment choices, careless conversations, or distractions disguised as harmless. But what we allow through our gates will either build us up or tear us down from the inside out.

So guard your heart fiercely. What you consume shapes what you believe. What you believe shapes how you live.

Prayer:
God, help me watch the gates of my heart with care. May I not grow numb to what grieves You. Keep me sensitive to Your voice and swift to shut out anything that doesn't honor You. Amen.

THURSDAY

Don't Fight Naked

"But put on the Lord Jesus Christ, and make no provision for the flesh, to gratify its desires." Romans 13:14 (ESV)

THURSDAY: *Don't Fight Naked*

No one goes to battle unclothed, yet many believers do just that spiritually.

We walk out the door unarmed, unprayed, and unaware. We try to manage the day's pressures, temptations, and demands without inviting the Lord into any of it. And then we wonder why we feel defeated by noon.

The flesh will always be ready to rise, but are you clothed in Christ?

Putting on Christ is an act of surrender and dependence. It means choosing His strength over yours, His wisdom over your reasoning, and His presence over self-sufficiency. It's not legalism; it's survival.

Don't make provisions for the flesh. Starve it. Clothe yourself in Christ.

> **Prayer:**
> *Lord, I can't fight today's battles without You. Cover me in Your righteousness. Let my thoughts be Yours, my words be Yours, and my steps be directed by You. Amen.*

FRIDAY

Still Standing

> *"...take up the full armor of God, so that you may be able to resist in the evil day, and having prepared everything, to take your stand."*
> Ephesians 6:13 (CSB)

After all is said and done, will you still be standing?

The sign of spiritual maturity is not how many Scriptures we quote or how high we raise our hands during worship. It's this: when the storm comes and the enemy strikes, are we still standing in faith?

There are days you won't feel victorious. You may feel bruised, shaken, or weary. But if you're still standing, still choosing truth, still praying, still worshiping, that's victory.

SATURDAY: *The Mind is a Battlefield*

Your strength is not from you. The ability to stand is from the One who holds you.

Prayer:
Father, thank You that I don't stand in my strength but in Yours. On the days I feel like collapsing, hold me up with Your power. And when the dust settles, let it be said — I'm still standing. Amen.

SATURDAY

The Mind is a Battlefield

"We take captive every thought to make it obedient to Christ." 2 Corinthians 10:5 (NIV)

Before defeat ever shows up in our behavior, it starts in our thoughts.

Long before a person gives in to fear, temptation, or insecurity, the mind has already been compromised. That's the real battlefield. The enemy knows that if he can plant a lie and get us to believe it, he doesn't have to do anything else. We'll self-sabotage from within. He doesn't need chains on your wrists, just a whisper in your mind.

That's why Scripture urges us to take every thought captive. Not a few. Not just the big ones. Every single thought. And we don't just trap them and observe, we bring them under the authority of Christ. We measure them against God's truth. Is this thought grounded in Scripture? Does it reflect the character of Christ? Or is it laced with fear, shame, doubt, pride, or bitterness?

You may not be able to stop every thought from entering your mind. Thoughts come like birds in flight, but you can choose which ones you allow to nest there. You can choose which ones to feed. If a thought doesn't align with the Word, don't entertain it. Don't let it rent space in your head. Evict it in the name of Jesus.

Prayer:
Lord, train my mind for battle. Let me not become a prisoner of unchecked thoughts. Help me to recognize what is not from You — to name it, reject it, and replace it with Your truth. Saturate my thoughts with Your Word, and help me walk in the mental freedom Christ purchased for me. Amen.

Sunday

The Power of Gathering

> *"And let us consider how to encourage one another in love and good deeds, not abandoning our own meeting together, as is the habit of some, but encouraging one another." Hebrews 10:24–25 (NASB)*

Sunday is a sacred invitation — to pause, to gather, to worship.

As you prepare your heart today, remember the importance of coming together with other believers. There's something beautiful about lifting your voice in worship alongside others, sitting under the Word, and letting God refresh your spirit through fellowship. Church is not just a building; it's a body. And you are a vital part of it.

So find your place, settle in, and be present in God's house.

Prayer:
Lord, thank You for the gift of the church, a place to grow, to serve, and to be renewed. Help me enter Your presence with gratitude and expectation. Amen.

WEEK 49

MONDAY

When Doubt Creeps In

> "Now the serpent was more crafty than any of the wild animals the Lord God had made. He said to the woman, 'Did God really say, "You must not eat from any tree in the garden"?'" Genesis 3:1 (NIV)

> "But when you ask, you must believe and not doubt, because the one who doubts is like a wave of the sea, blown and tossed by the wind." James 1:6-7 (NIV)

"Did God really say?"

That one question from the serpent in the garden was enough to plant the first seed of doubt. It's subtle, isn't it? Doubt doesn't scream; it whispers. But that whisper can cause even the strongest to waver.

I've experienced it firsthand. I remember starting a new job, eager and confident. I would complete a task and submit it, thinking I'd done everything right. But then my supervisor would glance at it and ask, "Are you sure?" And just like that, all my confidence would crumble. That simple question planted doubt.

We see it again and again in Scripture.

Moses, handpicked by God to lead His people, still asked, "Who am I that I should go?" Despite hearing God's voice directly, Moses wrestled with inadequacy.

The father of the sick boy in Mark 9:24 cried out, "I do believe; help me overcome my unbelief!" Jesus honored his honesty and healed the boy.

MONDAY: *When Doubt Creeps In*

Peter—bold, courageous Peter—stepped out of the boat to walk on water. But the moment he took his eyes off Jesus and looked at the storm, he began to sink. And still, Jesus reached out and caught him.

Even spiritual giants had their moments of doubt. The beautiful truth? God didn't disqualify them. He met them in their doubt, restored their faith, and strengthened them for the journey ahead.

So, what kind of doubt are you facing today?

Are you doubting God's provision?

His healing power?

His ability to restore?

His presence in your storm?

Let the Word remind you: God is faithful. His promises are true. And His love does not waver, even when your faith does.

But remember what James writes: Doubt makes us unstable, like a wave tossed by the wind. Faith and doubt cannot co-exist. One will silence the other.

Choose today which one you'll give voice to.

> **Prayer:**
> *Lord, how often doubt sneaks into my thoughts—sometimes quietly, sometimes forcefully. But You are steady, sovereign, and good. Help me silence every voice that questions Your truth. Strengthen my belief. Replace every doubt with confidence in You, my faithful and loving Father. In Jesus' name, Amen.*

TUESDAY

A Bible That's Falling Apart

"I have stored up your word in my heart, that I might not sin against you." Psalm 119:11

"The unfolding of your words gives light; it imparts understanding to the simple." Psalm 119:130

Tuesday: *A Bible That's Falling Apart*

> *"The grass withers, the flower fades, but the word of our God will stand forever." Isaiah 40:8*

> *"Your words were found, and I ate them, and your word was to me the joy and rejoicing of my heart." Jeremiah 15:16*

A.W. Tozer once said, "A Bible that's falling apart usually belongs to someone who isn't." That quote has stayed with me for years.

When I hold my husband's Bible, or my father's, I see pages torn and worn thin. The margins are filled to the brim with notes. Ink has bled through from years of study, and some letters are smudged, perhaps from tears that fell while reading God's promises in moments of sorrow. These Bibles are precious trophies of faith. They've been used, and more importantly, lived through.

I'm reminded of a story I heard in Sunday school:

A father sends his son off to college with a new Bible and one piece of advice: "Read it every day."

The son nods, says goodbye, and goes off to begin his new chapter in life.

Month after month, he calls home, asking for money. Each time, the father asks, "Son, have you read your Bible today?"

"Yes, Dad," the son replies, though he hadn't.

One day, the son receives the devastating news that his father has passed. Overwhelmed with grief, he finally opens the Bible for the first time, and tucked inside, between the pages, he finds envelopes with money, one for each month he had called. If only he had read the Word... he would have also received the provision.

What a powerful image. When we neglect the Word, we miss out, not just on wisdom or encouragement, but on the tangible blessings God may have hidden for us within its pages.

Did you eat His Word today?

Did you devour it like Jeremiah, who said, "I ate them, and Your Word was the joy and rejoicing of my heart"?

Or did you rush through a quick "one-minute devotion" hoping it would be enough?

Friends, reading the Word is our only spiritual ammunition to face the challenges of the day. Not a podcast, not a quote, not even a sermon—nothing replaces the living Word in your hands.

> **Prayer:**
> Lord, forgive me for the times I've taken Your Word lightly. Stir within me a hunger—not just for a verse, but for deep communion with You through Scripture. Let my Bible bear the marks of use, not neglect. May I be found, like Jeremiah, feeding on Your words and finding joy in every one of them. Amen.

WEDNESDAY

Salute Your Mother

"Her children arise and call her blessed; her husband also, and he praises her." Proverbs 31:28 (NIV)

All mothers have shed tears in their lives. But have you ever seen them cry while raising their children? Most of us haven't. Yet we all remember running to our mothers with every little scrape, every little boo-boo. Somehow, she always had a comforting word or a healing touch.

But does that mean she never felt pain? Absolutely not.

Does it mean her children never gave her heartache? Definitely not.

A mother often keeps her tears hidden, tucked away during quiet moments spent with her Lord. That's where she releases her pain. Her tears are not shed in front of the world, but before the One who sees and knows.

You and I are the products of those unseen tears.

So today, take a moment to honor the woman who carried you, fed you, nurtured you, and cried for you when no one else saw.

Salute the mother who gave her best so you could have a good life.

Salute the mother who didn't let you see her suffering but gave it all for your joy.

Salute the mother who knew where to shed her tears—in the presence of Jesus.

WEDNESDAY: *Salute Your Mother*

Salute the mother who was your biggest cheerleader even in your worst moments.
Salute the mother who stretched meals to feed many mouths and still wore a smile.
Salute the mother who knew what it meant to put others before herself.
Salute the mother who made your happiness her mission.
Salute the mother who was custom-made by God just for you.
Her sacrifices may have been quiet, but her love was thunderously loud in Heaven.

Prayer:
Lord, thank You for mothers—their strength, their wisdom, and their unseen tears. Bless every mother who continues to carry silent burdens. May she know that her prayers are not in vain and that her tears are stored in Your bottle. Help us honor and bless the women who have poured into our lives. Amen.

THURSDAY

More Valuable Than Sparrows

> *"Look at the birds of the sky, that they do not sow, nor reap, nor gather crops into barns, and yet your heavenly Father feeds them. Are you not much more important than they?"* Matthew 6:26 (NASB)

I have a bird feeder, and I love sitting by the window to watch the sparrows. Tiny and feeble, they brave the outdoors—rain, wind, snow, and sun. They don't plant seeds, harvest crops, or store food in barns. And yet, somehow, they're fed.

Who feeds them? Our Heavenly Father does.

If God is that mindful of the birds, creatures without voice, shelter, or plans, how much more is He mindful of us? We, His children. We, who were created in His image. In Matthew 6, Jesus asks this question plainly: "Are you not of more value than they?"

So today, if your heart is anxious, weary, or overwhelmed, snuff it all out with this truth: You are of more value.

More than the sparrows. More than the lilies. You are known, seen, and cherished.

> **Prayer:**
> Lord, remind me of my worth in Your eyes. When I feel small or forgotten, let the birds remind me that You are near, and that I am deeply loved. Amen.

FRIDAY

Keep It Real

> *"Finally, brothers and sisters, whatever is true, whatever is honorable, whatever is right, whatever is pure, whatever is lovely, whatever is commendable... think about these things." Philippians 4:8 (NASB)*

Here's one of my pet peeves: Society has conditioned us to be overly diplomatic and politically correct. We're taught to say just enough to keep the peace, to sugarcoat the truth, to avoid rocking the boat. But in all that careful editing, we lose something important—we lose our authenticity.

Why can't we just be real?

My kids love to tease me: "No mincing words with Mom!" And you know what? I take no offense. I'd rather speak the truth in love than hide behind a smoky mirror of polite pretense. There's something powerful about walking in truth, not brashly, not carelessly, but with clarity, courage, and compassion.

The Bible doesn't tell us to think on what's popular. It says to think on what is true, honorable, right, and pure. How can we do that if we're constantly walking on eggshells, afraid to speak with conviction? Jesus

FRIDAY: *Keep It Real*

Himself didn't tiptoe around the truth; He spoke with love but never diluted His message.

Realness doesn't mean being harsh. It means being anchored. It means letting your words be a reflection of your heart, seasoned with grace but rooted in truth. The world doesn't need more filters. It needs believers who are real, honest, and Spirit-led.

So let's keep it real, with kindness, with humility, and with truth.

Prayer:
Father, help me walk in truth today. Strip away any fear of offense, and teach me how to speak with grace and clarity. May my words reflect what is true, honorable, and pure. Keep me grounded in You, and help me never lose my voice in a world that craves silence. Amen.

SATURDAY

Assignment from Above

"And God spoke to Israel in visions of the night and said, 'Jacob, Jacob.' And he said, 'Here I am.'" Genesis 46:2 (NASB)

"Then I heard the voice of the Lord, saying, 'Whom shall I send, and who will go for Us?' Then I said, 'Here am I. Send me!'" Isaiah 6:8 (NASB)

When God places a thought on your heart, it's not random; it's a divine assignment. Whether it's a burden to pray for someone, a prompting to serve, or an idea that keeps resurfacing in your spirit, it's often heaven's way of saying, "I have something for you to do."

But here's the reality: we often hesitate. We question whether we heard Him right. We wonder if we're qualified. We stall, waiting for

SATURDAY: *Assignment from Above*

confirmation after confirmation, hoping the assignment will pass to someone else.

But if God gave it to you, He already factored in your weaknesses, your hesitations, and your history. He knows who He's calling, and still calls you anyway.

Picture God as the Divine VP of Purpose, carefully delegating specific tasks to specific people, not by accident but by intentional design. He assigns you not because you're the most talented, but because He knows you're available. He's just waiting for your response: "Here I am."

That's what Jacob said. That's what Isaiah said. That's what we are invited to say, too.

So today, if your heart stirs with something that seems bigger than you, don't run. Don't overanalyze it. Simply answer the call. God is not looking for perfect vessels, just willing ones.

Prayer:
Lord, I'm ready to receive my assignment. Give me ears to hear when You speak, and the courage to say "Here I am" without hesitation. Equip me with what I need to carry out what You place in my heart today. I may not feel ready, but I trust that You are. Amen.

Sunday

Worship and Fellowship

"I was glad when they said to me, 'Let's go to the house of the Lord.'"
Psalm 122:1 (NASB)

There's something sacred about Sunday mornings, the intentional pause, the gathering of God's people, the lifting of voices in praise, the Word going forth, and the reminder that we're not walking this journey alone.

Scripture encourages us not to forsake assembling together (Hebrews 10:25), and there's a reason for that. In a world that constantly pulls us

SUNDAY: *Worship and Fellowship*

in every direction, corporate worship centers us. It realigns our priorities, refreshes our spirit, and reminds us of the bigger picture — God is on the throne, and we are part of His body.

Church isn't just a building; it's a lifeline. It's where iron sharpens iron, where burdens are shared, where joy is multiplied, and where we get a glimpse of heaven on earth.

This morning, don't let sleep, schedules, or excuses rob you of what God wants to deposit in your spirit. Go to His house, not just out of habit, but with expectation. The pew you sit in today might be the place God chooses to speak directly to your heart.

Prayer:
Lord, thank You for the gift of Sunday, for fellowship, for worship, and for the church. Help me not to treat it casually but to value it deeply. I come with an open heart today, ready to meet with You.

WEEK 50

Monday

"But God..."

> *"I do not trust in my bow; I do not count on my sword to save me. But You give us victory over our enemies, You put our adversaries to shame." Psalm 44:6-7 (NASB)*

Life is a series of challenges, some expected and others catching us off guard. There are days when you might feel capable, strong, and in control. But then comes a moment—a diagnosis, a sudden loss, a failure—when your bow and sword (your skills, plans, or strategies) feel insufficient. That's when these two words change everything: But God.

"But God" reminds us that victory is not ours to claim by might or intellect. It is His to give. Our strength is limited, but His is limitless. Our view is partial, but His is panoramic. When "But God" becomes part of our narrative, pride dissolves, and faith is activated.

Even sweeping the floor or lifting your hand to wave is a "But God" story. Every move and every breath is proof of His enabling grace. Think of David facing Goliath, not in his strength, but in the name of the Lord. His story became history because of one confident "But God" moment.

Today, when you're tempted to rely on your tools or feel overwhelmed by what you lack, whisper these two powerful words: But God. Speak them over your fears, over your day, and every situation.

Live a "But God" day. Reframe your struggles through the lens of His power. Let those two words shift your perspective and renew your strength.

TUESDAY: *The Power of the Pause*

> **Prayer:**
> *Father, thank You that You are the God of "But God" moments. When my strength fails, You sustain. When I reach the end of myself, You begin to work. Teach me to rely on You in all things. May my life be a daily testimony of Your power, not mine. Amen.*

---------- TUESDAY ----------

The Power of the Pause

"Be still, and know that I am God." Psalm 46:10 (NIV)

In a world that applauds hustle and glorifies productivity, the word pause can feel foreign, even weak. But sometimes, the most powerful thing you can do is stop.

There's a holy strength in stillness. Not the kind of stillness that comes from giving up, but the kind that comes from giving in, surrendering to the God who holds your next breath, your next step, your next breakthrough.

Sometimes life presses pause for us. A diagnosis. A heartbreak. A closed door. A season where everything slows to a crawl. And we panic. We ask, Lord, why is nothing moving? Why am I stuck here?

But what if the pause isn't punishment... it's preparation?

What if, in the stillness, God is recalibrating your heart? What if He's removing distractions, healing wounds, strengthening your foundation, not so you can go back to how things were, but so you can rise stronger for what's ahead?

But what if the pause isn't punishment... it's preparation?

What if, in the stillness, God is recalibrating your heart? What if He's removing distractions, healing wounds, strengthening your foundation, not so you can go back to how things were, but so you can rise stronger for what's ahead?

TUESDAY: *The Power of the Pause*

When gold is refined in the fire, it must sit still under intense heat, not fighting the process. Only then can the impurities surface and be removed. Only then does the beauty emerge.

The same is true of us. We're so quick to act, to fix, to figure it out. But there's power in pressing pause and letting God do what only He can do.

Pause doesn't mean you're forgotten. It means He's doing a deeper work beneath the surface.

> **Prayer:**
> *Lord, teach me to embrace the pause. When life slows down, help me resist the urge to fill the silence. May I lean into stillness, trusting that You are at work even when I can't see it. Refine me in the waiting, and prepare me for what You've already prepared for me. Amen.*

WEDNESDAY

Still Standing

"Though the mountains be shaken and the hills be removed, yet My unfailing love for you will not be shaken." Isaiah 54:10 (NIV)

Earthquakes shake foundations. Storms topple trees. Even the strongest structures can crumble under the right pressure. But God's love? It never shakes.

Life will shake you — loss, disappointment, change, grief — they all rattle your heart and threaten your footing. But in those moments, God offers more than just sympathy. He offers stability. A place to stand when everything else is falling apart.

His promises are not mood-dependent or weather-sensitive. His love doesn't blow away in the storm. It is rooted in eternity, grounded in truth, and sealed with covenant.

WEDNESDAY: *Still Standing*

You may not feel strong today, but you are still standing because His love is still holding.
Take a deep breath and whisper this to your heart:
"I'm standing not because I'm strong, but because He is."

> **Prayer:**
> *Father, thank You that even when my world trembles, Your love remains. Help me anchor myself in Your unshakable truth. When emotions rise and circumstances shift, let me plant my feet on the solid ground of Your promises. Thank You that I am still standing, not by my strength, but by Your grace. Amen.*

THURSDAY

Don't Rush the Process

"He will sit as a refiner and purifier of silver..." Malachi 3:3a (NIV)

There's something sacred about the refining process. It's slow, deliberate, and incredibly personal. The Refiner doesn't walk away. He stays with eyes fixed, hands steady, until the impurities rise and the silver reflects His image.

We often want the fire to end quickly. We want instant relief, fast answers, and overnight growth. But transformation doesn't happen on our timeline. It happens on God's.

If the silver is pulled out too soon, it's still impure. If we try to skip the process, we miss the very beauty He's drawing out of us.

You may be in a season where the heat feels intense. But hear this: you are not being burned; you are being refined. And the One who watches over you is not impatient. He is invested. He sees what you will become.

So don't rush the process. Don't resent the flame. Let it do its holy work.

> **Prayer:**
> Lord, when I grow weary in the fire, remind me that You are near, not distant. That Your goal isn't to harm me but to purify me. Help me endure with trust, knowing You are shaping something beautiful in me. Refine me, Lord, until You see Your reflection. Amen.

FRIDAY

When Your Child Breaks Your Heart

"Honor your father and your mother, so that you may live long in the land the Lord your God is giving you." Exodus 20:12 (NIV)

There's a unique kind of heartbreak that comes when your own child, the one you carried, fed, protected, and prayed over... turns cold. Maybe it's in the way they talk back. Or the silence that's louder than words. Maybe it's the rolled eyes, the indifference, or that feeling that they've forgotten everything you poured into them.

It stings.

You wonder, Did I fail? But not every wound in parenting is a sign of failure. Even God's children walked away from Him, and He's the perfect Parent.

The world teaches independence. But Scripture teaches honor. And honoring doesn't end at 18. It doesn't get erased because of disagreements or differences. God didn't put an expiration date on respect.

If you're that hurting parent today, take heart: God sees it all. The prayers you've whispered. The tears you've cried when no one was looking. He's not done. He can work on hearts behind the scenes, even the ones that feel far gone.

And if you're the child who's drifted? Maybe it's time to text. Call. Apologize. No parent is perfect, but neither are you. Grace goes both ways.

> **Prayer:**
> Lord, this ache is deeper than I can explain. Remind me that I'm not alone in this grief. Help me love without bitterness and wait with hope. Soften their heart, Lord, and help me keep mine tender too. I trust You with this pain. Amen.

SATURDAY

Refined, Not Ruined

"I have refined you, but not as silver is refined. Rather, I have refined you in the furnace of suffering." Isaiah 48:10 (NLT)

There's painful beauty in the refining process.

We don't volunteer for the furnace. No one signs up to be tested through tears or molded through heartbreak. But it's in the heat of life's trials that our faith is forged.

God never wastes pain. He doesn't toss us into suffering to destroy us, but to purify us — to burn away the things that don't belong and reveal what was always of value beneath the surface.

Think of clay in the potter's hands. For the vessel to be shaped well, the clay has to be soft and pliable. But if it resists, stiffens, or keeps shifting on the wheel, the potter cannot form it properly. The same is true with us. If we resist God's shaping, squirming every time life presses too hard, the process takes longer, and the vessel remains unfinished.

Some wounds don't just heal; they transform. That sharp edge of pride? Burned away. The illusion of control? Melted. What remains is faith that's real, trust that's raw, and a dependence on Him that's unshakable.

You may not see it now, but there's something sacred forming in the fire.

You are not being ruined. You are being refined, shaped for something beautiful.

> **Prayer:**
> Father, this fire hurts. But if You're in it, I trust it has purpose. Purify my heart. Mold me like clay in Your hands. I don't want to come out bitter; I want to come out better. Stronger. Glowing with Your glory. Thank You for walking with me through the heat. Amen

SUNDAY

Worship and Fellowship

"I was glad when they said to me, 'Let's go to the house of the Lord.'"
Psalm 122:1 (NASB)

There's something sacred about Sunday mornings, the intentional pause, the gathering of God's people, the lifting of voices in praise, the Word going forth, and the reminder that we're not walking this journey alone.

Scripture encourages us not to forsake assembling together (Hebrews 10:25), and there's a reason for that. In a world that constantly pulls us in every direction, corporate worship centers us. It realigns our priorities, refreshes our spirit, and reminds us of the bigger picture — God is on the throne, and we are part of His body.

Church isn't just a building; it's a lifeline. It's where iron sharpens iron, where burdens are shared, where joy is multiplied, and where we get a glimpse of heaven on earth. This morning, don't let sleep, schedules, or excuses rob you of what God wants to deposit in your spirit. Go to His house, not just out of habit, but with expectation. The pew you sit in today might be the place God chooses to speak directly to your heart.

> **Prayer:**
> Lord, thank You for the gift of Sunday, for fellowship, for worship, and for the church. Help me not to treat it casually but to value it deeply. I come with an open heart today, ready to meet with You.

WEEK 51

Why We Gather: The Power of the Church

"They devoted themselves to the apostles' teaching and to fellowship, to the breaking of bread and to prayer." Acts 2:42 (NIV)

---- Monday ----

The Wheel of Teaching

"They devoted themselves to the apostles' teaching..." Acts 2:42a (NIV)

Unless you are taught, you cannot make wise choices.
    That's true in school, in life, and certainly in your walk with God. The early church knew this; they didn't grow by accident. They devoted themselves to learning. They sat under teachings. They listened, absorbed, and applied the truth.
    We live in a world overflowing with information, podcasts, opinions, and trending posts, but lacking in wisdom. That's why teaching rooted in God's Word is vital. It becomes the compass for every decision, the plumb line for every step.
    Don't skip the Word. Don't skim it like a checklist. Sit under it. Soak in it. Let it shape your character and renew your mind.

Prayer:
Lord, give me a heart that is eager to learn. Help me not just to hear Your Word, but to live it out with wisdom and courage. Amen.

TUESDAY

The Wheel of Fellowship

"...and to fellowship..." Acts 2:42b (NIV)

In this world, we cannot live in silos. God never meant for us to.

If that were the case, He would have left Adam alone in the garden. But He didn't; He created a helpmate. Why? Because community is God's design.

Fellowship isn't just about potlucks and handshakes. It's about connection. Accountability. Encouragement. We thrive in togetherness. Isolation may feel safer, but it's never stronger.

When you're in a godly community, you're reminded that you're not alone. Someone lifts your hands when they're weak. Someone prays when you have no words. Someone speaks the truth when your mind is flooded with lies.

Don't be alone. The church needs you, and you need the church.

> **Prayer:**
> *Lord, thank You for the gift of fellowship. Help me build authentic relationships that reflect Your love and strengthen my walk with You. Amen.*

WEDNESDAY

The Wheel of Breaking the Bread

"...to the breaking of bread..." Acts 2:42c (NIV)

Wednesday: *The Wheel of Breaking the Bread*

The breaking of bread was more than a meal; it was a moment. A time to remember. To reflect. To realign.

Communion is not just a ritual. It's a sacred pause. A chance to examine your heart, confess your sins, and remember the price Jesus paid for you. When we gather on Sundays and take the bread and cup, it's not a casual snack; it's a covenant moment.

The emblems speak. The bread reminds us of a broken body. The cup whispers of poured-out grace. It's an invitation to come clean, to come close, and to walk away forgiven.

Don't take it lightly. Let it reset your heart each time.

> **Prayer:**
> *Jesus, thank You for the cross. As I break bread in remembrance, help me never to forget what You did for me. Search my heart and draw me near. Amen.*

Thursday

The Wheel of Prayer

"...and to prayer." Acts 2:42d (NIV)

Who can survive without prayer?

It's the most valuable weapon a Christian can have. Prayer is more than words; it's warfare. It's not a ritual; it's a lifeline. A direct line to the heart of God.

When everything else fails, prayer doesn't. When you don't have the strength to fight, you can still kneel. And in that kneeling, heaven moves.

The early church knew the secret: revival doesn't come from strategy; it comes from seeking. Breakthrough doesn't come from hustle; it comes from humble cries. Power doesn't come from position; it flows from prayer.

So pray. Not as a last resort, but as your first weapon. Your first response. Your constant rhythm.

> **Prayer:**
> Lord, may prayer never become routine in my life. Teach me to pray with faith, boldness, and expectancy. Keep my heart connected to Yours. Amen.

FRIDAY

Serving Side by Side

> *"Each of you should use whatever gift you have received to serve others, as faithful stewards of God's grace in its various forms." 1 Peter 4:10 (NIV)*

Church isn't just about receiving; it's also where we show up to serve.

There's something powerful that happens when the body of Christ functions as it was designed. Each member, with their unique gifts, stories, scars, and testimonies, plays a part in building up the whole. The early church didn't just meet and listen; they served each other in love.

You may feel like your gift is small or unseen, but there is no such thing in God's eyes. Whether you're making coffee, holding babies, welcoming someone at the door, or praying behind the scenes, it matters. It all matters.

When we serve side by side, we reflect Christ Himself, who did not come to be served, but to serve. And in serving together, we strengthen the church, deepen relationships, and make space for God's grace to flow through us to others.

So don't just attend church. Engage. Contribute. Serve. There's a place for you in the story He's writing through your local body.

> **Prayer:**
> Father, help me see where I can serve others in love. Show me how to steward the gifts You've given me and use them for Your glory. Whether the task is big or small, help me serve with joy and purpose. Amen.

SATURDAY

The Power of Showing Up

> *"Now you are the body of Christ, and each one of you is a part of it." I Corinthians 12:27 (NIV)*

Sometimes, the greatest ministry you can offer is simply being there.

You don't need to have eloquent words or flashy gifts; your presence alone speaks volumes. When you walk through the church doors week after week, you remind others (and yourself) that faith is not a solo journey.

There are people watching you, quietly encouraged by your faithfulness. Maybe you're the only hug they'll receive all week. Maybe your smile softens someone's hardened heart. Maybe someone's prayer gets answered just because you showed up.

Consistency matters. Commitment matters. Your seat in the pew isn't just about you; it's about the Body. And when even one part is missing, the whole feels it.

So don't underestimate the power of your presence. God does something special when we come together, and the beauty of church is that no one walks in alone when we choose to walk in together.

Prayer:
Lord, thank You for the gift of community. Remind me that even when I feel tired, unseen, or disconnected, there's power in showing up. Help me stay rooted, faithful, and present in the life of Your Church. Amen.

Sunday

Let Us Not Give Up Meeting Together

"Not giving up meeting together, as some are in the habit of doing, but encouraging one another — and all the more as you see the Day approaching." Hebrews 10:25 (NIV)

God never meant for us to do life alone.

From the beginning, He designed us for a relationship with Him and with each other. When the early church gathered, it wasn't out of habit or obligation. It was out of deep need and joy. They knew that something powerful happened when believers came together in unity. And it still does.

Every Sunday gathering is a holy rhythm, a reset for weary souls. It's a place where burdens are lifted, hearts are mended, and hope is stirred again. It's where the Word is proclaimed, worship is lifted, and faith is rekindled. It's where we get reminded: we are not alone.

Don't let disappointment, distraction, or convenience rob you of the gift of fellowship. The world may say, "It's just one Sunday," but heaven sees it as sacred. You need the church, and the church needs you.

Prayer:
Lord, thank You for the blessing of gathering with other believers. Help me not to grow weary in showing up, and remind me of the joy, strength, and purpose found in fellowship. May I never take Your Church for granted. Amen.

WEEK 52

Monday

The God Who Restores

> *"I will restore to you the years that the swarming locust has eaten..."*
> Joel 2:25 (ESV)

There are seasons of life that feel wasted, years swallowed by pain, disappointment, or bad decisions. Maybe it was a broken relationship, a missed opportunity, or a long stretch of grief that clouded your joy. It's easy to wonder, "Can anything good come out of what I've lost?"

But God doesn't just soothe broken hearts; He restores what was lost. He takes the tattered strands of our story and weaves them into something beautiful. He doesn't give us back the exact thing we lost; He gives us back more: perspective, peace, purpose.

Joel 2:25 was spoken to a people who had experienced devastating loss — crops, livelihood, and hope — yet God promised not just survival, but restoration. That promise still stands.

Nothing is too far gone for God to redeem. Even the chapters you'd rather tear out can become the foundation of your testimony.

You may have lost time, but you haven't lost His plan. His ability to restore is not limited by the clock; it's defined by His power and love.

Prayer:
Lord, You are the God who restores. I bring You the lost years, the broken dreams, the heavy regrets. Breathe new life into places that feel barren. I trust that what I place in Your hands, You will renew. Thank You that my story is not over. Amen.

TUESDAY

Held in the Potter's Hands

"Yet you, Lord, are our Father. We are the clay, you are the potter; we are all the work of your hand." Isaiah 64:8 (NIV)

Have you ever watched a potter at work? The clay doesn't control the process; the potter does. The shape, the design, the refining, all come through the steady pressure and skilled touch of the potter's hands.

But what happens if the clay resists?

It wobbles. It warps. And sometimes it has to be reshaped entirely.

That's what it can feel like when we resist God's shaping in our lives. We want control, comfort, predictability. But true transformation happens when we remain pliable — yielded, trusting, surrendered.

The beauty is this: even when we've hardened or cracked, the Potter never discards us. He patiently reworks the clay, molding something even more meaningful from what the world might call ruined. He sees the end result while we're still spinning on the wheel.

Whatever season you're in, the spinning, the shaping, or the refining fire, know that His hands are steady. You are not being destroyed. You're being crafted.

Prayer:
Lord, help me to stay pliable in Your hands. Forgive me for the times I resist Your shaping work. I trust that You are forming something far greater than I can see. Mold me into a vessel that brings You glory. Amen.

WEDNESDAY

Give It to God — and Actually Go to Sleep

> *"Cast your burden on the Lord, and He will sustain you; He will never permit the righteous to be moved."* — Psalm 55:22

Every night as I'm winding down, two simple reminders stare back at me. A plaque on the wall reads, "Give it to God and go to sleep," and a pillow echoes the same message. Comforting words, right?

But here's the honest question I have to ask myself: Do I really give it to God and go to sleep? Do I hand over the worries, the what-ifs, and the things I can't control—and then actually rest? Truthfully, not always.

I might talk to Him about it. I might even shed a few tears and whisper a prayer. But somewhere in the quiet, I find myself still holding on...just in case. There's that subtle hesitation to fully release control. As if keeping one hand on the situation will somehow keep it from falling apart.

Yet God's Word couldn't be clearer:

"Cast your burden on the Lord, and He will sustain you; He will never permit the righteous to be moved." — Psalm 55:22

It doesn't say to toss your burden like a boomerang that comes back or place it gently while keeping a backup plan. It says to cast it—to throw it completely and let it land in His hands.

How much casting are we really doing? Or have we mastered the art of pretending to cast?

Tonight, let's stop rehearsing the worry and start releasing it. Let's surrender the weight we were never meant to carry and trust the arms that never sleep. His arms are always stretched wide, waiting to receive every burden we drop.

Let it go. Give it to God. And this time... actually go to sleep.

Prayer:
Lord, You see what I carry and how tightly I grip it, even when I say I trust You. Teach me to surrender, not in word alone but with a heart that truly lets

> go. Help me cast my cares—not recycle them. Tonight, I give it all to You. Please hold what I can't. Amen

---

THURSDAY

After the Breaking, Comes the Blessing

> *"He heals the brokenhearted and binds up their wounds." Psalm 147:3 (NIV)*

There's something sacred about brokenness. Not because it feels good, but because it invites us to need God in a deeper way. In the breaking, we come to the end of ourselves. And that's exactly where He begins.

When Jesus broke the bread at the Last Supper, He blessed it. The breaking came before the blessing. That pattern is seen throughout Scripture, and often in our lives too. Brokenness precedes breakthrough. Loss makes room for newness. Surrender brings clarity. Cracks let the light in.

Your story doesn't end with the fracture. God doesn't discard the broken; He binds, blesses, and uses those very pieces to display His grace.

You may carry scars. But scars don't mean the wound is still open; they mean healing has taken place. And healed people, when surrendered to God, can bring healing to others.

So don't be ashamed of your broken places. In God's hands, they become testimonies.

> **Prayer:**
> Lord, thank You that You don't waste my brokenness. Use it to make me tender, wise, and useful for Your Kingdom. Heal what still hurts and bring beauty from what was shattered. I trust You with my story. Amen.

FRIDAY: *The Cracks Let the Light In*

FRIDAY

The Cracks Let the Light In

> *"But we have this treasure in jars of clay to show that this all-surpassing power is from God and not from us." 2 Corinthians 4:7 (NIV)*

We try so hard to appear whole, to patch the cracks, hide the scars, and smooth out the broken edges. But what if the cracks weren't meant to be hidden? What if they're the very places where God's light shines through?

Jars of clay — that's what Scripture calls us. Fragile. Ordinary. Breakable. And yet, within us is a treasure: the presence of God. Not despite our cracks, but because of them.

A perfect vessel might try to take the credit. But a cracked one? It makes it clear, this light isn't mine. It belongs to the One who lives within me.

The world doesn't need to see perfect Christians. It needs to see real ones, held together by grace, still standing by mercy, glowing with the glory of the One who never let them go.

Don't be ashamed of your scars. They're not signs of failure; they're stories of survival. They whisper, I've been through fire, but I'm still shining.

Prayer:
Lord, thank You for using broken vessels like me. I surrender my cracks, my flaws, and my past to You. May Your light shine brightly through every scar and remind others that healing is possible in You. Amen.

SATURDAY

Wholeness Doesn't Mean Unbroken

"He heals the brokenhearted and binds up their wounds." Psalm 147:3 (NIV)

Wholeness doesn't mean going back to how things were before. It doesn't mean the pain never happened or that the cracks disappeared. In God's Kingdom, wholeness looks different; it looks redeemed.

You might carry the memory of what broke you. You may even still feel the tenderness in places God has touched. But wholeness is when those wounds stop bleeding and start breathing hope. When the place of pain becomes a place of praise.

The Japanese art of kintsugi repairs broken pottery with gold, making the object more valuable and beautiful than before. That's what God does with us. He doesn't toss us aside. He gathers every shattered piece and puts us back together with the gold of His grace.

So, if you've walked through betrayal, loss, illness, or deep sorrow, and you're still standing, you are living proof of restoration.

Not unbroken, but whole. Not untouched but undeniably held.

> **Prayer:**
> *Father, thank You for mending what I thought could never be repaired. Help me to see beauty in the places I once only saw brokenness. May my life be a testimony of Your healing love. Amen.*

SUNDAY

The Power of Gathering

"And let us consider how to encourage one another in love and good deeds, not abandoning our own meeting together, as is the habit of some, but encouraging one another." Hebrews 10:24–25 (NASB)

Sunday is a sacred invitation — to pause, to gather, to worship.
    As you prepare your heart today, remember the importance of coming together with other believers. There's something beautiful about lifting your voice in worship alongside others, sitting under the Word, and letting God refresh your spirit through fellowship. Church is not just a building; it's a body. And you are a vital part of it.
    So find your place, settle in, and be present in God's house.

Prayer:
Lord, thank You for the gift of the church, a place to grow, to serve, and to be renewed. Help me enter Your presence with gratitude and expectation. Amen.

SPECIAL WEEKS/DAYS

HOLY WEEK DEVOTIONALS

He Knew, and He Still Rode In

"When He approached Jerusalem, He saw the city and wept over it."
Luke 19:41 (NASB)

Palm branches waved. Hosannas rang out. The crowd celebrated a King.
But Jesus wept.
Why?
Because He knew. He knew their cheers would turn to jeers. Their "Hosanna!" Would soon become "Crucify Him!"
He knew the betrayal, the lashes, the cross that awaited. And still, He rode in on a donkey, fulfilling prophecy.
He knew... and still, He came.
This is love, not just in words, but in action. Jesus didn't run from suffering. He stepped into it for our sake.
As Holy Week begins, let's remember: Our Savior is not detached from pain. He's acquainted with it. He's walked through it. He conquered it.
Let this week draw you near to the One who chose the cross out of love for you.
Jesus, You knew—and still, You came. You saw the cost and still said yes.

Prayer:
Thank You for riding in. Thank You for staying on the path when You could have turned away. My heart bows in gratitude and awe. Amen.

When He Rode in on a Donkey

> *"Rejoice greatly, daughter of Zion! Shout in triumph, daughter of Jerusalem! Behold, your King is coming to you; He is righteous and endowed with salvation, humble, and mounted on a donkey."*
> Zechariah 9:9 (NASB)

Palm Sunday arrived not with trumpets, but with tears. Not with pageantry, but with palms. The King of kings chose a donkey, not a warhorse, to make His entrance into Jerusalem.

In those days, a king who rode a donkey came in peace. A king who rode a horse came for war. Jesus was declaring something powerful without uttering a word: I have come not to crush, but to save.

Imagine the scene. The people shouting "Hosanna!" Had expectations. They hoped He would overthrow the Roman government. They were ready for revolution. But Jesus came to redeem something far greater than politics; He came to redeem the human heart.

And that same heart still misses the point sometimes. We want Jesus to fix everything out there, but He's far more interested in what's going on in here—in our motives, our wounds, our hidden places.

Holy Week invites us to slow down. To pause and reflect not just on the what of Jesus' journey, but on the why. It wasn't the nails that held Him to the cross; it was love.

What areas of your life do you need to surrender as you walk into this sacred week?

Where do you need His peace to replace your striving?

Will you allow the humility of the donkey to challenge the pride of your own expectations?

Let us not miss the Savior in the crowd. He is still the Prince of Peace. Still the humble King. Still, the Lamb who takes away the sin of the world.

> **Prayer:**
> *Lord Jesus, thank You for riding in low so that You could lift us high. Help me not to miss You this week. As I walk through Holy Week, let me walk slowly, intentionally, and with a heart of surrender. Teach me to see the cross not as defeat, but as the greatest declaration of love. I worship You, my humble King. Amen.*

THANKSGIVING DEVOTIONAL

The Leper Who Returned

> *"Now one of them, when he saw that he had been healed, turned back, glorifying God with a loud voice, and he fell on his face at His feet, giving thanks to Him." Luke 17:15-16 (NASB)*

Ten lepers were healed that day, but only one returned. One out of ten.

That verse often arrests me. It makes me wonder how many blessings I've rushed through without stopping to say thank you. Gratitude isn't just polite; it's powerful. It's transformative.

The one who returned didn't just whisper "Thanks." He praised God loudly, fell on his face, and gave honor to the One who made him whole.

Jesus notices thankfulness.

We often associate gratitude with things that look like blessings: a job, healing, a miracle. But gratitude is even more powerful when we thank God in the middle of the unknown or through the loss. Gratitude doesn't erase our pain, but it reframes our perspective. It reminds us that God is still near and still good.

This Thanksgiving, be the one who returns. Be the one who thanks Him not just for the blessings, but for His presence. Be the one who kneels low and praises loud.

Prayer:
Lord, thank You. For the healing I've seen, and even for the places I'm still waiting. You've been faithful. I don't want to be the nine who walked away—I want to live a life of thankfulness. I fall at Your feet in worship today. Amen.

Gratitude Inventory

> *"They looked to Him and were radiant,*
> *And their faces will never be ashamed." Psalm 34:5 (NASB)*

THANKSGIVING DEVOTIONAL: *Gratitude Inventory*

I sat down in my usual corner and looked around. An overwhelming sea of gratitude began to well up in my heart. As an immigrant, I arrived in this country with just two suitcases, and now I'm surrounded by "stuff." God gently turned my eyes from the material to the spiritual. He used my abundance to pose a deeper question: Are you rich in the things that truly matter?

The verse came to mind: "Seek first the Kingdom of God, and all these things shall be added unto you." So I paused to reflect:

Am I truly seeking His Kingdom?
Has this become routine?
Do I linger long enough to hear His voice?
Am I asking for more of Him—more love, more joy, more peace?

It hit me, I take inventory of groceries, bills, and appointments. But when was the last time I took inventory of my spiritual life?

What's missing? And why?

Unless the things of this world grow strangely dim, we can never fully experience the beauty of who He is.

As the old hymn reminds us:
"Turn your eyes upon Jesus...
Look full in His wonderful face...
And the things of earth will grow strangely dim
In the light of His glory and grace."

Prayer:
Lord, help me to take an honest inventory of my heart. Let me not be consumed by earthly gain, but drawn deeper into spiritual richness. May my eyes stay fixed on You, and may my gratitude overflow, not for what I own, but for who You are. Amen.

CHRISTMAS DEVOTIONAL

The Gift That Changed Everything

> *"For a Child will be born to us, a Son will be given to us; and the government will rest on His shoulders; and His name will be called Wonderful Counselor, Mighty God, Eternal Father, Prince of Peace."* Isaiah 9:6 (NASB)

They expected a king in robes. They got a baby in swaddling cloth. They hoped for someone to overthrow Rome. They received Someone who would overthrow sin.

God's greatest gift didn't come wrapped in extravagance but in vulnerability. A manger. Straw. Humble beginnings. And yet, that gift changed everything.

We decorate and celebrate, but Christmas at its core is about this: God came close. He didn't shout from heaven; He stepped into the mess with us.

Have you ever unwrapped a gift slowly, treasuring every layer? May we do the same with the miracle of Jesus. His love. His humility. His nearness. The world may try to steal our attention with glitter and noise. But let's pause and worship.

> **Prayer:**
> Lord Jesus, thank You for coming close. For choosing the cradle before the crown. For entering our broken world to make us whole. This Christmas, I celebrate the greatest gift ever given—You. Amen.

 NEW YEAR'S EVE DEVOTIONAL

Anchored in Gratitude

> *"When you have eaten and are satisfied, you shall bless the Lord your God for the good land which He has given you." Deuteronomy 8:10 (NASB)*

As the year draws to a close, we often look ahead. We set goals. We make resolutions.

But before we rush into what's next, let's pause to remember.

This year may have held joy or sorrow, or both. You may have walked through heartbreak, healing, or something in between. But you're here. Still breathing. Still believing. Still clinging to the One who holds all things together.

Take a moment and look back, not with regret, but with gratitude. Even the wilderness had its manna. Even the storm had His whisper.

The Israelites were told to bless the Lord after they were satisfied. Sometimes we forget to thank Him once we've come through. But gratitude roots us. It anchors us. It sets the tone for the year ahead.

Prayer:
Lord, thank You for carrying me through this year. For every step, both the joyful and the painful. I bless You now for what You've done and for who You are. Help me to walk into the new year anchored in gratitude. Amen.

NEW YEAR'S DAY DEVOTIONAL

Let It Go

> *"Do not call to mind the former things, or consider things of the past. Behold, I am going to do something new..."* Isaiah 43:18–19 (NASB)

New Year's Day. A clean slate. A chance to begin again. But how can we step into the new if we're still clinging to the old?

That heartbreak? Let it go.
The bitterness? Let it go.
The fear of failure? Lay it down.
The shame you've carried too long? Hand it over.

God doesn't consult your past to plan your future. He's the God of fresh starts, and He delights in doing something new.

This doesn't mean we forget everything. It means we release what's holding us back so we can walk forward in freedom. Like Paul said in Philippians 3:13, "Forgetting what lies behind and reaching forward to what lies ahead..."

Let this be the year you stop rehearsing your past and start anticipating His promises.

Prayer:
Father, help me release what I've been holding onto. I want to walk into this new year unburdened, unshackled, and fully surrendered. Do something new in me. I trust You with what's ahead. Amen.

www.ingramcontent.com/pod-product-compliance
Lightning Source LLC
Chambersburg PA
CBHW022057090426
42743CB00008B/633